A Crocker Genealogy

VOL. 2

Andrea Leonard

HERITAGE BOOKS
2014

HERITAGE BOOKS

AN IMPRINT OF HERITAGE BOOKS, INC.

Books, CDs, and more—Worldwide

For our listing of thousands of titles see our website
at
www.HeritageBooks.com

Published 2014 by
HERITAGE BOOKS, INC.
Publishing Division
5810 Ruatan Street
Berwyn Heights, Md. 20740

Heritage Books by the author:

A Crocker Genealogy, Volumes 1 and 2

*Records of the Proprietors of the Common Lands in the
Town of Barnstable, Massachusetts, 1703–1795*

International Standard Book Numbers
Paperbound: 978-0-7884-0776-5
Clothbound: 978-0-7884-6002-9

PREFACE

Hardly had A CROCKER GENEALOGY, VOL I, been released when more information about the family began arriving in my mailbox. New babies generated several letters, as did marriages and deaths. Errors motivated some people to offer corrections. Most exciting, entirely unknown branches of the family popped to the surface.

One criticism of the earlier book pointed out that I had neglected in many instances to note sources of my information. This work may not serve as a reference for tracing descendancy that will be accepted by certain organizations and family societies such as Sons and Daughters of the American Revolution or the Mayflower Society; when possible, in this sequel, sources are given. I hope those wishing to prove eligibility to join such groups will be helped by these leads.

In two lines, one designated (Blank.), the other, (P-), a direct connection is missing, but in each instance the relationships are supported by family Bible entries, church, grave, or town records; yet "missing links" exist. They are included here in the hope that the missing link will be found as a result of this publication.

I am indebted to and wish to thank each contributor of the valuable data within this book; the details they have provided have enabled me to compile Volume II of A CROCKER GENEALOGY. I am most grateful to my sister-in-law, Catherine Harris Leonard, who proof-read these pages.

In this volume you'll discover some individuals have more "flesh on their bones" than those in Vol I; I hope your pleasure in Vol II is enhanced by these notes which are attributed to those people who have generously shared them with me.

-- Andrea Leonard

References for Sources

GA   - Gail Adams, Westchester CA 90045
NA   - Nancy Adams, Sarasota FL 34231
LTB - Loring T Briggs, Onancock, VA 23417
JOB - James Oliver Brooks Jr,
JMcKC- John MacKay Cammett, New York City NY 10025
SHC - Stuart Hyland Cammett, Grosse Pt Park MI 48230
PB   - **CEMETERY INSCRIPTIONS, TOWN OF BARNSTABLE**, Paul Bunnell
PC   - **OSTERVILLE, VOLS I & II** Paul Chesbro, Osterville MA 02655
CFC - Charles F Crocker, Marstons Mills MA 02648
JRC - **CROCKER GENEALOGY**, (Pub. 1966) James Russell Crocker
TC   - Thomas Crocker, Esq, Alexandria VA 22314
TTC - Terri Tallman Corbett, Centerville MA 02632
TAC - Tracy Ashley Crocker, Minnetonka MN 55305
RJG - Rev Robert J Goode Jr, Warsaw IL 62379
JG   - James Gould, PhD, Barnstable Historic Commission 02601
FWF - Col Franklin W Fish Jr, Claremont CA 91711-3732
         (Governor, Mayflower Society, Pomona Valley Colony)
ANCH- Anne N Clarke Harmon, Osterville MA 02655
MTH - Marion (Thomas) & Peter Hickman, Cotuit MA 02635
DL   - Donald Leary, Largo FL 34641-5109
JL   - Jack T Leonard, Salem MA 01970
LBL - Leona Buggert Leonard, New Ulm MN 56073
SL   - Stuart Lloyd, Berkeley Heights NJ 07922
         (Former Historian of NJ Mayflower Society)
LL   - Lane Lovell, Edgartown MA 02539
DM   - David Martin, Washington DC 20011
EWMcN- Edith Woodbridge McNair, Madison NH 03849
FLM - Fredrick L Millner, Trenton NJ 08610-2724
         Genealogist, Hinckley family
GCN - Gail C Nightingale, Osterville MA 02655

(Continued)

iv

References for Sources (Continued)

HYE - Hye Family Genealogies, Five Volumes
AO - **GENEALOGICAL NOTES BARNSTABLE FAMILIES**, Amos Otis
SCP - Col Stanton Crocker Parker
LMP - Leland M Puckett, Cave City AR 72521-9776
EPR - Ethel Parker Riedell, Osterville MA 02655
SCR - Susan Crocker Rosenthal, Schenectady NY 12308
    (Mayflower Society #4511-60-580)
BWS - Barbara W Shaw, Lavalette NJ 08735
CS - Cheryl Stanfield, Lake Odessa MI 48849
VCS - Virginia C Stinets, Osterville MA 02655
RLT - C.P.O. Robert L Tallman, U S Coast Guard, San Diego CA
GWT - Garfield W Toolas, So Dennis MA 02660
JTV - Joan Thomas Vos, Marstons Mills, MA 02648
WAW - **CROCKER GENEALOGY**, William Adolf Walter (1901-1966)
LGW - Linda Goettman Wilson, Bowie MD 20715

    Each of the people listed offered to share their own
    research and family records with me, and generously
    supplied additional information when asked. Without
    their input, this sequel would not have been written.--A.L.

AL - A Leonard, 63 Leonard Rd, Osterville MA 02655
    Member, D.A.R, #477802

    NOTE: The same identification numbering system
    is used in Vol II as that in Vol I.

    NOTE-Tracy A Crocker followed his ancestral lines
    back to Charlemagne and Lady Godiva; if they
    are HIS forebears, they are also OURS.

TABLE OF CONTENTS:

A CROCKER GENEALOGY - VOLUME II

PAST HISTORY - THE ENGLAND CONNECTION

Thomas Crocker Esq of Alexandria VA conducted his own personal
search for the background of William Crocker, the progenitor of our
Crocker family, and gave permission to quote the following "Study of
the English Crocker Family." He writes in the first person:

I have long been fascinated by the mystery of Deacon William
Crocker, the first Crocker in America: Who was he and why did he
emigrate? Much has been written on the Crocker family in America but
virtually nothing on where they came from or who they were in England.
Most of the family genealogies say William Crocker came from Devon or
England, but beyond that, a brick wall of silence. Therefore I sought
to penetrate the wall of silence, and my discoveries reveal both
interesting and unexpected results.

I. The Search for the English Connection

I started my search with the well-known source, GENEALOGICAL
NOTES OF BARNSTABLE FAMILIES [Amos Otis]. From that book I gleaned the
following facts about the patriarch of the Crocker family in America:

1. William Crocker emigrated in 1634, perhaps on the same ship as
    the Rev John Lothrop. (If it were the same ship, it would have
    been the Griffen which departed London July 21, 1634 and arrived
    in Boston September 18, 1634).

2. William Crocker first settled at Scituate, just south of Boston,
    and in 1639 moved to Barnstable on Cape Cod, where he remained
    the rest of his life.

3. William Crocker joined Lothrop's congregation December 25, 1636,
    in Scituate more than two years after he emigrated. This is a key
    fact: William Crocker was not originally a Puritan but presumably
    was an Anglican who converted to Puritanism once here, perhaps

through the influence of his first wife whom he had married earlier in 1636.

4. William's older brother John Crocker also emigrated to America. There is a definite record (UK Pub. Rec. Off. E190/876/11) of a John Crocker who, embarking on the Speedwell, departed Weymouth, England, April 22 1637 together with his "wife and boy." (In this context "boy" was used to mean servant). John was thus married in England before he left. The probate from his will when he died in 1669 in Barnstable shows his wife to have been named "Joane" or "Joan." There was also a Francis Crocker, presumably a relation, who emigrated to Barnstable about the same time.

5. William Crocker had seven children, the first two of which he named Elizabeth and John. This also is a key fact because these are recurring names in the English line of Crockers.

6. William Crocker was a hard-working, prosperous farmer who at his death in 1692, aged "about 80," was probably the wealthiest man in Barnstable. To judge from his will, William Crocker was literate and, most unusual for a Puritan, kept a black slave. He also was made a deacon only a few years before he died. His pious son Job had been a deacon for some years before that.

7. William Crocker's brother, John, was apparently a somewhat mean-spirited and litigious farmer and tavernkeeper. He was described as a "good liver," i.e., prosperous. He did not belong to Lothrop's church, that is, he remained an Anglican.

These are the basic known facts about our patriarch in America and his immediate family. Building on that, I examined the extensive genealogical records maintained by the Mormon Church seeking English birth or baptismal records of two Crocker brothers, an older John and a younger William. The Mormons have transcripts of records of every parish in England which effectively show a record of every Crocker who lived in Devon at this time.

Therefore, I examined all parish records for Devon, England, from 1600 to 1625 looking for a record of these two brothers. There is, incidentally, virtually no question that the Crocker brothers came from Devon, not only because of references to this fact but also because there are thousands of entries for that name in Devon. To this day they fill pages of the Devon telephone book, unlike directories for any other shire. Moreover, a check of the Mormon records for the neighboring shires of Cornwall, Dorset, and Somerset shows only a few Crockers and those only after 1700.

As a result of this search, I found only two sets of brothers named John and William Crocker. The first, and less likely candidates, are a John Crocker, son of Matthew Crocker, baptized September 8, 1605 in Exeter, Devon. He had a younger brother William baptized April 28, 1616, also in Exeter. The church in which they were baptized, Holy Trinity, served a poor part of town to judge from the number of illegitimate and prison-born children in the records. No further records of Matthew, John or William Crocker follow the records of baptisms, i.e., they probably died or moved away, conceivably to America; however, I do not believe these are "our" two brothers for two reasons.

First, there were 11 years between them in age, which would have made it unlikely the older would have followed the younger in emigrating to a savage wilderness like America at that time. Second, they were Exeter city boys who hardly would have prospered as farmers under the conditions of 17th century Massachusetts.

The second alternative is a pair of brothers, John, son of Hugh Crocker, baptized July 21, 1612, at Ermington, Devon, and his brother William, baptized February 11, 1615, at Modbury, Devon. Modbury is several miles from Ermington. Hugh had married the boys' mother, Thomasine Michell (pronounced "Mitchell"), January 14, 1610 at Ermington, where she was from. Quite significantly both Ermington and Modbury are just a few miles up the main road leading eastward from Yealmpton, site of Lineham House, the Crocker family seat after 1402.

I am convinced these are our two brothers because of the following factors:

1. The age spread was closer (only three years).

2. They grew up in a rural area and would have had experience in farming.

3. William would have been in his late 70s (and thus close to "about 80) at his death in 1692.

4. I could find no further records of William in England (thus suggesting that he left).

5. At age 19 in 1634 William, a second son with no prospect of inheriting the family farm because of primogeniture, would have been just the right age and recklessness to emigrate to America.

6. The Ermington parish records show a John Crocker as having a wife named "Joan" and two children, William (named after John's brother?) christened February 8, 1634 and Joan christened June 11 1637. Neither child appears to have survived infancy (although I have not yet confirmed this with Ermington burial records) and there is no further mention of this family in Ermington records after 1637, thus suggesting they may have left.

   All this makes sense. John Crocker, being the oldest son, would have stayed in England to help run and eventually inherit the family farm under primogeniture. Notwithstanding this plan, if his two children died he would have had a possible motive to emigrate to America and join his brother. Indeed this may even explain the clear record of his being a somewhat mean and bitter man. The only discrepancy, which I cannot explain, is the record showing John Crocker emigrating on the Speedwell in 1637 several months before the daughter Joan was christened. Dating, however, like spelling of names, was less than perfect in this period.

7. William named his first two children Elizabeth and John, which admittedly are common names but nonetheless recurrent in this line of English Crockers.

8. The brothers William and John from Modbury/Ermington had a cousin named Francis Crocker, who (either himself or his son) may be the Francis who joined them in Barnstable, reputed to be a relation.

Assuming that "our" William is indeed the son of Hugh, it means that William came from a rather prominent family at that time in Devon and may have had reason to keep his Anglican, and indeed royalist, background quiet in Puritan New England.

II. The Lineham Crockers

Hugh Crocker, father of William and John (hereafter Hugh the Younger), was most probably the third son of Hugh Crocker of Lineham, his older siblings being John and Francis, the former taking Lineham by primogeniture. Although Hugh the Younger did not inherit Lineham, he without question would have grown up in the house.

To digress for a minute about Lineham: Located just north of Yealmpton, Devon, Lineham is an estate of several thousand acres of prime farm land. It commands a sweeping view of the countryside and is a most pleasing place. The current house, a small Palladian structure, was built in 1699 by Courtenay Crocker. However remnants of the old medieval manor house remain in the garden and pool area of the present house, including several arches, remains of a chapel, and a large stone fireplace and mantel. In this house Hugh the Younger grew up.

Lineham supposedly came into the Crocker family through marriage into the Churchills around 1400, as described more fully below. Lineham has had a somewhat unhappy history since passing out of the Crocker family in the 18th century and has gone through so many owners in the last 20 years as to gain something of a reputation in the village of Yealmpton as a "cursed" house. As discussed below, the Crockers did not originally come from Lineham, which is near the south coast of Devon, but from Crocker's Hele on the north side of Devon, just beyond Dartmoor.

Returning to our story, Hugh the Younger had no prospect of inheriting Lineham because he was a younger son. He married Thomasine Michell from nearby Ermington, a small village with a church, still standing, with a notably crooked steeple. Thomasine was buried on April 1, 1628 in the churchyard at Ermington. Her grave cannot be identified today because no tombstones survive at Ermington from this period. The Michell family was solid locally but not a particularly prominent family from what I can determine.

Hugh the Younger's father, Hugh the Elder, was the oldest son in his generation and thus inherited Lineham through primogeniture. His younger brother George Crocker inherited and lived at Crocker's Hele, as shown by George's will of 1630. Thus, that original Crocker family property descended in the family from Saxon times down to at least 1620. Indeed, when I visited this past August (1989) the current owners said they had found in a safe in the cellar old letters to family remaining at Crocker's Hele from a John Crocker (possibly William's brother?) who had emigrated to America. Unfortunately, they had given the letters to a lady named Crocker from Ilfracomb, Devon, whose full name and address they could not recall.

The Lineham line runs back from Hugh the Elder through some seven John Crockers, all important men in Devon and married into important West Country families such as the Strodes, Yeos, and Churchills. Direct ancestors of Hugh the Elder are mentioned prominently in the various muster rolls leading up to the Spanish Armada and were responsible for providing soldiers for the defense of England.

Hugh's greatgrandfather John Crocker was High Sheriff of Devon in 1509 under Henry VIII; the Crockers, however, apparently did not prosper politically under the Tudors. Crockers had been significant local backers of the House of York, the Tudors' predecessor dynasty, with which history amply shows the Tudors wanted to make a clean break.

John, the High Sheriff's father, Sir John Crocker, was the most important in the line. The following facts can be stated with certainty from various sources:

1. Sir John, born in the early 1400s, lived to a reasonably old age, dying March 7, 1508. He is interred in the parish church in Yealmpton; his grave site is marked by a brass effigy showing him in full armor, his dog at his feet, his broad sword and misericord at his side (admittedly a rather stylized knightly pose).

2. As evidenced by his will, Sir John owned extensive lands throughout Devon, including most importantly, Lineham, Hemerdon, and Crocker's Hele. He held his properties primarily by virtue of service to the Courtenay family (the Earls of Devon who were his liege lords) and directly to the king.

3. He was cupbearer to the Yorkist King Edward IV, whom history has treated as a generally effective and courageous monarch. His service as cupbearer accounts for the cup on the family shield.

4. He participated in Edward IV's 1474 invasion of France. He never fought, however; Louis XI of France met Edward IV at the bridge at Picquigny and sued for peace. Essentially he bought off the English with payments and honors. Among the many of Edward's retainers honored by Louis was Sir John, who was granted three fleurs-de-lIs by Louis to add to his shield.

5. Sir John was exiled (presumably to France) by Richard III after Richard usurped the throne from Edward IV's son, whom he later murdered in the Tower of London. The exile well may have resulted from Sir John's support of the West Country rebellion against Richard in 1483, which was prominently led by the Courtenays, although this is purely my own speculation.

6. Sir John was described in contemporary sources as one of the leading warriors of the West Country; he led a cavalry troop in besieging the rebel Perkin Warbeck at Exeter in 1497, thereby earning the respect of Henry VII who had defeated Richard III in 1485 to establish the Tudor dynasty (this good grace may account for his son's appointment as High Sheriff in the early years of Henry VIII's reign, but entree was short-lived, as noted above).

Sir John's father, also supposedly a Sir John, fought under Henry V in the major English victory at Agincourt in 1415. Either this John Crocker or, possibly, his father is buried in the village church at Yealmpton and his gravesite is marked by a plaque in the floor reading in Latin, "Here lies John Crocker, Knight, husband of Alis and Alicia, who died March 1433."

In 1402 the John Crocker who died in 1433 and is buried at Yealmpton became the possessor of Lineham, supposedly through inheritance from his mother Agnes Churchill, who had married his father, yet another John Crocker, of Crocker's Hele. Reportedly, Agnes was daughter of Giles Churchill, whose brother William established the line of the Duke of Marlborough and Sir Winston Churchill, although I have not confirmed this through multiple sources. (Note: November 1995: I have since confirmed this. We are cousins of Sir Winston.)

This takes us back to the Crocker's original ancestral home, Crocker's Hele. This property is in good, rolling farmland bordering the River Torridge just west of the village of Meeth, north of the market town of Hatherleigh. It is not quite as lush countryside as that at Lineham in South Devon. The farm still exists and is marked by a sign reading "Crocker's Hele."

Lying on a rather steep slope leading down to the river, its name in the Domesday survey of 1087 was "Helescane," which means "steep slope inhabited by bees." The current owners told me that to this day the slope is alive with bees. Nothing remains of the original house (the current relatively modest home being built about 1700) except for an ancient medieval door preserved in the entryway. Also the owners tell me that the enormous hedgerows that delineate the driveway are probably over 1000 years old.

Crocker's Hele is on the direct route of a known Saxon sub-invasion of the sparsely populated Celtic kingdom of Dumnonia in 732. Given the fact that Crocker is a Saxon name and local lore places the Crockers in Devon before the Norman Conquest, it is perhaps not unreasonable to assume that they settled at Crocker's Hele as part of the Saxon invasion/migration of that vicinity around 732.

There are several other places associated with the Crocker family in Devon, incuding Crockernwell, a truly fly-bitten crossroads on the edge of Dartmoor (but listed as "Crockernwell" with a full description in the Domesday Book of 1087), and Crockerntor, a hill on the moor that I have yet to visit; these, however, appear to be of marginal importance. By examining the geographical distribution of the villages of the hundreds of persons named Crocker in the 1600-1625 records that I studied, there are two clear loci: the area around Crocker's Hele and the area around Yealmpton.

Indeed, this examination shows them literally branching out like spokes from these two hubs, following old roads on the map of Devon. The migration of Hugh Crocker the Younger from Yealmpton several miles up the road to Ermington and thence several more to Modbury is a perfect case in point. The inescapable conclusion is that there are two broad lines of Devon Crockers: the "newer" line from Lineham and the "older" line (from which the newer line was descended) from Crocker's Hele. This geographic evidence tracks exactly with the birth and will records noted above. In the absence of any better information, I can only conclude that William Crocker, founder of the line in America, was directly in descent of both these lines.

As to my observations on all of the above, the record is, in a sense, one of the rise and fall of a family. The Crockers of Crocker's Hele were undoubtedly a prosperous farming family by the measure of the times. They were not members of the Norman ruling, or even knightly, classes in the Middle Ages but rather of old Saxon background. Their lands were ample but not major, and Crockers played a political role only on a very local level in what is to this day an extremely rural area of Devon.

Commencing in the late 1300s and early 1400s, however, their role began to change for two reasons. First, the oldest Crocker sons for several generations entered into a series of advantageous marriages with the local Anglo-Norman gentry and knightly families (Churchills, Fortescues, Yeos, Strodes, etc.) and the marriage with the Yeos, or even more likely the Bonville's, purportedly gave their children descent from King Edward I (although I have never confirmed this) and they began to accumulate substantial and widespread lands in Devon.

Lineham House was only one of a number of manors they owned; although they resided there, it was not the largest or most valuable of their properties.

Second, the oldest sons assumed the obligations of knight service and distinguished themselves in battle and at court in the tempestuous years of the 15th century, which brought both the Hundred Years War and the Wars of the Roses. They were sufficiently identified with the Yorkist cause and their liege lords, the Courtenays, to be rewarded when they succeeded and punished (e.g., through exile) when they failed. With the ascendancy of the Tudors and a marked abatement in warfare after 1485, however, they no longer played such a role.

As knighthood was waning generally at this time, they, like many others, allowed their knightly obligations and titles to lapse and settled into what was broadly the "squirearchy" of their local areas. Although the oldest sons were generally designated "gentleman" in the parish records, many younger sons married out of that class, moved away (one became mayor of Exeter and played a role supporting Charles I in the Civil War, while others went to Ireland) or, like our ancestors, emigrated to America.

Thus, within the hundred years or so following Sir John's death in 1508, the Crocker family dissipated its prominence and waned with the decline of feudalism. Those remaining at Lineham continued to marry into prominent local families until the direct male line ran out in the 18th century and the property passed from the family. (TC)

DEACON WILLIAM CROCKER

William Crocker was born in England c. 1612 (AO) and died in Barnstable Massachusetts in September 1692. He married his first wife, Alice, in 1636; her maiden name is unknown. Mother of all William's children, Alice died after 1683. William married 2d Patience (Cobb) Parker, widow of Robert Parker, daughter of Patience (Hurst) & Elder Henry Cobb, who was baptized in Barnstable 3-13-1641/2, died in 1727.

(For additional detail, see Vol I)
(For English Genealogy (TC), see Vol II, p A-1)

Last Will & Testament of Deacon William Crocker of Barnstable
From **GENEALOGICAL NOTES OF BARNSTABLE FAMILIES**
by Amos Otis (1888)

The 6th day of September Anno Dom. 1692 I, William Crocker of Barnstable, being sick and weak in body but through ye mercy of God of disposing mind and memory, and knowing ye uncertainty of this life on earth, and being desirous to settle things in order, do make this my last will and testament in manner and forme following, viz:

first and principally, I give and committ my soul to God in Jesus Christ my Saviour and Redeemer throw whose pretious death and merrits I hope to find ye free pardon and remition of all my sinnes, and everlasting salvation, and my body to ye earth from whence it was taken, to be buried in such decent manner as to my Executor hereafter named, shall seem meet and convenient, and as touching my worldly estate which God hath in mercy lent unto me, my will is to bestow ye same as hereafter is expressed, and I do hereby revoke and make void all wills by me formerly made and declared and appoint this to be my last will and testament.

Imprimus my will is that all those debts and duties which I owe in right or conscience to any person or persons whatsoever, shall be well and truly contented and paid when convenient by my Executor.

Itt. I give and bequeath unto Patience my loving wife besides ye liberty to dispose of all ye estate which she brought with her or had at ye time of our intermarriage, and besides ye forty pounds I then promised to give her in case she should survive me, I give unto her my best bedd and bedstead with all ye ffurniture thereto belonging.

Itt. I give and bequeath to my eldest son John Crocker, my now dwelling house and lands both upland and fresh meadows adjoyning and belonging thereunto now and of late under my occupation and improvement to have and to hold to him his heirs and assignes forever he or they paying to ye s'd Patience my wife twenty pounds of ye fores'd forty pounds she is to receive, and I do also hereby confirm to him my son John his heirs and assignes forever all those parcels of land I heretofore gave unto him and are well known to have been in his quiet possession for sundry years; I further also give and bequeath to him my son John my two oxen which he hath had in his posession some years.

Itt. I give and bequeath unto my son Job Crocker besides ye land I heretofore gave him and know to be in his possession, twenty acres of that fifty acres at ye ponds which I purchased of John Coggin to have and to hold to him my son Job his heirs and assignes forever and that he chuse it on which side of s'd land he please.

Itt: I will and bequeath to my sons Josiah and Eliazer Crocker besides those lands I heretofore gave to each of them and are in their particular knowne possession, all my upland at the marsh together with all ye marsh adjoining thereunto, (except such particular parcel or parcels thereof as I have heretofore given and is possest of late by any other or is in these presents hereafter mentioned,) to be equally divided between them ye s'd Josiah and Eliazer to have and to hold to them their heirs and assignes forever; Each of them ye s'd Josiah and Eliazer paying seven pounds & ten shillings apiece to ye s'd Patience in paying of ye forty pounds above mentioned. And I further will and bequeath to my sons Josiah and Elizaer to each of them one cow.

Itt. I will and bequeath unto my son Joseph Crocker (besides ye two parcels of upland and one parcel of marsh which I heretofore gave him and is known to be in his possession ye house and land as he hired of me and now lives on) that is to say, so much of my s'd land as he hath now fenced in; together with that parcel of marsh which he hath from year to year of late hired of me; to have and to hold to him ye s'd Joseph his heirs and assignes forever: he or they paying five pounds to ye s'd Patience to make up ye full of s'd forty pounds I promised to her as above s'd.

Itt. I give and bequeath all ye rest of my lands att ye ponds to my grandsons, viz: to Nathaniel, ye son of John Crocker, Samuel, ye son of Job Crocker, and Thomas, ye son of Josiah Crocker to be equally divided between them and to their and each of their heirs and assignes forever.

Itt. my will is and I do hereby constitute and appoint my trusty and well beloved son Job Crocker to be my sole executor to see this my last will and testament to be performed, with whom I leave all ye residue of my estate in whatsoever it be, to be equally distributed amongst all my children unless I shall signifie my minde to have such part or parts thereof to be disposed to any in particular.
In witness whereof I have hereunto sett my hand and seal.

On my further consideration I signifie my mind before ye ensealing hereof and it is my will that Mr. Russell shall have my two steers which are att Isaac Howlands and that Mr. Thomas Hinckly shall have my nagro boy if he please he paying fourteen pounds to my Executor for him.

William Crocker (Seal)

Signed Sealed and declared
In presence of
Samuel Chipman,
Mercy Chipman

Samuel Chipman and Mercy Chipman whose hands are sett as witnesses to this will made oath in Court October ye 19: 1692, that they did see the above said William Crocker now deceased sign seal and declare this above written to be his last will and testament.

Joseph Lothrop: c l.

Examined and duly compared with ye original will and entered October ye 22, 1692.

Attest: Joseph Lothrop, Recorder.

To better understand Deacon William Crocker's division of lands and property in his last will and testament, we find that Amos Otis in his book, Genealogical Notes of Barnstable Families, explains that:

Deacon William Crocker's son Job had inherited the estate which had been his uncle John's homestead; his father, therefore, gives him a larger proportion of his estate that is not connected with the West Barnstable farm; son John had the great lot of his uncle John, on which he had a house -- therefore no immediate need existed that he be provided for. For his other four sons, Deacon William had provided houses, or they had already built homes on land he had given them.

Referring to lands at "the ponds," Deacon Crocker had purchased of John Coggin fifty acres of land in a part of Barnstable then called the Indian Ponds, now a part of Marstons Mills. The ponds, today known as Hamblin's, Middle, and Mystic, are headwaters of a stream we have now named Mills River in that village.

Josiah Crocker, son of Deacon William, was a substantial farmer who resided in the old stone house built by his father. He inherited the southeasterly part of his father's estate in West Barnstable and owned acreage in other parts of the town of Barnstable. (AO, WAW, TAC)

Josiah's wife, Melatiah Hinckley, whom he married in Barnstable 10-23-1668, was born Barnstable 11-25-1648, and died 2-2-1714/15. She was the daughter of Governor Thomas Hinckley by his first wife, Mary Richards. Melatiah survived Josiah, and her will, dated 1-21-1713/14, names her five sons and three daughters then living.

# # #

Please be advised that this book is a sequel to A CROCKER GENEALOGY
VOL. 1. To trace each addition or correction included in this volume,
you will need to refer to Vol. I.

Notes, corrections and additions in A CROCKER GENEALOGY, VOL. II,
are emtered in numerical order corresponding to the identification
numbers assigned in A CROCKER GENEALOGY, VOL. I., with page numbers
supplied where insertions should be made. Minor corrections are
underlined.

First Generation

INSERT ADDITION: I, p 1 (SCR, JRC)
1. *William Crocker's wife, Alice, was buried Barnstable MA 5-4-1684.
   His second wife's mother was Patience (Hurst) Cobb

William Crocker and his brother, John Crocker, according to Amos
Otis, (GENEALOGICAL NOTES OF BARNSTABLE FAMILIES, VOL. I, p 200) "are
said to have come over in 1634, either in the same ship with the Rev.
Mr. Lothrop or in another that sailed about the same time." Lothrop's
church records show John Crocker as an inhabitant of Scituate in 1636.
He probably moved soon after 1639 to Barnstable. "His wife's name was
Joan or Jane. The date of his marriage does not appear on the record."
Otis assumes John did not marry until late in life; (see p A-4, this
volume, for Thomas Crocker's account of his research in Devon) and we
know he left no family when he died in 1669 for, "after providing for
his widow, he gave his estate to the sons of his brother, William, and
appointed his nephew, Job, his executor."

Otis describes John as a very different man from his brother,
Dea. William Crocker. "He was illiterate, kept a public house, where
it was customary in early times for a certain class of people, found
in all communities, to assemble to drink and indulge in low and
vicious conversation. Such company and such associations never
improved the temper or moral character of a man, or add anything to
his respectible standing in society. That he belonged to Mr. Lothrop's
church does not appear. He was one of the pioneer settlers of Scituate
and Barnstable. He was not a perfect man. His ashes rest in the old
burying-ground beside those of the fathers where it will be well to
let them rest in peace." --(Otis, Vol. I, p 204,)

2.

Although the 'ordinary' or public house kept by William Crocker's brother, John, no longer exists, Crockers of later generations, descendants of William, operated other taverns in Barnstable Village, and one of these stands to this day and can be found on Route 6-A almost directly across the Old King's Highway from Sturgis Library, repository of a most complete collection of early American genealogical materials and a mecca for genealogists. (See p 7.)

Second Generation

INSERT ADDITION: I, p 1 (JRC)
II. *John Crocker Sr's 1st wife, Mary (Bodfish) born 1639

NOTE: My thanks to Ms Judith A Elfring, Registrar, The Pilgrim John Howland Society, Yarmouth ME 04096, for the following correction:

"According to NEH&G Register, Elizabeth (Tilley) Howland & John Howland I (MAYFLOWER) had ten (not nine) children, namely: Desire, John II, Hope, Elizabeth, Lydia, Hannah, Joseph, Jabez, Ruth, and Isaac. John Howland II was born Plymouth MA 2-24-1626. John Howland I born Cambridgeshire, England, son of Henry & Margaret Howland. Margaret came from Huntingdonshire."

INSERT ADDITION: I, p 2 (WAW, JRC, DL)
16. *Eleazer Crocker I born Barnstable, died Barnstable before
     9-17-1723. His 2d wife, Mercy (Phinney) was sister of
     Benjamin Phinney, who married Martha (Crocker) (175.)

INSERT ADDITION: I, p 2 (E McN)
17. *Joseph Crocker was a Sgt in the Indian Wars. His wife,
     Temperance (Bursley) was sister of Mary, wife of John
     Crocker Sr (11.)

John Bursley, born in England, died Barnstable 1660, is recorded at Wessaguscus (Weymouth) 1629 and at Barnstable in 1639. His wife, Joanna (Hull), daughter of Rev Joseph Hull of Barnstable, married 2d Dolar Davis.

Third Generation

NOTES: See I, p 3 (AO)
111. <u>Elizabeth Crocker</u>: According to Amos Otis,(AO), pg 211, Elizabeth
(111.) married in <u>1678</u> Dea Richard Childs and died <u>1-15-1716;</u>
however, AO, pg 184, also states Elizabeth died <u>1-15-1696</u> (after
seven children), and Dea Richard Childs married 2d Hannah _____
and had 3 more children.

"<u>Deacon Richard Childs</u>," Amos Otis (AO) says, was "probably son
of the first Richard of Barnstable"..."probably the Richard
Childs who married 10-15-1649 Mary Linnell," born 1584, died
1662, daughter of Peninah (Howes) and Robert Linnell.

The Rev Robert J Goode (11131.13111.111.) (RJG) of Plymouth MA,
a descendant of Dea Richard Childs and his wife, Elizabeth
(Crocker) Childs through two lines of the Childs family (both
included below), fills in blanks in the Crocker record:

INSERT ADDITION: I, p 3 (RJG)
111. *Elizabeth Crocker born 10-7-1660, died <u>1-15-1696</u>, married <u>1678</u>
Dea Richard Child born March 1653, died 1716

NOTE-I, p 1 & 4, re Deacon Job (14.) & Thomas (143.) Crocker: Excerpt
from NEH&G Register II, Vol. XIV, 1860, Cape Cod and Martha's
Vineyard Memoir by Judge Sewall (1702): "I met Thomas Crocker
(who married the widow of John Lothrop) and Lt Howland." (John
II). Judge Sewall also mentioned a visit with Mr Isaac Robinson,
then 92 years old. Robinson had been the pastor of the church at
Leyden, Holland. Further, he noted Rev Thomas Walley had died
3-24-1677/8. Mary, daughter of Rev Thomas Walley, married Deacon
Job Crocker. (14.)

CORRECTION: I, p 5:
144. *Mary born 6-29-1681, died 9-10-1759, <u>married John Howland III</u>
born 12-31-1674, died March 1738. He was son of John Howland Jr,
who was born Plymouth MA 2-24-1626

NOTE-I, p 5 (FLM) <u>Deacon John Crocker</u> (145.) born 2-24-1683, died
   2-7-1773, married 2d 6-22-1721 Mary Hinckley born May <u>1687</u>, <u>died</u>
   <u>7-27-1744</u>. Hinckley family historian, Fredrick L Millner (FLM),
   Trenton NJ, questions the identity of Mary; Was she daughter of
   Bethia (Lothrop) & Dea John Hinckley? Or daughter of Sarah (Cobb)
   & Benjamin Hinckley? In Otis' genealogy, Mary daughter of Bethia
   (Lothrop) & John Hinckley married Samuel Jenkins, NOT John
   Crocker. Other sources differ. At this time no hard evidence
   proves which Mary married Ens Dea John Crocker. After lengthy
   study, Millner concludes that Dea John Crocker's 2d wife, Mary
   Hinckley, was not the daughter of Bethia (Lothrop) and Dea John
   Hinckley, but who her parents were, or whether she was the widow
   of a Hinckley, is still uncertain. After review, I agree.
   [Millner lists 39 Marys in the first six Hinckley generations.]

   Millner also suggests that this Mary (Hinckley) Crocker and Nancy
   were the same person. Bunnell's <u>CEMETERY INSCRIPTIONS OF THE TOWN</u>
   <u>OF BARNSTABLE</u> gives date of death of Mrs Mary Crocker, wife of
   Deacon John, 7-27-1744. From Amos Otis (I,p 239): "it appears
   that he [Dea John] married a 3d wife Nancy, her grave stone
   records her death July 27 1744, age 56." Was Mary called "Nancy,"
   perhaps, to distinguish her from other Marys?

<u>INSERT CORRECTIONS</u>: I, p 5 & 6 (JRC, WAW,TAC)
147. *Elizabeth Crocker born 5-15-1688 married Rev Benjamin Allen
       <u>son of James & Elizabeth Allen</u>

154. Mary Crocker born 9-20-1677, <u>died 8-31-1756</u>

157. *<u>Josiah Crocker's children are listed in Generation Four, etc.</u>

NOTE-I, p 6 & 8, Tracy Ashley Crocker (17181.15151.12.) Minnetonka MN
       descends from both Josiah (15.) & Joseph (17.); in all sources
       Mary (154.) born 8-10-1677, <u>died 8-31-1756</u>, Josiah's daughter,
       married 11-5-1705 William (171.) born 8-25-1679, died <u>June</u> 1741.
       Both were born, married and died in <u>Barnstable MA</u>. (AO,WAW,TAC)

INSERT ADDITIONS: I, p 7 (JRC, SCR)

167. *Eleazer Crocker II born 8-3-1693 (twin of Ruth), married
     Haverhill MA 4-7-1720 Judith Sanders born there 6-17-1696, died
     Willington CT 8-26-1776, daughter of Hannah (Tewksbury) & James
     Sanders (who married at Haverhill 10-20-1687). Eleazer taught
     school; the family resided in Windham, Willington, Glastonbury,
     and Tolland, all CT towns. Date of his death is unknown.

169. *Abel Crocker born Barnstable MA 6-15-1695, died Carver MA
     7-17-1781, married Barnstable MA 4-16-1718 Mary Isham born
     Barnstable MA June 1687, died Carver 11-5-1782, daughter of
     Jane Hyde (Parker) & John Isham of Osterville MA. Jane H Parker
     was the daughter of Robert Parker whose widow (Patience Cobb)
     was Deacon William Crocker's second wife.

INSERT ADDITION: I, p 8 (JRC)

16(11). Mercy Crocker born after 1717, married 10-26-1737 Ebenezer
        Hatch born Falmouth MA 3-22-1708/9, the son of Bethia (Nye)
        & Jonathan Hatch

INSERT ADDITION: I, p 8 (SCR, JRC)
Children of Sgt Joseph Crocker (17.)
  & Temperance (Bursley) Crocker:

171. *William Crocker born 8-25-1679, died June 1741 (WAW)

172. *Ensign Timothy Crocker born 4-30-1681, died 1-31-1737
     bur W Barnstable MA

INSERT ADDITION: I, p 9 (SL,DL,WAW,JRC)
175. *Martha Crocker born 2-22-1689, married June 1709 Benjamin
     Phinney I, son of Mary (Rogers) (MAYFLOWER) & John Phinney,
     brother of Mercy Phinney who married Mary's Uncle Eleazer (16.)
     [Note: Martha did not marry twice. (SL, see 1525.)]

Fourth Generation

INSERT ADDITION: I, p 11 (RJG)
Children of Elizabeth (Crocker) (111.) Childs
& Deacon Richard Childs:

1111. Samuel Childs born 11-6-1679

1112. Elizabeth Childs born 1-23-1681/2, died in infancy

1113. *Thomas Childs born 1-10-1682, died 4-11-1770, a cordwainer, married 1710 Mary Hamblin, born 1681.

1114. Hannah Childs born 1-22-1684

1115. Timothy Childs born 9-22-1686

1116. *Ebenezer Childs (Dea) born Mar 1691, died 1-17-1756 in Nova Scotia, buried West Barnstable, married 1719 Hope ____

1117. Elizabeth Childs born 6-6-1692

1118. *James Childs born 11-6-1694, died 11-2-1779, married Elizabeth Crocker (1425.) born 1702/3, daughter of Sarah (Parker) & Samuel Crocker. See also 145(10).

1119. Mercy Childs born 5-7-1697

111(10). Joseph Childs born 3-5-1699/0, married 4-23-1724 Deliverance (?) (? born 1711/12 daughter of James & Ruth (Lewis) Hamblin)

CORRECTION: Fred Millner of Hinckley Heritage Club looked into descendancy of Joseph Smith Jr who married Reliance Crocker (1125) and advises this Joseph Smith is not of the Mormon family of Smiths.

INSERT ADDITION: I, p 13 (AO, Vol I, p 224)

Cornelius Crocker Sr, (1426.), proprietor of Crocker Tavern on Old King's Highway (Rte 6-A) in Barnstable Village, son of Sarah (Parker) & Samuel Crocker, was bound, when but a lad, as apprentice to a tailor; he afterwards had a tailor shop of his own. Cornelius, because he had a club foot, was unable to perform work requiring much phyical labor. He bought and had rebuilt, however, the ancient grist mill on Mill Creek, and also owned Crocker's Wharf and a fish house on the harbor where he gave employment to quite a number of local men. As a result, he was influential in the neighborhood and the town.

Like many 18th century entrepreneurs, Cornelius Crocker acquired several businesses and various pieces of real estate. A moderate Tory during the Revolution, he became one of the wealthiest men of his time in Barnstable's East Parish; he believed the colonies were mistaken in adopting policies that he foresaw would lead to war with England. Otis states, "His political principles and interests were antagonistical, and prudence dictated that he should commit no act that would render his large estate liable to confiscation." Like many a businessman, today, his politics were dictated by expediency.

Not the least of Cornelius's holdings was the property later known as "Lydia Sturgis's tavern," where he ran a public house for many years. Always kept in good repair, the structure was built to accommodate those attending the courts, and it became, according to Amos Otis, a favorite resort for travellers.

"Tories," Otis states, "were few in number in Barnstable. Among the more moderate of those were men of wealth, of respectability, and influence. They were citizens, and so long as they did not give aid or comfort to the enemies of the country, and contributed their share to the public expenses, they were entitled to the protection of the laws, though their political opinions might not have been in accordance with the views of a majority of the people." Such a man was Cornelius Crocker Sr.

"Treason," writes Otis, "should be nipped in the bud; but perfect freedom to debate on matters of policy is the unalienable right of a free people."

Unalienable rights, however, did not always prevail. Otis recounts the
tale of Abigail (Davis) Freeman, widow of David, lived in an ancient
dwelling where she kept a small grocery store located next to the
Court House. Talkative and outspoken, Abigail refused to surrender her
small stock of tea to be destroyed by the Vigilance Committee and
freely expressed her tory principles. Ducking stools for the cure of
scolds and unquiet women had gone out of use but the then modern
invention of tarring, feathering, and riding on a rail were in vogue.

When a group of young men upon whom Widow Nabby had vented her spleen
determined they must act, Otis says, they entered her house after she
had retired for the night, "took her from her bed... smeared her with
tar and covered her with feathers. From a nearby fence they procured
a rail across which she was set astride. Either end of the rail was
supported on the shoulder of a stout youth, and she was held in
position by a man walking alongside, holding her hand..." After she
promised to meddle no more in politics, they released her.

BOTE-Stuart Lloyd (SL) traces his lineage from both Thankful (Crocker)
(1525.) Morse, daughter of Hannah (Green) & Thomas Crocker, and Martha
(Crocker) (175.) Phinney, daughter of Temperance (Bursley) & Sgt
Joseph Crocker. Sources: Falmouth Vital Records and MORSE GENEALOGY
by J Howard Morse & Miss Emily W Leavitt (NY 1903).

Lloyd, historian of NJ MAYFLOWER SOCIETY for ten years, says Martha
Crocker (175.) did NOT marry 2d Capt Theodore Morse. [See I, p 18,
Thankful (1525.) & p 24, Zaccheus Phinney Sr (1755.)] Morse married
1st Thankful (1525.) & 2d, Susannah (Davis) Phinney, widow of Zacceus
Phinney Sr (1755.) Lloyd's correction is confirmed by another descendant, Edith McNair, Madison NH. The relationships among the
individuals involved are complicated, so are detailed here.

Theodore Morse, master mariner and a strong Tory, settled in
Falmouth MA; he received a captain's commission from the king.
He so violently expressed his sentiments that his Whig opponents
took him to Cambridge MA but returned him to Falmouth unharmed.
Theodore Morse married 1st Thankful Crocker (1525.); he married
2d in Falmouth 2-12-1763 Susanna (Davis) Phinney born 10-2-1725,
daughter of Annah (Dimmick) & Jabez Davis, widow of Zaccheus
Phinney Sr (1755.) whom she had married 3-2-1742/3. He died 1754.

CORRECTION: I, p 18, (SL)

1525. *Thankful Crocker born Falmouth MA 8-20-1717, died there
7-1-1762, married Falmouth 4-26-1739 Capt Theodore Morse born
Plymouth MA 8-20-1714, died Falmouth 12-19-1794, son of
Elizabeth (Doty) (MAYFLOWER) & Joshua Morse. He married 2d
1-12-1763 Susannah (Davis) Phinney born 10-2-1725, widow of
Zaccheus Phinney (1755.)

Capt Theodore Morse and his 2d wife, Susanna (Davis) Phinney
Morse, had two children, Berecynthia Morse b 1764 and & Calvin
Morse b 1766. These two children were not Crockers.

ADDITION: I, p 20, (CS)

1635. *John Crocker IV born Barnstable 1-11-1721-2, died Barnstable
6-14-1776, called "Cape Breton John," married Barnstable
2-14-1750 Mary Bursley

CORRECTIONS: I, p 21 (WAW, JRC, DL)
Children of Sarah (Crocker) Bursley (165.)
  & Joseph Bursley I:

1651. *Joseph Bursley II born 3-8-1714, married Bethia Fuller born
9-1-1715, died 2-2-1794, daughter of Thankful (Gorham) &
Lt John Fuller

1653. Mercy Bursley born 7-10-1721, died 5-19-1793, married 5-22-
1757 John Goodspeed, died 7-26-1786, son of Susannah (Allen)
& Benjamin Goodspeed

1661. Lydia Bursley died 1-19-1824; her husband, Benjamin Lucas,
was born Plymouth MA

INSERT ADDITION: I, p 21 (JRC)
Children of Theophilus Crocker (166.)
  & Lydia (Eddy) Crocker:

1662. Theophilus & Mercy (Hayford) Crocker had Theophilus Jr born
8-17-1761, married 10-27-1785 Mary/Polly Allen, probably
daughter of Joanna (?) & Capt Oliver Allen

10

INSERT ADDITION: I, p 21 (SCR, JRC)
Children of Eleazer Crocker II (167.)
& Judith (Saunders) Crocker:

1671. *Joseph Crocker born Haverhill MA 3-4-1720/1, married and had
son Joseph born Willington CT 12-21-1753

1672. *Benjamin Crocker born Haverhill MA 3-3-1722/3, died Willington
CT 8-32-1776, married at Willington CT 11-18-1745 Elizabeth
Fenton born Willington CT 2-21-1726/7, died Willington CT
9-5-1776, daughter of Ann (?) & Capt Francis Fenton born Woburn
MA 7-22-1690. Elizabeth (Fenton) & Benjamin Crocker had 11
children; their 3rd son was Eleazer III (16723.)

1673. *Ebenezer Crocker born Windham CT 1-2-1724/5

1674. John Crocker born Windham CT 8-23-1727, died 11-19-1727

1675. *Hannah Crocker born Windham CT 6-27-1729, married Elijah
Whiton

1676. Ruth Crocker born Windham CT 12-7-1732, died 9-8-1737

1677. John Crocker born Windham CT 8-3-1735, died Willington CT
8-16-1743

1678. *Sarah Crocker born Windham CT 8-9-1739

INSERT ADDITION: I, p 21, (JRC)
Children of Ruth (Crocker) Fuller (168.)
& Samuel Fuller:

1681. Sarah Fuller born 4-16-1719, died unmarried

1682. Barnabas Fuller born 9-1-1721, married Deborah (?)

1683. Eleazer Fuller born 2-9-1722/3, twin, married 1756 Elizabeth
Hatch

1684. William Fuller born 2-9-1723 (twin of Eleazer)

1685. Joshua Fuller born Barnstable MA 10-3-1727, married Joanna
Taylor

1686. Lot Fuller born 1733, died 1811, married Rachel (?)

INSERT ADDITION: I, p 22 (JRC, DL)
Children of Abel (Dea.) Crocker (169.)
& Mary (Isham) Crocker:

1691., 1692., & 1693.: already listed, Vol I, p 22

1694. Mary Crocker born 7-25-1727, married Plympton MA 5-30-1771
Dea Thomas Savery born 1736, son of Percilla (Paddock) &
Thomas Savery, his 3d wife.

1695. Elijah Crocker born 5-8-1729, died probably before 1784, unm

1696. *Sarah Crocker born 6-13-1733, died 7-25-1813, married Plympton
MA 8-1-1751, Elijah Perry of Middleboro, born @ 1728, died 1812

1697. *Joseph Crocker born Plympton MA 9-25-1737, married 1st
Barnstable MA 1-3-1760 Relief Lovell, married 2d Plympton MA
6-4-1767 Margaret Jackson, married 3d Plympton MA 1774 Deborah
Ransom.

INSERT CORRECTIONS: I, p 23 (JRC)
Children of William Crocker (171.)
& Mary (Crocker) (154.) Crocker:

1716. Mary Crocker born 8-12-1714, died 11-11-1785

1717 Joseph Crocker born 1718, died 4-7-1741, unmarried

1718 Benjamin Crocker born 3-20-1720, died 2-27-1785

INSERT ADDITION: I, p 23 (JRC)
1721. Jerusha Crocker born 12-12-1711, died 1-29-1742, married Elijah
      Deane born (Raynham) Taunton MA 1700, died 4-29-1750, son of
      Mary (Kingsby) & Thomas Deane.

INSERT ADDITION: I, p 24 (JRC)
Children of Joanna (Crocker) Fuller (174.)
  & Joseph Fuller:

1741. Rebecca Fuller born 12-29-1709, died 7-30-1732 unmarried

1742. Bethia Fuller born 3-2-1712, died 7-1-1737 unmarried

1743. Temperance Fuller born 4-24-1714, married Abraham Blossom

1744. Timothy Fuller born 4-3-1719, married 1st Jane Lovell,
      married 2d Hannah (?)

1745. Matthias born 9-3-1723, married Lydia Blossom

1746. Bathsheba Fuller born 8-10-1726, died June 1749

1747. Lemuel Fuller (See I, p 24, # 1741.)

INSERT ADDITION: I, p 24 (SL, DL, WAW, JRC)
Children of Martha (Crocker) Phinney (175.)
  & Benjamin Phinney:

1751. *Temperance Phinney born 1710, died ___, married 1733 James
      Fuller born Barnstable 5-1-1711, son of Benjamin, grandson of
      Samuel Fuller Jr; Samuel Fuller Sr was on the MAYFLOWER in 1620

CORRECTIONS: I, p 24 (JRC)

1752. Melatiah Phinney born 1712, married 5-18-1732 Josiah Morton

1753. Barnabas Phinney born 1715, married Mehitable (?), had son 1746

1754. Silas Phinney born 1718

1755. *Zaccheus Phinney born 1720, died 1754, married Falmouth 10-2-1742 Susannah Davis born 10-2-1725, daughter of Anna (DimmIck) & Jabez Davis of Falmouth (E McN)

1756. Seth Phinney born 6-27-1723

Fifth Generation

INSERT ADDITION: I, p 25, (RJG)
Children of Thomas Childs (1113.)
& Mary (Hamblin) Childs:

11131. *David Childs born 7-20-1711, married 1-29-1734 Hannah Cobb,
daughter of Hannah (Davis) born 1683 & Gersham Cobb born
8-4-1675

11132. Jonathan Childs born 11-27-1713

11133. Silas Childs born 3-10-1715; removed to R I, said to have
settled in Warren, had many descendants

11134. Hannah Childs born 7-29-1720, married 3-6-1748 Prince Taylor
of Lebanon CT

11135. Thomas Childs born 9-10-1725

11136. Benjamin Childs born 12-4-1727, died early, married Rebecca,
daughter of Stephen Davis of Barnstable, removed to Portland,
ME; had Thomas, Isaac, & Rebecca, all of whom died early.
Benj.'s widow left her estate to her siblings in Barnstable.

11137. Mary Childs born 4-1-1733

INSERT ADDITION: I, p 25 (RJG)
Children of Ebenezer Childs (1116.)
& Hope (_____) Childs:

11161. Elizabeth Childs born 7-18-1720, died 9-18-1720

11162. *Ebenezer Childs Jr born 4-10-1723, married 1st 1-15-1745
Hannah (1582.) born 10-10-1718, died 2-23-1755 age 37;
daughter of Hannah (Hall) & Ebenezer Crocker; he married 2d
1756 Abigail Freeman

11163. Richard Childs baptized 8-1-1725

11164. Mary Childs baptized 9-3-1727, died 6-15-1762

11165. Mercy Childs baptized 1-4-1730

INSERT ADDITION: I, p 25 (RJG, AO, PB)
Children of James Childs (1118.)
  & Elizabeth (Crocker) (1425.) Childs:

11181. *Samuel Childs born 7-15-1723, died 11-29-1784, married Mary
Hinckley born 4-12-1729, died 3-16-1793, daughter of Phoebe
(Holmes) & Thomas Hinckley

11182. *James Childs born 4-22-1725, died 4-3-1772, married 6-5-1755
Mary Parker born 1733, died 5-26-1796, daughter of David
Parker Esq

11183. Elizabeth Childs born 12-20-1730, died @ 1754, married
5-19-1748 Daniel Crocker (145(10).) born 3-1-1725/6, died
11-12-1788, son of Mary (Hinckley) & Dea John Crocker.

11184. Sarah Childs born 4-9-1736, died of small pox 12-16-1796,
married 5-2-1754 Dea Jonathan Crocker (145(12).) born 11-22-
1731, died of small pox 12-4-1796

11185. Thankful Childs born 8-4-1741, married 3-27-1760 Joseph
Lawrence of Sandwich

11186. Richard Childs born 3-22-1743/4, died 5-22-1805 unmarried.

INSERT ADDITIONS & CORRECTIONS: I, p 26 (GA)
11272. *Abigail Crocker, born Barnstable 9-19-1724, died probably East
Haddam CT about 1771, married 1st Colchester CT 2-23-1744 John
Williams born probably Colchester CT 7-22-1718, died
6-17-1754; she married 2d 4-23-1755 Enoch Arnold

SPECIAL NOTE: Author's request: Ref: Hinckley Family Bible. Any clues
about Reuben Crocker's forebears will be appreciated. There were
at least two Reuben Crocker's and there may have been a third.
Mary (Polly) Bassett's lineage is also unknown. Oliver Hinckley's
bible records the death of Polly Bassett and newspaper clippings
record parentage of Louisa Crocker at the time of her marriage to
Oliver Hinckley. BLANK. serves as an ID number. (AL)

INSERT ADDITION: I, p 30, (JG, PB, PC Vol II, p 270 & 372, 1860 cens.)
BLANK. Reuben Crocker born before 1777, died 3-16-1860, married 1st
Mary/Polly Bassett?, died 4-11-1825; he married 2d Widow Susan
Childs

CORRECTION: I, p 30 (FF)
11532. *Desire Crocker born 8-9-1727, died 1-22-1804, married
10-3-1747 Cornelius Sampson born 1726, died 3-1-1796, son of
Rebecca (Cooke) & Benjamin Samson

INSERT ADDITIONS & CORRECTIONS: I, p 30 (LGW),
14211. *Noah Crocker born 9-12-1724, died Lee MA 4-10-1807, married
Falmouth MA 1-29-1756 Content Davis born 10-12-1729, died Lee
MA 7-23-1794 daughter of Bathsheba (Smith) & Jedidiah Davis

IINSERT ADDITIONS & CORRECTIONS: I, p 32 (CFC)
Children of Benjamin Crocker (142(10).)
& Abigail (Jenkins) Crocker: (Abigail, born Falmouth MA)

142(10)1.*Joseph Crocker Dea born 4-15-1746, died 7-3-1825, married
Mary Hinckley born 8-9-1748/9, died 7-24-1841, daughter of
Sarah (Howland) & Edmond Hinckley (who married 12-6-1744.)
[Sarah Howland was daughter of Isaac Howland born West
Barnstable 7-23-1689, died there 11-8-1751, married
5-15-1719 Elizabeth Jennings.]

142(10)2. Benjamin Crocker Jr born 9-17-1749

142(10)3. Timothy Crocker born 10-3-1751

142(10)4. Abigail Crocker born 11-19-1753

142(10)5. Bathsheba Crocker born 11-11-1755

142(10)6. Peter Crocker born 1-11-1758

142(10)7. Josiah Crocker born 4-17-1760

INSERT ADDITION: I, p 33 (PC, Vol II p 193)
14326. *Thomas Crocker born 1-23-1740, died ?, married Reliance
(Goodspeed) born 6-29-1746, daughter of Reliance (Tobey) &
Jabez Goodspeed

INSERT ADDITION: I, p 36 (FF)
145(10)9. *Temperance Crocker born 7-28-1776, died 1-5-1812, married
See   *Ezra Crocker born Cotuit MA 3-21-1775, died 10-18-1858, son
15841.4.   of Sylvia (Thacher) (17244.) & Alvan F (15841.) Crocker

INSERT ADDITION: I, p 38
Loring Crocker I (14(10)49.) - From A Pilgrim Returns to Cape Cod,
Edward Rowe Snow, The Yankee Publishing Co, Boston MA, 1946

"The greatest advance in salt-making came with Loring Crocker's
Common Fields Salt Works at Barnstable. Crocker built a water
reservoir which automatically fed the various vats. Three of the
seven vats he called the first, second, and third water rooms.
The next three were the pickle rooms, and the last, the salt
room. Epsom Salts and Glauber Salts were both by-products of the
process. Prices per bushel went as high as 82 cents, and at one
time the sum of two million dollars was invested in Cape Cod salt
works. Outside competition, unfortunately for the Cape's
industry, ruined the trade, and one by one the salt works were
given up and their lumber sold for building purposes elsewhere."

INSERT ADDITION: I, p 39 (SL, EMcN)
Children of Thankful (Crocker) Morse (1525.)
& Capt Theodore Morse:

15251. Chloe Morse born 1-17-1740, died 9-16-1760

15252. Micah Morse born 12-1-1741, died young

15253. Asarelah Morse (Rev) born 1-17-1745; removed to Granville, NS,
died there, married Hepsebeth Ball

15254. *Susannah Morse born 7-21-1746, died 6-16-1829, married at
Falmouth MA 1-5-1769, her step brother, Benjamin Phinney
(17551.) born Barnstable MA 1744, died Lexington MA 1843, son
of Susanna (Davis) & Zaccheus Phinney Sr (1755.) [Susanna
(Davis) Phinney married 2d 1763 Theodore Morse, his 2d wife,
making Benjamin Phinney (17551.) step-brother to Susannah
Morse (15254.), both Crocker descendants.]

Benjamin (17551.) and Susannah (Morse) Phinney moved to Nova
Scotia during the Revolutionary War. Some of their children,
among them Elias born 1778, died 1849, were born in Nova Scotia.
After the war the family moved from Nova Scotia to Lexington MA.

INSERT ADDITION: I, p 39 - HISTORY OF ROPES FIELD, COTUIT (JG)
Ebenezer Crocker (15843.) inherited Ropes Field in Cotuit which,
according to James Gould, Historian (27 July 1995), had been
granted in 1708 to his grandfather Ebenezer (158.) and his great
uncle Josiah Crocker (157.). The field has been farmland since
the first European settlement in the area. In the Proprietors'
Records of 1708 the area is called "Attaquin's field," so it was
probably farmed by a member of that Indian family that later ran
the famous Attaquin Hotel in Mashpee.

The field was part of the farm of Major Ebenezer Crocker who, in
1783-1793, built the first house in nearby Cotuitport; he was a
state representative and a major in the Revolution. On his death
his son, Rev Nathan (Nathaniel Bourne Crocker (15843.2.), Providence minister and trustee of Brown University, inherited the property. Later the farm went to his brother, Braddock (15843.3.)
who built the first wharf and store at the foot of the land. His
daughter, Mary Bourne Crocker (15843.31), married Capt Alexander
Scudder, Cotuit's first postmaster. He went off to the Gold Rush
in 1849, after selling the land to the village's first summer
resident, Samuel Hooper.

It was Hooper who built the yellow farmhouse. Under him this field was part of the farm worked by farmer William Webb and his son, James. Deeds of this era refer to the area nearby as the orchard field without telling the crop which was probably apples. Hooper was for many years U.S. Representative in Washington and entertained many national figures including cabinet members and Senator Charles Sumner. On Hooper's death in 1874 his daughter, Isabella Balfour, who lived in Scotland, inherited the farm. She rented it to General "Jack" Reed, a Republican party leader.

In 1893 Isabella Balfour sold the field and farm to Elizabeth Jackson Lowell, daughter of one of the founding editors of The New York Times. She gave her name to the Cotuit High School, the Ball Park, and Lowell Avenue. On her death in 1904 the farm went to her daughter, Alice Ropes, wife of Harvard Divinity School Professor James Hardy Ropes. Under the Ropes family the field was farmed until 1932 by John B Morton, a farmer from western Massachusetts. Fred Gordon (see 16346.6612.) was the last farmer, from 1932-1964, when this was part of the Ropes Chicken Farm.

Since 1964 the field has been mowed regularly and used occasionally as pasturage for horses. The Cotuit Mosquito Yacht Club has used it as a refuge for boats during hurricanes. In 1996, by popular subscription, the field was acquired and placed in perpetual conservation under the Mary Barton Trust of Cotuit.

The Historical Commission of the Town of Banstable has designated the Ropes farm as one of the two last remaining complete farms in the town, a rare relic of the era when farming and fishing were the mainstays of life on Cape Cod. -- James W Gould

References: Cotuit Historical Paper #8 (1957); National Register for Cotuit CTB 41, LR5; Proprietors Records, p 74.

INSERT ADDITION: I, p 40 (CFC)
15846. *Kenelm Sunday Crocker b Barnstable 8-14-1757, died 6-8-1797, married Falmouth MA 11-24-1785 Martha Bourne, born Falmouth MA 12-19-1760, died 2-8-1837, daughter of Persis (Davis) & John Bourne V of Falmouth MA

INSERT ADDITION: I, p 41 (PH)
16325. *Bursley Crocker married Mary/Molly Pitcher born 1755 died
Marstons Mills Oct 1849

NOTE-Charles F Crocker (16346.6631.) & (17181.6211.) Marstons Mills MA
has supplied a great deal of additional information. His sources,
like most in this book, are family records as well as census and
local Vital Records. He descends from three of Deacon William's
sons: Job (14.), Eleazer (16.) & Sgt Joseph Crocker (17.).
NOTE: When a female Crocker descendant marries a male Crocker
descendant the male's I.D.# is used for their children.

INSERT ADDITION: I p 41 (CFC)
16333. Deborah Crocker born 3-30-1745, married 5-2-1765 Nye Jones
born 2-10-1741, died Nantucket MA 3-8-1837, son of Mariah/Mary
(Fuller) & Jedidiah Jones

INSERT ADDITIONS: I, p 42 (JRC, CS)
16337. Jonathan Crocker born 3-23-1756, died 12-8-1835, married
6-26-1820 Clarissa Fowler born 1778 of Renssalaer NY

16341. Ansel Crocker I born 8-27-1739 married Mercy Meiggs

16343. *Thomas Crocker Capt born 9-19-1743, died 11-9-1800 married
Jane ____, died 7-5-1795; had daughter Ruth born @ 1804, died
9-13-1825, by a 2d marriage.

INSERT ADDITION: I, p 42 (JRC, CS) (*P- = probably!)
Children of John (Cape Breton) (1635.)
& Mary (Bursley) Crocker:

16351.*Francis Crocker born @ 1753, died 4-24-1815, married 2d Abigail
(?) born @ 1773, died 3-6-1849, both bur W Barnstable MA

*P-16352. *Mary/Marcy/Mercy Crocker born 10-30-1756, died Lee MA
(See   3-18/28-1795, married Paul Ewers born Sandwich MA 9-9-1752,
14212.1.) died Dryden Twp, Tompkins Co NY 7-17-1835, his 1st wife

16353.   Abraham Crocker 4-6-1758

16354.   Anna Crocker born 8-13-1760

INSERT ADDITION: I, p 43 (JRC)
Children of Joseph Crocker I (1671.)
 & ?   (   ) Crocker:

16711. *Joseph Crocker II born Willington CT 12-21-1753, died there
        10-5-1776, married Willington 12-21-1775 Zerviah Case born
        Tolland CTY 11-2-1756, daughter of Ensign William Case. She
        married 2d Willington CT 9-24-17789 Nathaniel Fenton

INSERT ADDITION: I, p 43 (SCR)
Children of Benjamin Crocker (1672.)
 & Elizabeth (Fenton) Crocker:

16721. to 1672(11). Brothers Seth, Nathaniel, & Eleazer moved to
        Cambridge, Washington Cty NY, after the Revolution. Eleazer later
        moved to the Hill farm in Saddle Mountain, now White Creek NY

16723. *Eleazer III born Tolland CT 4-10-1754, died Cambridge NY
        9-10-1820 of typhoid fever, married Cambridge NY 6-26-1777
        Susannah Hinckley born Cambridge NY 11-30-1755 (twin of John
        who died 12-25-1755). She died there NY 6-28-1836, daughter of
        Susannah (Harris?) & John Hinckley.

Eleazer Crocker III served during the Revolution at the battles
of Bunker Hill, Concord, Lexington, and Saratoga; he was at New
York when the British evacuated that city. He was a sentry at the
foot of Bunker Hill the night the earthworks were being built. In
the morning upon discovery of the works, the bombardment began;
the British fired over his head. When New York City was captured
by the British, Eleazer and a companion, both sick with fever,
were hidden by friends in a "meat box" until after dark, then
taken in a small boat to the New Jersey shore. His companion died
before they reached safety. In NJ a Dutchman cared for Eleazer.

Among Susannah (Hinckley) & Eleazer's children (genealogies dis-
agree on names & number), Francis (16723.4.) is consistently
listed. Siblings: Judith, (Mrs. McNitt); Roena, (Mrs Eliahim
Akin); Elizabeth; Benjamin; Eleazer; Athela; Vorania; and Betsey.

[Susannah (Harris?) Hinckley born 2-23-1720, died 12-19-1813, married Falmouth MA 9-13-1742 John, son of Mary (Goodspeed) & Ichabod Hinckley; they had 13 children.]

HINCKLEY FAMILY: The earliest recorded Hinckley was Robert Henkele, born Lenham, County Kent, England. The family had lived there since 1300. Robert Henkele of Lenham left a will dated 1522. His son was John Henkle; while no will was found for him, the will of his son, John Hynckleye of Harrietsham, born about 1512, was dated 1577.

John Hynckleye married Johane (?) and had one daughter and two sons; the younger son, Robert, born 1537 at Harrietsham, England, died 1606/7. He had three children by his 1st wife, Elizabeth. By his 2d, a widow, Mrs Katherine Lease, born @ 1550, died about 1606, whom he married on 10-2-1575, he had eight children of whom Samuel born 1589, died 1662, was fifth son. At his death Robert Hinckley, a gentleman with extensive holdings in the Harrietsham area, left Samuel and all his siblings with a good start in life.

Samuel Hinckley: Samuel's share of his father's estate helped him start his farm at Tenterden. It is most likely sale of this farm provided the necessary capital for adventure in the New World.

Samuel married in May 1617 Sarah Soole born Hawkhurst England 1600, died Barnstable MA 8-18-1656. Samuel & Sarah left England with their three daughters on ship HERCULES, Capt John Witherly, in March 1635, arriving Newton (now Cambridge MA) in May. Samuel Hinckley died Barnstable MA 10-31-1662. They had eight more children subsequent to coming to the New World. Among them were John, father of Susannah Hinckley who married Eleazer Crocker III and Thomas, who became Governor of Plymouth Colony.
(Hinckley notes derived from records of SCR.)

INSERT ADDITION: I, p 43 (JRC)
Children of Rebecca (Crocker) Dunham (1691.)
& Silvanus Dunham:

16911. Patience Dunham born 1740, married Perez Shaw

16912. Israel Dunham born 1740, married Hannah Whiting

16913. Sylvanus Dunham born 1744, married Mary Tribble

16914. Rebecca Dunham born 1745, married John Chase

16915. Dimron Dunham born 1747, married Lydia Shaw

16916. Silas Dunham born 1749, married 1st Mary Tilson,
married 2d Lydia Poldon

16917. Susanna Dunham born 1751, married Arthur Cobb

16918. Elijah Dunham born 1753, married Eunice Thomas

16919. Isaac Dunham born 1755, died 5-18-1776

1691(10). Molly Dunham born 1757, married John Morton

1691(11). Asa Dunham born 1759, married Lydia Cobb

1691(12). Eleazer Dunham born 1761, married Jane Bryant

INSERT ADDITIONS: I, p 44. (TC, JRC)
16927.   *Rhonda Crocker born _____, married Plympton MA 11-20-1777,
(See   her 1st cousin Daniel Perry born 5-16-1752, died 1828, son
16961.) of Sarah (Crocker) (1696.) & Elijah Perry

16928. *Rowland (Roland) Crocker born Carver MA 4-8-1757, died Conway
NH 2-8-1839, married 1-16-1781 Mehitable Merrill born 1756,
died Conway NH 10-31-1836, daughter of Sarah (Hazen) & Capt
Nathaniel Merrill. Rowland served in Revolutionary War.

16929. Susannah Crocker born 2-13-1762, married Plympton MA
        11-20-1783 Lt Lemuel Cole of Carver MA, son of Ruth
        (Sampson) & Joseph Cole.

1692(10). Infant died /

Children of Daniel Crocker (1692.) (JRC)
   & Abigail (Roberts) Crocker:

1692(11). Elijah Crocker

1692(12). *Daniel Crocker born Yarmouth N.S.CAN 3-16-1767, married
           1795 Elizabeth Dennis, daughter of Sarah (Grant) & Ambrose
           Dennis of Marblehead MA & Yarmouth N.S. CAN

1692(13). Abigail Crocker born 7-22-1768, died 1837, married Yarmouth
           NS CAN 11-12-1789 James Frost of Argyle NS 1756, died 1825

1692(14). Eleazer Crocker born 6-20-1769

1692(15). Hannah Crocker born 10-3-1770, married 1st Yarmouth NS CAN
           4-28-1791 Capt Ezekiel Ellis, son Ebenezer Ellis; married
           2d John Rogers, son Cornelius Rogers, brother of Benjamin
           who married her sister Deborah

1692(16). Lydia Crocker born 3-7-1772

1692(17). *Sarah Crocker born 12-25-1774, died 1-11-1865, married
           Capt John Valpey

1692(18). Deborah Crocker died 9-20-1858, married 1801 Capt Benjamin
           Rogers, son of Cornelius Rogers, brother of John who
           married her sister Hannah

1692(19). Mary Crocker died 1-24-1862, married 4-27-1796 Capt Philip
           Hemeon, died 1860, son of Capt Philip Hemeon

1692(20).*Joseph Crocker born Yarmouth N.S. CAN 8-23-1781, died
           6-16-1869, married Sarah Porter, daughter of Nehemiah Porter

INSERT ADDITION: I, p 45 (JRC, NA)
Children of Mary (Crocker) Savery (1694.)
  & Dea Thomas Savery:

16941. Samuel Savery

16942. Nathan Savery

16943. Isaac Savery

INSERT ADDITION: I, p 45 (DL, JRC)
Children of Joseph Crocker (1697.)
  & Relief (Lovell) Crocker:

16971. Relief Crocker born @ 1762/6, married Abner Highland

Children of Joseph Crocker (1697.)
  & Margaret (Jackson) Crocker:

16972. *Abel Crocker born Plympton MA 3-16-1768, died St Albans ME
        6-8-1840, married 1-1-1800 Lydia Bates, died 1-5-1870,
        daughter of Aquilla (Braley) & Solomon Bates of Hanover MA.

        Abel Crocker, a pioneer of Greene ME, was in Greene as a teenager
        prior to the town's incorporation in 1788. He ran the grist mill,
        known as Crocker's Mills, on Allen Stream. His was the first
        grist mill in town, erected by or shortly before 1786. It carried
        two sets of stones and did a good business. He removed to
        St. Albans in 1830.

Children of Joseph Crocker (1697.)
  & Deborah (Ransom) Crocker:

16973. *Warren Crocker born N Yarmouth ME 10-25-1775, died Wayne ME
        9-19-1844, married Polly (?) born Winthrop ME 6-7-1785, died
        Wayne ME 4-30-1866

16974. Joseph Jr born

16975. James

INSERT ADDITIONS: I, p 46 (JRC)
17117. Benjamin Blish bpt 7-18-1742, married Susannah Baxter

17141. William Crocker b 2-6-1744, died young   )
                                                    (reversed)
17142. Mary Crocker born 3-25-1745, married Enoch Kembly)

INSERT ADDITION: I, p 47 (JRC)
Children of Alice (Crocker) Beals (1715.)
   & Stephen Beals Sr:

17151. Stephen Beals Jr born 11-13-1737

17152. Alice Beals born 11-2-1739

17153. Abner Beals born 9-13-1741, died 12-9-1742

17154. Hannah Beals born 6-261743, died 1745/46

17155. Abner Beals born 7-28-1745

INSERT ADDITION: I, p 50 (RJG, PC Vol II, p 289-90)
Children of Temperance (Phinney) Fuller (1751.)
   & James Fuller:

17511. *Martha Fuller (MAYFLOWER) born 1734, died 10-3-1808, married
         12-24-1761 James Lovell II born 1732, died 4-20-1816, son of
         Abigail (Gorham) & James Lovell I. Buried Osterville MA (PB)

INSERT ADDITION: I, p & 50 (SL, EMcN)
Children of Zaccheus Phinney II (1755.)
& Susanna (Davis) Phinney:

17551. Benjamin Phinney born 1744, died Lexington MA 1843, married
        Falmouth MA his step-sister, Susannah (Morse) born 7-21-1746,
        died 6-16-1829, daughter of Thankful (Crocker) (1525.) &
        Theodore Morse.

17552. *Timothy Phinney born 1746, died 1838, married Barnstable MA
        3-23-1767 Temperance Hinckley born 1748, died 1825, daughter
        of Mehitable (Sturgis) & Ebenezer Hinckley II. [Ebenezer
        Hinckley was born 1712, son of Ebenezer I and grandson of
        Mary (Fitzrandolph) & Samuel Hinckley II; his wife Mehitable
        (Sturgis) Hinckley was born 1720, died 1773.]

17553. Barnabas Phinney born 1748

17554. Zaccheus Phinney III born 1751

(This page purposely left blank)

NOTES

Sixth Generation:

INSERT ADDITION: I, p 51 (RJG)
Children of David Childs (11131.)
& Hannah (Cobb) Childs:

11131. *David Childs born 2-7-1735/6, married 4-4-1758 Hannah Davis,
1.   daughter of Mary (Phinney) & Job Davis. [Mary (Phinney) Davis
     born ___, daughter of Susannah (Linnell) Phinney born 1673 &
     Ebenezer Phinney born 1674. Job Davis born 1700, died 1751,
     son of Hannah (Linnell) born 1660 & Dolar Davis born 1660,
     died 1710.]

11131. Jonathan Childs born 12-25-1737, married 3-19-1787 Thankful
2.   Howland. Removed to Sandwich MA

11131.3. Asenath Childs born 2-28-1738/0, married _____ Linnell

11131.4. Anna Childs born 8-18-1742, died unmarried

11131. Josiah Childs born 9-7-1745, married 1st Temperance Lewis,
5.   daughter of George Lewis. After she died he married 2d
     Abigail, daughter of Nathaniel Sturgis.

Josiah Childs was with his uncle, Capt James Churchill, in the
French War and, during the Revolution, was one of the Home Guard
detailed for the defense of the coast. Although entitled to a
pension, he did not obtain it. He was employed fifteen winters in
trading voyages to the Carolinas. (AO, page 186)

11131. Edward Childs born 9-13-1749, married Mary, daughter of Seth
6.   Lothrop.

Edward Childs was employed for many years by the eccentric
Abner Hersey who, in one of his early wills, named Edward to
receive 100 Ls. The doctor asked Edward how he intended to use
the bequest; Edward's response "fit out my daughters and marry
them off," displeased the doctor who could not tolerate even
neatness in dress; indignant, he altered his will, and Edward
lost the money. (AO page 187)

INSERT ADDITION: I, p 51 (RJG)
Children of Ebenezer Childs Jr (11162.)
   & Hannah (Crocker) (1582.) Childs:

11162.1. Ebenezer Childs III born 11-3-1747, bpt West Church 11-9-1747

11162.2. Josiah Childs born 8-8-1749

11162.3. Hannah Childs born 9-10-1751

11162.4. David Childs born 3-2-1754

Children of Ebenezer Childs Jr (11162.)
   & Abigail (Freeman) Childs:

11162.5. Jonathan Childs born 5-13-1757

11162.6. Abigail Childs born 12-26-1758

11162.7. Hope Childs born 1-21-1761

11162.8. Mary Childs baptized 4-10-1763

Children of Samuel Childs (11181.)
   & Mary (Hinckley) Childs:

11181.1. Samuel Childs Jr born 7-7-1753

11181.   Elijah Childs bpt 10-21-1764, died 12-20-1828, married
  2.   11-10-1785 Mary Gorham born 9-11-1766, daughter of Thomas
       Gorham born 8-13-1728 & his 2d wife, Widow Rebecca Jones of
       Yarmouth, married 1765 (AO p.444). Elijah & Mary had Samuel
       Childs (Dea) and other children. Elijah was for many years
       master of the Barnstable and Boston packet sloop ROMEO.

11181.3. Ebenezer Childs born 1-18-1766, died unmarried

INSERT ADDITION: I, p 51 (RJG)
Children of James Childs (11182.)
  & Mary (Parker) Childs:

11182.1. Elizabeth Childs born 5-6-1756

11182.2. Daniel Childs baptized 8-10-1760

11182.3. Mary Childs baptized 2-15-1761

11182.3. Sarah Childs baptized 12-30-1764

11182.4. James Childs baptized 5-24-1767

INSERT ADDITION: I, p 51 (GA)
Children of Abigail (Crocker) Williams (11272.)
  & John Williams:

11272. *Anne Williams born Colchester CT 3-22-1753, died Union, Broome
1.   Cty NY 12-25-1815 (obit: Owego Gazette 1-2-1816), married
       3-30-1775 (or 4-1-1775) Amos Patterson born Watertown MA
       1-19-1749, died Union, Broome Cty NY 3-5-1817, son of Lydia
       (Marean) & Joseph Patterson (Sources: Patterson genealogies)

       Amos Patterson served in the Revolution with the state militia
       for short periods. He was a partner in the "Boston Purchase Co,"
       organized to buy a huge tract of land in New York. Anne Williams'
       ancestry includes four "Mayflower" ancestors.

INSERT ADDITION: I, p 51 (AL)
Children of Reuben Crocker Sr (blank.)
 & Mary/Polly (Bassett?) Crocker:

blank. *Louisa Crocker born Cotuit MA 11-19-1797, died Osterville MA
  1.   8-20-1881, married Cotuit MA Oliver Hinckley, born Centerville
        MA 4-10-1792, died Osterville MA 10-5-1888, son of Eunice
        (Goodspeed) & Prince Hinckley. She descended from Roger Good-
        speed; he, from Samuel Hinckley I.

Oliver Hinckley spent his boyhood at the home of his parents near
Great Pond (Wequaquet Lake) in Centerville MA. As a youth he ap-
prenticed to Jesse Crosby, carpenter, who turned out small boats
for local fishermen. His boat shop was located on the shore of
North Bay in Osterville, where he, his sons, and generations of
their descendants continued small-boat construction long after
Jesse Crosby Sr's death in 1804. In fact, until the late 1980's
Crosbys operated boat yards in Osterville.

Oliver Hinckley learned his trade from Jesse Crosby Jr who encouraged the younger man to establish his own shipyard. Oliver
bought bay-front property just north of the Crosby shops and
began building vessels much larger than those of the Crosbys;
on the brow of the hill just above his shed he built a house.

The best route to Nantucket Sound from Hinckley's yard was around
the north end of an island which lay between the villages of
Osterville and Cotuit, through Cotuitport harbor, and out the
natural break in the barrier beach where Mills River drained into
the sea. In 1817, at the age of 25 years, Oliver married Louisa
Crocker, daughter of Mary and Reuben Crocker of Cotuitport. The
young couple moved to Bay Street, Osterville, to occupy their new
house that, to this day, overlooks the Crosby yards to the south
and North Bay to the west. There, only a few steps from his
dooryard, Oliver Hinckley built sea-going vessels for thirty
years, while Louisa raised a large family of children.

Between 1817 and 1845 Hinckley's shipyard launched 23 vessels; three were brigs designed for foreign voyages; the rest schooners for the coasting trade. A preserved roll, written in Mr Hinckley's hand, is probably typical of what records would show for similar yards in other villages of Barnstable--indeed in most New England coastal towns. This is the list giving date built, type of ship, name, tonnage, and for whom it was built)

1817	schooner	HALLETT	60 tons	
1818	schooner	GLIDE	75 tons	
1819	schooner	LOUISA	80 tons	
1821	sloop	ECHO	100 tons, George Lovell	
1822	brig	RANGER	160 tons, Joseph Eldredge	
1824	schooner	MIRROR	110 tons, Z D Bassett	
1825	brig	CALO	160 tons, Thomas Percival	
1827	schooner	ALPHIM ... 55 tons, Isaac Hodges		
1828	schooner	TALENT	80 tons, John Cammett	
1829	schooner	BALANCE	70 tons, Z D Bassett, Matthew Cobb, and George Lovell	
1831	schooner	PAGE	150 tons, Z D Bassett	
1833	schooner	FRANK	68 tons, Samuel Wiley	
1834	brig	CORINNA	200 tons, Z D Bassett, Matthew Cobb, and George Lovell	
1835	schooner	OLIVER	106 tons, David Fuller	
1836	schooner	MARINER	92 tons, Freeman Adams	
1837	schooner	LOUISA	101 tons, Lot Hinckley	
1839	schooner	AUGUSTA	87 tons, Leander Nickerson	
1839	schooner	SPY	69 tons, Jonathan Parker	
1840	schooner	UTICA	89 tons, Andros Bearse	
1842	schooner	COTUIT	for David Nickerson	
1845	schooner	EARL	for Benjamin Hinckley	

Uncounted Barnstable mariners of an earlier century shipped aboard vessels that sailed from port never to be heard from again. Barnstable's old town and church records reveal the sad frequency of "lost at sea." The ships Oliver Hinckley built proved as vulnerable as any others, despite the prudent care and quality workmanship performed in his yard.

Hyannis Captain Simeon Baxter, whose wife and three small children awaited his return, took command of the fine new Hinckley brig, CORINNA, in 1834. Captain Baxter, then but 31 years old, was also made part owner of the new ship. They brought her around to Hyannis, rigged her out, and shipped her crew. Cleared for a foreign port, the CORINNA sailed out of Hyannis harbor one fine June day, a spanking north wind filling her new white sails. Never reported, she made no port save that of missing men.

On a lighter note Captain Thomas Percival of Barnstable had a new brig, the CALO, 160 tons, built for himself in 1825 at Oliver Hinckley's yard. According to a well-circulated story of the time, Captain Percival set out to name her CALHOUN after John C Calhoun, then vice-president of the United States, but, after receiving news of Calhoun's "undignified course" as president of the Senate, Percival ordered the painter, who had gotten as far as "C A L" in lettering the brig's name, to add only the letter "O" and let it stand. So widely did this story circulate that Captain Percival published a denial of its truth in the Barnstable County Gazette in 1826 -- which is how we know of it.

Oliver Hinckley celebrated his 96th birthday 4-10-1888; at his death he was survived by five of his seven children (two of whom were Methodist Episcopal ministers), 30 grandchildren, and 24 great grandchildren, all of whom are Crocker descendants.

blank.2. infant born 10-19-1798, died

blank.3. *Bassett [MAYBE BETSY B? - (NA)] Crocker born 10-25-1800

blank.4. Bassett Crocker born 6-1-1809, died 7-1-1809

blank.   Reuben Crocker Jr born 1810, died 1889, married 1st 1827
  5.   Temperance Crocker died 1840; had Phoebe born 9-14-1837 & Sarah born 2-14-1839; married 2d 1844 Dorcas H Childs born 1817, died 12-11-1868; had son Anacosta & daughter Rosemary.

blank. *Ignatius Crocker born 6-6-1813, died 10-17-1881, married 1st
6.   Osterville MA 1834 Mehitable West, born 6-15-1815, died
8-3-1851, daughter of Hannah (Saunders) & Stephen West;
married 2d Mary (West) born 11-28-1817, died 8-1-1890 (PB)

blank.7.   Bassett Crocker born 4-13-1816

INSERT ADDITION & CORRECTION: I, p 52 (FF)
Children of Desire (Crocker) Sampson (11532.)
  & Cornelius Sampson:

11532.1. *Crocker Sampson born 4-29-1749, died 1823, Harvard 1771,
married 6-27-1784 Rebecca Hawley born 1762, died 1844

11532.2. Joseph Sampson born 2-10-1751

11532.3. Rabedsah (Robediah) Sampson born 10-2-1752, died 12-17-1779

11532. *Josiah Sampson Esq born 5-9-1753, died 7-14-1829, bur Marstons
4.   Mills Cem, married 1st Mary Crocker born 1759, died 3-16-1795;
married 2d Sarah born 1755, died 2-12-1844

11532.5. Priscilla Sampson born 12-28-1755, died 9-20-1776
11532.6. Anne Sampson born 2-16-1758, died 10-2-1836
11532.7. Lucy Sampson born 10-29-1763, married 1783 Thomas Jackson
11532.8. Cornelius Sampson Jr born 12-7-1771, died 6-23-1794
11532.9. Desire Sampson born 1-22-1776, died 12-18-1828

INSERT ADDITION: I, p 53 (LGW)
Children of Noah Crocker (14211.)
  & Content (Davis) Crocker:

14211. *Ruth Crocker born Sandwich MA 10-23-1759, died Mt Morris NY
1.   6-24-1837, married (prob 1776) John Percival II born Sandwich
MA 11-6-1754, died Gaines NY 6-13-1837, son of Lydia (Fuller)
& John Percival I. John Percival II of Lee MA served in the
Revolutionary War. Lydia Fuller was a MAYFLOWER descendant.
(See Addenda re Percival; II, p C-1 through C-10.)

John Percival II descended from James Percival, first of the name in New England, who settled in Sandwich in 1670, and whose son John married Mary Bourne. John Percival II, within a month of the outbreak of the War of Independence, (Battles of Lexington & Concord, 4-19-1775), enlisted at Lenox MA 5-16-1775 as a private in Capt Goodrich's Company, Col John Paterson's MAssachusetts Regiment. He was at the Battle of Bunker Hill (6-17-1775) and volunteered in the same company under Col Benedict Arnold's expedition to Quebec, fought in the Battle of Quebec, and joined the retreat through Montreal, Crown Point and Ticonderoga to reach home in June 1776. He and Ruth Crocker probably married later that year or early in 1777.

In June 1777 John Percival II re-enlisted for six months in Capt Rowley's Company, Col Ashley's Massachusetts Regiment; he was a guard at the Battle of Saratoga 9-19-1777 and again at Saratoga when American troops defeated Burgoyne's invasion from Canada. Burgoyne surrendered his entire force of about 5,000 men 10-17-1777, the first major American Victory in the Revolutionary War. John remained at Lee MA until 1798 when he moved to Sherburne, Chenango Cty, NY; he purchased land in 1799 in the part of that town which split in the early 1800s and became Smyrna. He was one of the first deacons of the newly organized (1824) First Congregational Church of Smyrna NY.

(This John Percival is not to be confused with Captain John "Mad Jack" Percival born West Barnstable MA 4-3-1779, died 9-17-1862, son of Mary (Snow) of Harwich & Capt John Percival of Barnstable, although they were probably quite closely related.)

INSERT ADDITION: I, p 53, (CS) (See (16352.), II, p 20)
14212. *Susannah Hamblin born Barnstable MA 2-15-1765, died Tompkins
2.   Co NY 5-22-1820, married Lee MA 2-18-1796 Paul Ewer born
        Sandwich MA 9-9-1752, died Tompkins Co NY, his 2d wife.

See   Paul's 1st wife was Marcy/Mary/Mercy Crocker whose parentage
(P-   is uncertain, but (1635.), q.v., is likely. After Marcy died
16352.) Paul married Susannah and they moved to Scipio, Cayuga Co, NY;
        later they moved to Dryden, Tompkins Co NY.

CORRECTION: I, p 56 & 74
14324. Lemuel Nye III (N-17638) born Barnstable MA 1780, died
8. 2-19-1830, married Temperance Crocker. Lemuel Nye III may have
    married a Temperance Crocker [as recorded, Nye Genealogy 1977
    (Vol I, p 230)] but she could not have been daughter of Martha
    (Nye) & Prince Crocker born 9-6-1772; his daughter Temperance
    born 1-24-1815, (not 1776), died 1839, probably unmarried.

Lemuel Nye Jr born 1733 married 10-25-1757 Rebecca Crocker born
11-30-1735, died 6-4-1817, daughter of Rebecca (Hamblen) & Thomas
Crocker. (NYE Genealogy, p 133)

Lemuel Nye Sr born 3-21-1698, married (intentions 4-30-1728)
Sarah Jenkins, born 12-1-1706, daughter of Experience (Hamblen) &
Thomas Jenkins (NYE Genealogy, p 91). Lemuel Nye I married 1737
another Sarah Jenkins, born 12-1-1706, daughter of Mary (Ellis),
of Middleboro & a different Thomas Jenkins. (AO II, p 97)

INSERT ADDITION: I, p 56 (JG, TAC, PC Vol II, p 193)
Children of Thomas Crocker (14326.)
& Reliance (Goodspeed) Crocker:

14326. *Lydia Crocker born 1773, died Nantucket 10-29 1846, married
1. 1795 Master Mariner Isaac Hodges Sr, born 1-2-1770, (1850
    Census, Nantucket MA) died 18__, son of Lydia (Phinney)
    Hinckley-Hodges & Hercules Hodges. Isaac Hodges Sr & Nymphas
    Hinckley were half-brothers. Isaac Hodges Sr married 2d at
    Nantucket 6-6-1847 Deborah (Chadwick) Coffin, widow of Andrew
    Coffin. Deborah was the daughter of Wickliffe Chadwick.

    Lydia (Phinney) Hinckley married 1st Benjamin Hinckley III. He
    died 4-15-1765, age 37. Their son, Nymphas, born 9-13-1753, died
    12-12-1832, married 10-16-1782 Chloe Jenkins. Both are buried
    Osterville, MA. A daughter, Abigail born 1756, died young.

INSERT ADDITION: 1, p 91 & 114 (JG)
    Hercules Hodges I born England 1743/4, died 6-20-1821, buried
    at Osterville MA. After coming to Cape Cod he married 10-26-1766
    at the East Parish Church in Barnstable MA Lydia (Phinney)
    Hinckley, widow of Benjamin Hinckley. Hercules's occupation was
    Mariner. He and Lydia were parents of Chloe Hodges who married
    Luther Crocker (See 17151.15.)]

    Papers supplied by James Gould, Barnstable Historical Commission,
    state: "In a book on 'Prisoners of War on the Old Ship JERSEY,'
    Hercules Hodges' name is listed three times. Someone wrote in the
    margin of that book, "Hercules ran away from London as a youth to
    ship to America. He served in the Revolution and may have been
    well off for he received no pension."

    Lydia Phinney born Centerville MA 7-21-1729, daughter of Reliance
    (Goodspeed)* & Thomas Phinney Jr, died after 1780 and before her
    father's will was probated in 1784. Hercules Hodges I probably
    married again; Lydia was age 37 and he, 23, when they married.

* Reliance Goodspeed born 9-18-1701, married 3-18-1726 Thomas
    Phinney Jr-- "The English ancestry of Roger Goodspeed of Barn-
    stable, Mass."--G Andrews Moriarty, Jr. (Register, October 1928)

    Nymphas Hinckley's half-brother, Capt Isaac Hodges Sr [son of
    Hercules Hodges I, above] born 1770, died ?, married 1795 Lydia
    Crocker (14326.1.) born 1773, died 1846, daughter of Reliance
    (Goodspeed) & Thomas Crocker. I, p 33 & above, (PC Vol II, p 193)

INSERT ADDITION: I, p 57
    Joseph W Crocker (145(10)7.3.) From Shipmasters of Cape Cod,
    Henry C Kittredge, Houghton Mifflin Co 1935; "Account of a voyage
    from Shanghai to New York in 80 days as shown by a journal kept
    by an anonymous Cape man who made the passage under Captain
    Joseph W Crocker and later held a master's ticket himself.
        "The ship Swordfish, Captain Joseph W Crocker, Master, left
    Shanghai December 12, 1859; was 11 days down the China Sea
    and out clear of Java Head; 55 days from Java Head to the

Equator west of the Cape of Good Hope; becalmed about the
Equator five days, gaining about 60 miles during the five
days; 14 days from that point to New York and anchored in
the North River at 2:30 A.M. March 2nd, 1860, 80 days from
Shanghai. ... During the passage passed 102 vessels. Sailed
16,122 nautical miles during the 80 days, and five of the
days made only 60 miles. Someone may say we could not get by
the quarantine in the night, but we did--called the Doctor
at 1:00 A.M. and paid the extra fee; and he let us pass,
thereby saving half a day." -- A Shipmaster.

NOTE-For the following information I thank Col Franklin W Fish of
Claremont CA, a MAYFLOWER descendant (Governor, Pomona Valley
Colony) and member of the John Howland Society. Col Fish has
traced his Fish lineage to the 1500s in England. Three Fish
brothers, Nathaniel (his ancestor), Jonathan & John landed at
Lynn MA in 1637, and that same year helped found Sandwich, the
first incorporated town on Cape Cod.

INSERT CORRECTIONS & ADDITIONS: I, p 58 (FF)
Children of Prince Crocker (145(10)8.)
  & Martha (Nye) (N-12713-1) Crocker:

145(10)8. *Bathsheba Crocker born Barnstable MA 4-20-1805, died
   1.   there 11-17-1836, married 11-6-1826 Franklin Fish born
            Barnstable MA 10-26-1801, died San Francisco CA 3-5-1876,
            son of Mary (Parker) & Heman Fish. [Mary Parker born Barn-
            stable MA 2-1-1777, died 5-8-1855, daughter Mercy (Jenkins)
            & Daniel Parker MD born 3-25-1734/5, died 2-18-1809, son of
            Mary (Hawes) born Yarmouth MA 3-23-1703/4 & David Parker
            born Barnstable 2-17-1700/01, died there 6-24-1788.]

            (See I, p 55, 14324.3. Asa Nye married Mercy Parker, sister
            of Mary Parker, wife of Heman Fish.)

145(10)8.2. Patience Wood Crocker born 2-4-1807

145(10)8.3. Nathan Nye Crocker born 12-30-1810, bur Yarmouth Cem

38

145(10)8.4. Temperance Crocker born 1-24-1815

INSERT ADDITION: I, p 63, (BWS)
Children of Abner Crocker (16324.)
  & Martha (Crocker) (17143.) Crocker:

16324.2. Sarah Crocker born 1779, married Benjamin Wright
          See 16324.21. See also 16344.32.

CORRECTION: Change ID#s from 16323. to 16325.
INSERT ADDITION & CORRECTIONS: I, p 62 & 63 (PH)
Children of Bursley Crocker (16325.)
  & Mary/Molly (Pitcher) Crocker:

16325.2. *Abigail Crocker born Barnstable 3-19-1782, died 6-1-1844,
See   married 6-20-1801 Shubael Hamblin Crocker (16344.2) born
16344.2. Marstons Mills MA 10-7-1779, died there 1-19-1846, son of
          Lydia (Hamblin) & Isaac Crocker III

INSERT ADDITION: I, p 63 (JRC)
Children of Thomas Crocker Capt (16343.)
  & Jane (?) Crocker: (Correct order unknown)

16343.1. Davis Crocker born @ 1773

16343.2. Thomas Crocker born @ 1782, died 5-15-1850, age 68

16343.3. Betsy Crocker married John Ryder of Barnstable

16343.3. Mary Crocker married Robert Bacon of Boston

16343.4. Anselm Crocker born @ between 1780-90

16343.5. Desire Crocker born between 1780-95

16343.6. Lucy Crocker born between 1780 and 1795

NOTE-CORRECTION & ADDITION: I, p 63 (PH)
Mr & Mrs Peter Hickman (Marion (Thomas) of Cotuit, MA, and her
sister, Mrs Hans Vos (Joan Thomas), descendants, and Mrs H Duncan
Shaw of New Jersey supply specifics of Crocker/Hamblin/Hinckley/
Scudder relationships in their families.

Children of Isaac Crocker III (16344.)
& Lydia (Hamblin) Crocker:

16344.2. *Shubael Hamblin Crocker born 10-7-1779, died 1-19-1846,
married 6-28-1801 Abigail Crocker (16325.2.) born 3-19-1782,
died 6-1-1844, daughter of Mary/Molly (Pitcher) & Bursley
Crocker. Both bur at Marstons Mills MA.

HAMBLEN FAMILY: AO notes on Hamblins: (variously spelled Hamblen,
Hamlen, Hamlin, Hamline, and Hamling), James I probably came
from London (See New England Historic & Genealogy Journal, David
Hamblen). James Hamblen I was an early member of Mr Lothrop's
church in Barnstable MA. His son, Bartholemew, was bpt 4-24-1642,
but baptisms of his older children, James and Hannah, do not
appear; they probably were born in England and came over later.

James Hamblen I was in Barnstable in 1639; he died 1690, naming
in his will his wife Anne and his sons James II, Bartholemew, and
his daughter Hannah. Also had John, Sarah, Eleazer, and Israel.

James Hamblen II (2, James 1) born probably in London, married
11-20-1662 Mary Dunham, probably the daughter of Dea John Dunham
of Plymouth. They had fourteen children; she died 4-19-1715.

Bartholemew Hamblen (2, James 1) served in King Philip's War,
married 1-20-1673, Susannah Dunham, perhaps sister of Mary, wife
of James Jr. They had ten children.

John Hamblen (2, James 1) married August 1667 Sarah, daughter of
Austin Bearse, had 9 daughters, 3 sons. He died 1718, age 73.

Eleazer Hamblin (2, James 1) also a soldier in King Philip's War, married 10-15-1675 Mehitable, daughter of John Jenkins; had six children born in Barnstable.

Israel Hamblin (2, James 1) born 6-25-1652 James's I youngest son born 6-25-1652, married 1st Abigail, perhaps a daughter of Joshua Lumbard. After five children she died about 1700; he married 2d Jemima ? and had three more children.

NOTE-Israel Hamblin & his 2d wife, Jemima, had a daughter, Ann, born 4-10-1706, married 1750 a Mr Tilson and moved to Middleboro. Descendants of the Hamblin families are, indeed, numerous.

INSERT ADDITION: I, p 65 (JRC)
Children of Francis Crocker (16351.)
  & Abigail (?) Crocker:

16351.1. Abigail Crocker born ?, married _____Russell

16351.2. Francis Crocker II born 1810, married Susan ____

16351.3. Erastus Crocker born @ 1813, died at sea 9-1-1831, age 18

INSERT ADDITION: I, p 65 (CS)
Children of Marcy/Mary/Mercy (Crocker) Ewers (P-16352.)
  & Paul Ewers:

P-16352.   John Crocker Ewers born Lee MA 9-2-1783, died Dryden Tp,
1.   Tompkins Co NY 7-12-1866, married Dryden Twp Tompkins Co
           NY 1825 Jane Talmadge

P-16352.   *Tillotson/Tilson Ewers born Lee MA 1785, died Unadilla Twp
2.   Livingston Co MI 1-15-1851, married Hannah (?) born @ 1783,
           died Unadilla Twp, Livingston Co MI 10-5-1848

P-16352.   Mary/Polly Busley/Bursley Ewers born Lee MA 1787, married
3.   Seneca Co NY 9-13-1827 Gilbert Honeywell

P-16352.4. Jane Ewers born Lee MA 6-7-1789, married _____ Chadwick

P-16352.5. Abigail/Nabby Ewers born Lee MA 1791, married ___Barber

P-16352. Martha Ewers born Lee MA 1793, married 1st ____ Halsey,
6.   married 2d _____Hart

P-16352. *Paul Ewers born Lee MA 3-18-1795, died Dryden Twp, Tompkins
7.   Co NY 7-2-1880, married Scipio Twp, Cayuga Co NY 12-29-1819
Alice Southmaid

INSERT ADDITION: I, p 65 (JRC)
Children of Theophilus Crocker (16621.)
& Mary/Polly (Allan) Crocker:

16621.1. Orion Lorenzo Crocker born @ 1785/6
16621.2. Theophilus Crocker born

INSERT ADDITION: I, p 65 (JRC)
Children of Joseph Crocker II (16711.)
& Zerviah (Case) Crocker:

16711.1. Joseph Crocker born Willington CT 9-12-1776

INSERT ADDITION: I, p 66 (SCR)
Children of Eleazer Crocker III (16723.)
& Susannah (Hinckley) Crocker:

16723. *Francis born at Willington CT 7-5-1790, died Culpepper VA
4.   12-10-1861, married Cambridge NY 10-11-1810 Anna Woodworth
born 11-15-1795, died Washington DC 3-9-1874, daughter of
Major Lott & Asenath Elizabeth (Heath) Woodworth

NOTE-Different sources give Eleazer & Susannah Crocker from four to
to seven children, but all agree that Francis (16723.4.) was
their youngest son.

Colonel Francis Crocker is described as being about 5'10", well-
proportioned and erect, with brown hair, blue eyes, light com-
plexion, high forehead with medium breadth, and weight of 175
pounds. His intellect was quick, active, and of a speculative

nature; he was of a determined will and could become unyielding, when his mind became established, to the point of obstinacy. He was a democrat and a Presbyterian. (SCR)

In his early manhood, Francis served as an officer in the New York State Cavalry, at that time one of the best organizations of its kind in northern New York. In business Francis proved himself a shrewd speculator in livestock and was considered one of the best judges of stock in the local markets. After a series of entrepreneurial ventures--all fairly successful--Francis moved to Fairfax County VA and purchased a farm and saw mill which he operated until after the Civil War broke out. (SCR)

Loyal to the Union, Francis was taken prisoner by Rebels and died in captivity after having been sadly mistreated, according to reports his family later received. His wife's father, Major Lott Woodworth and his own father, Eleazer, were both present at the surrender of Lord Cornwall at Yorktown. Lott's father, William, a captain in the army during the Revolution, was a descendant of Walter Woodworth, immigrant from Kent County, Eng, in 1635. (SCR)

Anna Woodworth married Francis Crocker when she was 16 years old. Described as being very beautiful, of medium size, symmetrically proportioned and having round plump features, she had black hair, dark blue eyes, red cheeks, and possessed an active intellect, quick perception, and a sweet disposition. (SCR)

INSERT ADDITION: I, p 66 (JRC)
Children of Rebekah (Crocker) Cobb (16926.)
  & Joseph Cobb:

16926.1.   Joseph Cobb born @ 1775, married Susanna Weston, daughter of Jabez Weston. They had a son Joseph born 1805.

16926.2.   Crocker Cobb born _____, married Mary Thompson

16926.3.   Heman Cobb born _____, married Betsey Whitmarsh

16926.4. Arthur Cobb born 1-11-1786, died Greensbush NY Mar 1813 in
War of 1812; married 8-4-1809 Sally Eddy born @ 1787, died
6-12-1832, buried Cobb Hill, Barnstable MA

16926.5. Rebecca Cobb born 1791, died 2-23-1826

INSERT ADDITION: I, p 66 (TC, JRC)
Children of Rowland Crocker (16928.)
  & Mehitable (Merrill) Crocker:

                                        (birth order uncertain)
16928.1. Samuel Crocker

16928.2. Thomas Crocker

16928.3. Roland Crocker

16928.4. Calvin Crocker

16928.5. John Crocker

16928.6. Ira Crocker

16928. *Enoch Crocker born Conway NH 1-8-1793, died Cape Elizabeth ME
7.   married 8-29-1827 Ellen Elizabeth Day born Portland ME
       2-16-1801, died Portland ME 9-16-1887, daughter of Hannah
       (Smith) & Brigade Major Ezekiel Day

INSERT ADDITION: I, p 66 (JRC)
Children of Daniel Crocker (1692(12).)
  & Elizabeth (Dennis) Crocker:

1692(12). *Dennis Crocker born @ 1796/7, died 12-18-1837, married
1.   Mary Cook

1692(12).2. *Daniel Crocker born @ 1799, married Ruth Hilton

1692(12). Abigail Crocker born @ 1802, died 1-12-1864, married
3.   Capt Ambrose Kelley, son of Samuel Kelley

44

1692(12).   Eleazer Crocker born @ 1805, died 12-8-1888, married
    4.   Wealthy Cook

1692(12).   Sarah Crocker born @ 1807, died 11-2-1837, married
    5.   William J Hatfield, son of Abram Marsh Hatfield

1692(12).   Hannah Crocker born @ 1810, married Andrew Gavel, son of
    6.   Dea John Gavel

1692(12).   Almira Crocker born @ 1812, died 1-27-1849, married
    7.   2-9-1837 Capt Thomas Flint Jr, son of Capt Thomas Flint

1692(12).8. Rowland H Crocker born 12-18-1814

INSERT ADDITION: I, p 66 (JRC)
Children of Eleazer Crocker (1692(14).)
  & Molly/Mary (Robbins) Crocker:

1692(14).   Lydia Crocker born 7-28-1792, died 6-1-1837, married
    1.   1-6-1811 Dea William Crocby, son of Charles Huckins Crocby

1692(14).   Zilpha Crocker born ___, died 12-26-1842, married
    2.   Abijah Raymond, son of Daniel Raymond

1692(14).3. Eleazer born ___

1692(14).4. Ruth born ___, married ___ Pike of Eastport ME

INSERT ADDITIONS: I, p 66 (JRC)
Children of Sarah (Crocker) Valpey (1692(17).)
  & Capt John Valpey:

1692(17).   Abigail Valpey born 10-17-1796, married Methaniel
    1.   Churchill, son of Ephraim Churchill

1692(17).   Hannah Valpey born 6-20-1797, married George T Hunter,
    2.   son of Sheriff George Hunter

1692(17).3 Benjamin Valpey born 9-4-1802

1692(17).4. John Valpey Capt born 10-6-1804, married _____ MacLaren

1692(17). Calvin Valpey Capt born 3-18-1806, married Elizabeth
5.   Gardner

1692(17).6. Sarah Valpey born 1808, married John Horton

INSERT ADDITIONS: I, p 66 (JRC)
Children of Joseph Crocker (1692(20).)
& Sarah (Porter) Crocker:

1692(20).1. Joseph Crocker born 4-14-1804

1692(20).2. Watson Crocker born 9-21-1806, died October 1846

1692(20). Rebecca Crocker born 8-14-1809, died 5-17-1890, married
3.   1st ------ Israel of Westport, married 2d Timothy Wetmore,
son of John Wetmore

1692(20). Mendal Crocker born Sept 1810, died 4-27-1880, married
4.   Mary _____

1692(20).5. Ruth Crocker born 5-29-1811, died 1-18-1827

1692(20). Mary E Crocker born 10-19-1814, died 4-17-1900, married 1st
6.   John M Israel, married 2d William Denton, both of Westport

1692(20).7. George C Crocker born Nov 1816, died Nov 1828

1692(20).8. Nehemiah Crocker

1692(20). *Samuel Crocker Capt born N.S.CAN 7-29-1820, lost on
9.   schooner Brilliant of Yarmouth N.S. off Cape Hatteras Jan
1863. Married 1st Mary Augusta Bain, adopted daughter of
Joseph Bain; married 2d Frances Mary Wetmore, daughter of
Timothy Wetmore

1692(20).(10). Sarah E Crocker born 8-29-1823, died 1-23-1887, unm

INSERT ADDITION: I, p 67 (JRC)
Children of Rhonda (Crocker) (16927.) Perry
& Daniel Perry (16961.):

16961.1. Silva Perry

16961.2. Hannah Perry

16961.3. Amy Perry

16961.4. Juphin Perry

16961.5. Rebecca Perry

CROCKER CEMETERY ASSOCIATION OF ST ALBANS, MAINE
From "History of St. Albans, Maine,"
by Gladys M. Bigelow and Ruth McGowan Knowles
HERITAGE BOOKS, Publisher

"A unique organization still active after more than 60 years is the Crocker Cemetery Association. On land once owned by the Crocker family, this well-kept cemetery is located on the Dexter Road next to Sidney Mower's property and is still in use as a resting place for the descendents (sic) of the original owners.

"On the afternoon of September 11, 1915, eight East St. Albans citizens met with Nettie Mower to discuss starting a neighborhood cemetery. The meeting was called to order by G G Mower. The first officers were President, G G Mower; Vice President, P W Libby; Secretary, Carrie E Fisher; Treasurer, C M Page; Executive Committee, G G Mower, P W Libby, Carrie E Fisher, C M Page, E G Crocker, Mrs C M. Page; Entertainment Committee, Nettie Mower, Hattie Smith, Hattie Bragg, Lucy Crocker, Lillie Libby.

"The first meeting was held at the East Saint Albans Library on October 22, 1915. Clifford Bragg was added to the Executive Committee. Monthly meetings were to be held on the Thursday evening nearest the full moon. The meetings were to open at 7:30 sharp and were to be followed by a social hour. Yearly dues of 25 cents were decided upon. The group voted to mow the cemetery twice a year.

"Surrounded by a neat iron fence, this peaceful plot is a tribute to those early families who began the project and to their descendants who have so faithfully met annually to preserve it. (All Crocker and Bates descendants.)

"Besides the officers elected at the first meeting, the membership list included: H W Cole, E E Badger, Mr & Mrs T W Smith, H B Fisher, John Page, Mrs G Page, Mrs Flora Blanchard, Mrs May Higgins, and Mrs S B Crocker.

"Members in 1980-81 are Ivan & Evelyn Crocker, Philip & Muriel (Crocker) Nelson, Winfred & Phyllis Wiers, Sidney Mower, Eva Springer, Victor & Ruth Springer, Zala Nelson, Wendall Patterson, Blaine & Nellie (Crocker) Tibbetts, Norman & Arline Cain. 1980-81 Officers are President, Blaine Tibbetts; Vice President Wendall Patterson; Secretary Muriel Nelson; Sexton, Joseph Tripoldi."

* * *

48

INSERT ADDITION: I, p 67 (JRC) (DL)
Children of Abel Crocker (16972.)
& Lydia (Bates) Crocker:

16972.   *Mahalia Crocker born Greene ME 7-9-1801, died 1-15-1845,
  1.   married Capt Greene Sprague born 8-8-1804, died 6-19-1888,
         son of Anna (Marrow) & William Sprague

16972.2.   Wheaton Crocker born Greene ME 11-1-1802, died 1804

16972.   *Eleazer Crocker born Greene ME 7-8-1804, died March 1883,
  3.   married Sarah Gray of Manmouth (?) ME (?). He was one of
         St Alban's most respected citizens; was selectman 1840-45,
         1847 & 1850; served two years in the state legislature, and
         one year as a state senator.

16972.   Carlisle Crocker born Greene ME 5-4-1808, died St Albans ME
  4.   4-20-1885, unmarried

16972.   *Lovell Jackson Ransom Crocker born Greene ME 1-12-1810, died
  5.   5-1-1872, named for his grandfather's three wives, married
         Dexter ME 12-6-1832 Hannah Smith Small born Dexter 12-20-1811.
         She died Mankato MN 4-7-1895. She was daughter of Hannah
         (Smith) & Ebenezer Small. This family moved from Maine to
         McKean Cty PA in the early 1850s, and from there to Wisconsin
         and Minnesota.

16972.   Lydia Bates Crocker born 10-8-1811, died 11-12-1877. She was
  6.   an invalid and bedridden for many years. She married Capt
         Joseph Sprague.

16972.   *Aurilla (Aurelia) Anna Crocker (twin) born Greene ME 7-7-1813,
  7.   died 1-25-1862 Chelsea MA, married Dexter ME 12-6-1832 Josiah
         Small born 1-1-1810, brother of Hannah (Small), wife of her
         brother, Lovell Jackson Ransom Crocker, above, and son of
         Hannah (Smith) & Ebenezer Small, pioneers of Dexter ME

16972. Aquilla (Allura?) Crocker (twin) born 7-7-1813, died 7-10-1878
8. married her cousin, Sewall Bates. They lived in St Albans Me. No children.

16972.9. James Granville Crocker (twin), born 3-17-1815, died 1834

16972.(10) Silenus G Crocker (twin) born 3-17-1815, died 1822

16972.(11). Eleanor Jane Crocker born 4-10-1817, died 9-21-1818

16972.(12). Marietta L Crocker born @ 1820, died 3-4-1870

16972.(13).*Deborah A Crocker born 3-22-1823, died 1897, married
Alonzo Denning (Deming?). He died 1865.

INSERT ADDITION: I, p 67 (DL) (JRC)
Children of Warren Crocker (16973.)
& Polly (?) Crocker:

16973.1. Hariot Crocker born Wayne ME 4-30-1807

16973.2. Philander Crocker born Wayne ME 3-6-1808

16973.3. Walter Crocker born Wayne ME 3-6-1812

INSERT ADDITION: I, p 68; (TAC) (WAW) (PB)
17181. *Morton Crocker, eldest son of Mary (Hinckley) & Deacon Joseph
1. Crocker, born 10-11-1770, died Richmond IN 3-27-1851, married
Barnstable MA 12-11-1794 Elizabeth Delap Scudder, born Barnstable 10-12-1773, died 8-3-1842, daughter of Rose (Delap)
& Ebenezer Scudder. Elizabeth Delap Crocker is buried in
Barnstable MA.

INSERT ADDITION: I, p 68: (JRC)
17181. *Joseph Jr born 8-17-1774, died 5-17-1865, married 1st Patty/
3. Martha Atwood born 1778, died Brewster MA 8-4-1816; married
2d Priscilla Berry born 1789, died Brewster 12-18-1834;
married 3d 6-27-1839, Jerusha (Hillman) Taylor of Yarmouth MA
She died 9-13-1861

50

INSERT CORRECTION: I, p 68 (CFC)
17181.6. *Ezekiel Crocker III born 4-10-1781, died Marstons Mills
        (Newtown) 11-3-1829, married Deborah born 1-18-1792, died
        Newtown 7-31-1895, daughter of Zylpha (Meiggs) & Lemuel
        Jones [who married @ 1790]. Zylpha Meiggs was the daughter
        of Temperance (Crocker) & Ralph Meiggs, born 8-8-1746.]

INSERT ADDITION: I, p 70, (RJG) (PC Vol II, p 289-90)
Children of Martha (Fuller) Lovell (17511.)
   & James Lovell II:

17511.1. Temperance Lovell born 1765, died 1845, married ___ Jeffers

17511. *Abigail Lovell born March 1765, died 12-1-1845, married 1782
  2.   Benjamin Hallett I born 1-18-1760, died 12-31-1849, son of
        Mercy (Bacon) & Jonathan Hallett. Served in Revolution.

17511. *Puella Lovell born 1766, died 1825, married 1789 Lemuel
  3.   Lewis born Hyannis MA 9-17-1761

17511.4   Martha Lovell born 1767, died 1842/3, married David Hallett

17511. *James Lovell III born Osterville MA 1770, died there 1855,
  5.   married Osterville 1800 Abigail Lovell born Osterville 1780,
        died there 1825, daughter of Olive (Jenkins) & Daniel Lovell.
        James Lovell married 2d 1827 Clarissa (Hallett) Wing born 1790
        died 6-3-1870, daughter of Sarah (Holmes) Hallett, widow of
        Lot Wing. They had a daughter Clarissa Lovell born 1828.

INSERT ADDITION: I, p 70 (SL)
Children of Benjamin Phinney (17551.)
   & Susannah (Morse) Phinney (15254.):

17551.1. (17551.1.through .9; surname Phinney

17551.6. Elias Phinney born Nova Scotia 1778, died 1849

INSERT ADDITION: I, p 70 (EMcN)
Children of Timothy Phinney (17552.)
& Temperance (Hinckley) Phinney:

17552. *Sturgis Phinney M.D. born Barnstable MA 1789, died 1841,
1. married in New Bedford MA 12-4-1816 Alice born 1797, died
1873, daughter of Rebecca (Ingraham) of New Bedford & Lewis
Tobey, a sea captain from Sandwich MA

INSERT ADDITION: I, p 70 (JRC)
Children of Temperance (Crocker) (1636.) Annable
& Joseph Annable (17711.):

17711. Asenath Annable born East Haddam CT 2-4-1756, died Middle-
1. field MA 12-14-1825, married East Haddam CT December 1777
Matthew Smith born East Haddam 5-12-1753, died Middlefield MA
7-30-1833, son of Sarah (Church) & Matthew Smith Sr.

NOTE-Joseph Annable was son of Jonathan Annable (1771.), grandson of
Remember (Crocker) Annable (177.)

INSERT ADDITION: I, p 71 (RJG)
Children of David Childs (11131.1.)
  & Hannah (Cobb) Childs:

11131. Susannah Childs born 7-30-1762, married 8-30-1784 Joseph Cobb
11.
11131. Asenath Childs born 9-22-1765, married 1st Josiah Clark,
12.   married 2d _____ Wild, lived in Boston

11131.13. Job Childs born 9-8-1767, married 11-24-1785 Jane Claghorn

11131. Hannah Childs born 11-17-1769, married 4-4-1788 Josiah Gorham
14.
11132.15. Anna Childs born Nov 1771, died unmarried (had Polly Allyn)

11132. Josiah Childs born 12-14-1773, married _____, removed to
16.   Westborough, and later to Boston

11132.17. David Childs born 7-8-1775

11132. Shubael Davis Childs born 12-16-1777, married ___, died in
18.   Chelsea MA

11132.19. Benjamin Childs born 8-11-1779, died young in Georgia

11132. Edward Childs born 3-9-1783, married 1st Jane Goodeno,
1(10). 2d Cynthia Goodeno, 3d ?

INSERT ADDITION: I, p 71 (GA)
Children of Ann (Williams) Patterson (11272.1.)
  & Amos Patterson:

11272. *Lucy Patterson born Richmond MA 9-18-1781, died Union, Broome
11.   Cty NY Nov (6 or 12 or 20) 1864, married Jonathan Day born
       Richmond MA 3-23-1779, died Oswego NY 12-14-1849, son of
       Jerusha (Miller) & Thomas Day

INSERT ADDITION: I, p 75, (JRC, PC Vol 2, p 270)
Children of Ignatius Crocker (Blank.6.)
  & Mehitable (West) Crocker:

Blank.61. Sylvester H Crocker born 9-10-1837, died 11-1-1850

Blank.62. Eliza A Crocker born 9-19-1839, died 4-25-1840

Blank.63. John H Crocker born 5-9-1841, died 6-17-1841

Blank.64. *Mercy A Crocker born Cotuit MA 8-3-1843, died Osterville MA
           1-6-1917, married Cotuit MA 1862 Isaac Lovell born Oster-
           ville MA 6-14-1824, died there 12-24-1905, son of Jerusha
           (Bartlett) & Robert Lovell.

Blank.65. Henry C Crocker born 5-1-1847, died 10-26-1847

Blank.66. Sylvester Crocker born 8-3-1854

Blank.67. William B Holbrook Crocker born 12-20-1855, married
           S. Adnea (_____)

INSERT ADDITION: I, p 72 (LGW)
Children of Ruth (Crocker) Percival (14211.1.)
  & John Percival II:

14211.11. Betsy Percival born Lee MA 10-20-1777, married Elias Ladd

14211.12. Lydia Percival born Lee MA 2-12-1779. married James Elmore

14211. John Percival III born Lee MA 4-25-1781, died Mt Morris NY
  13. 1-14-1858, married Catherine Parsons born 6-26-1790 of Chester
       VT, died Mt Morris NY 3-7-1871

14211. Ruth Percival born Lee MA 4-25-1783, died Lee MA, married
  14. Henry Gardiner (perhaps of Gardiner's Island)

14211.15. Samuel Percival born Lee MA 8-27-1785, married Cinda ____

14211.16. James Percival born Lee MA 6-5-1788, married Sarah

14211. Montgomery Percival born Lee MA 9-25/27-1790, married
  17. Eunice Clark/Cook

14211. *Hannah Gates Percival born Lee MA 1-12-1793, died Rochester NY
  18. 7-29-1861, married 9-19-1811 Marsena Allen born Gill MA
     9-8-1789, died Mt Morris NY 6-18-1861, son of Deborah W
     (Pardee) & Apollos Allen. Marsena had moved at age 8 to
     Sherburne (now Smyrna) NY. Both Hannah and Marsena joined the
     Sherburne West Hill Congregational Church on the 2nd Sunday of
     July 1816. On 6-26-1824 Marcena joined with others in organiz-
     ing the Congregational Church of Smyrna. He was elected Deacon
     1825. Marsena was a miller by trade. In 1834 he moved to
     Mt Morris, Livingston Co, NY

Apollos Allen, father of Marsena and son of Noah Allen Sr, moved
from Gill MA to the section of Sherburne NY which later became
Smyrna. The first ancestor in New England of this line of Allens
was Edward of Ipswich MA who is said to have come from Scotland
in 1636. He certainly was of Ipswich in 1660 and perhaps earlier.
He married there 1658 Sarah Kimball.

Prior to 1678 he moved to Suffield, now in CT, then under the
jurisdiction of MA. They had seven sons and five daughters. He
had received a grant of land and chosen his property in a fine
location on the Connecticut River opposite the present village of
Thompsonville. Sarah (Kimball) Allen died Suffield 6-12-1696.
Edward Allen died Suffield 11-22-1696.

John Allen Sr, second son of Sarah (Kimball) & Edward Allen,
moved to Deerfield MA, purchasing property at the "Bars" in 1689.
John Sr married in 1682 Elizabeth Pritchard. Both were killed by
Indians who raided Deerfield 5-10/11-1704.

One of John Allen Srs four sons, John Jr born 1-19-1684, married
Abigail Severance and settled in Greenfield MA where he died
11-30-1761 leaving six daughters and two sons of whom Noah
born 6-24-1727 was the Noah Sr who moved to Sherburne in 1797.

A lieutenant of Minute Men, he led a company to Cambridge on the
Lexington Alarm. He died 2-17-1802 and was buried at Sherburne
West Hill. He had married 10-16-1753 Ruth, daughter of Josiah
Martindale of Guilford VT. They lived at Greenfield, later at
Gill MA, and had five daughters and three sons. Noah Jr and his
brother, Apollos, both moved to Sherburne with their parents.

Ruth (Martindale) Allen was an original member of the Congregational Church on Sherburne West Hill. Her great-grandson, Orsen
Parda Allen, wrote of her: "After great-grandfather Noah's death,
his wife, Ruth Martindale, returned to Guilford VT. She was quite
a remarkable woman, working on to the last. I was told by a
grandson, Jesse Wilkins of Green River, Guilford, that three
weeks before her death she spun a run and a half of yarn in one
day. A letter written by her dated May 3, 1815, begins 'Most
Amiable Grandchildren.' I think it quite probable that my father
went to Vermont with his grandmother, but finally went back to
Smyrna."

Apollos Allen born Gill MA 12-14-1756, died 9-18-1807, married
Deborah W P Pardee of Farmington CT. She died 11-8-1804. He was
an influential citizen, much interested and active in public
affairs.

14211.19. Content Percival born Lee MA 2-28-1796, married ____ Baker

14211.   Abigail (Nabby) Percival born Lee MA 2-22-1798, married
  1(10). Daniel Sherman

14211.1(11). Almira Percival born (prob Mt Morris) NY 8-1-1801

14211.1(12). Sally Percival born NY 10-3-1803, died young in NY

INSERT ADDITION: I, p 72 (CS)
Children of Susannah Hamblin (14212.2.)
  & Paul Ewers:

14212.   Charles Ewers born Lee MA 1798, died Erie Co NY 12-04-1871,
  21.   married Dryden Twp, Tompkins Co NY 3-1-1820, Lua Barthalomew

14212.   Alvah Ewers born Lee MA 4-1-1799, died Detroit MI 7-13-1851,
22.   married Detroit MI 4-28-1829 Jane Geddes

14212.   Jesse Ewers born Lee MA c 1801, died Augusta Twp, Washtenaw Co
23.   MI 2-8-1870, married MI Abigail _____ born CT 1795, died
Augusta, Washtenaw Co MI 1-5-1885. Jesse's Ewers is not named
in Lee MA Vital Records; his probate file names all his
siblings and known living children, including his half-
brother, Tillotson, and Tillotson's son Joseph Crocker Ewers.

INSERT ADDITION: I, p 75 (JG) (PC Vol II, p 193)
Children of Lydia (Crocker) Hodges (14326.1.)
  & Isaac Hodges Sr:

14326.   *Hercules Hodges II born 1796, died 4-19-1831 in Pensacola FL
11.   1831, married 12-23-1817 at West Barnstable by Rev Enoch Pratt
Esther Parker born 1799, died 1880, daughter of Sarah (?) &
Jehiel Parker. No children.

Esther (Parker) Hodges married 2d in 1833 Capt Francis E West
born 1795, died 1872. They had one son, Capt Francis Hodges West,
born 1834, died 11-14-1865 Cartagena, Colombia, SA, of yellow
fever. He married 1856 Josephine Scudder born 1835, died 1881,
daughter of Olive (Lovell) & Erastus Scudder. Their daughter
Olive (West) born 1856, died 1889, married Capt Henry P Crocker
(11324.15.) See I, p 71 & 102

14326.   *Isaac Hodges Jr born Osterville MA 3-9-1798, Master Mariner,
12.   died 10-7-1872, married 1st 5-29-1820 Hannah Parker born
Osterville 1801, died there 1859, daughter of Sarah & Jehiel
Parker. He married 2d widow Susan (Folger) Stockman born 1809,
died 1901, daughter of Daniel & Mary (Brown) Folger. She had
a son, Wm Watson Stockman, 1842-1918, by her first marriage.

14326.   *Sarah Lucy Hodges born Osterville MA 10-30-1799, died
13.   6-19-1879, married 10-26-1824 Samuel Wiley born 1798, died
9-23-1885, son of Ruth (?) & David Wiley

14326. George Hodges born 10-16-1801, died Mobile AL 10-1-1839 of
14. yellow fever, married Nantucket 6-17-1827 Maria Loring

14326. Lydia Hodges born Osterville MA 6-9-1803, married Nantucket
15. 4-26-1827 Henry C Brown, son of Betsey (Allen) & Benjamin
Brown. They had four children.

14326. *Chloe Hodges born Osterville MA 5-7-1805, died Chicago IL
16. 8-14-1878, buried Rosehill Cemetery, Chicago, married at
Nantucket 5-7-1827, Luther Crocker (17181.15.) born at
Barnstable MA 11-14-1802, died 8-18-1883, son of Elizabeth
Delap (Scudder) & Morton Crocker.
[See I, p 114, Hercules Hodges Crocker (17181.151.)]

14326.17. Joseph Hodges, twin, born 1-4-1807, died 1807

14326.18. Benjamin Hodges, twin, born 1-4-1807, died 1807

14326. Sylvester Hodges born 2-9-1808, died Osterville MA May 1889,
19. married Barnstable (VR) 5-291834 Tryphosa Bearse born 1814,
daughter of Hannah (Green) & Solomon Bearse.

14326. Sophia Hodges born Osterville MA 2-24-1810, died Richmond IN
1(10). 12-7-1870, buried Earlham Cemetery, married Nantucket MA
2-26-1829 Edmund F A Fanning born 1808, died Nova Scotia
1848. See Will, Lt Gen Gov Edmund Fanning, Pr. Ed. Isl., N.S.
Widow Sophia (Hodges) Fanning was living with her sister
Chloe & Luther Crocker in Richmond Indian, 1850 Census.

INSERT ADDITION: I, p 77, Elijah Crocker (145(10)4.15.)

Captain Elijah Crocker's experiences as master of ships mirrored those
of most deep water men of his era, but by chance Elijah contributed
more than most of his contemporaries. While en route from Hong Kong to
San Francisco in 1869, he discovered in the Pacific Ocean a previously
uncharted cluster of rocks rising directly between the two ports.
Thick weather prevented an accurate observation, but, according to
Henry C Kittridge's SHIPMASTERS OF CAPE COD, "by dead reckoning they
lay in latitude 31.50 north, longitude 139.23 east, bearing NNW from
Smith's Island, distant forty-two miles."

Cape Cod sent many a man to sea for a living for, indeed, but few choices offered for a lad whose education was limited to local schooling. Men aspiring to a profession, if they could afford the time and college tuition, became doctors, lawyers, or preachers. Most men, however, faced hard-scrabble farming of the Cape's sandy soils or the challenges, dangers, and hardships of life aboard ship. To an enterprising youth seeking fortune and adventure, the sea promised opportunity for both.

When as young as 12 or 14 years, some youngsters signed on as cabin boys or cooks' helpers, and rose to command before reaching their majority. Captain Elijah, born in Barnstable at the height of the age of sail, must have watched the Boston packets come and go, heard the yarns of whaling voyages, and may have begun his own career aboard a coasting schooner plying the waters from Nova Scotia to Florida and the Caribbean, or even ports of Central and South America.

Elijah entered his twenty-first year in 1848 when gold was discovered in California. Gold fever gripped thousands, driving them to the west coast--some by sea, some overland. Everyone venturing to book passage aboard a ship could count on a harrowing voyage of three to four months. Calms and storms, wild winds, and heavy weather in southern latitudes strained even the sturdiest vessels, and since dreams of a canal across the isthmus of Panama remained just that, a dream, sailing for San Francisco from the east coast of the United States meant going around the horn.

We may assume Elijah navigated those hazardous waters more than a few times before he married in 1857 at age 29. Quite likely he found sailing the Pacific lucrative, for the China trade presented good profits for shipowners. Even though whaling days were drawing to a close, Pacific shipping between San Francisco and Asiatic ports took on new importance as steamships slowly replaced sailing vessels. Steamships needed supplies of coal.

Many ports on the east coast of Africa, India, the Maylay Peninsula, and Australia were already controlled by European nations. Contacts with officials in British, French, Dutch, Portuguese, and Spanish colonies depended upon political relations between the United States and those European countries. Some places remained independent of

European control, and required arrangements with aboriginal leaders of their populations.

Among the outstanding successes were the agreements reached with the Sandwich Islands, now our state of Hawaii, where Honolulu became a major coaling station, and in the Phillipines which, in those times, were a Spanish colonial possession.

Negotiating with officials to arrange for purchases of coal to power steamships and naval vessels in the Pacific and Indian Oceans was but one reason to send a ship to the Far East. Trade in goods -- spices, exotic woods, fabrics, ceramics -- was important, too.

When Captain Elijah Crocker discovered the previously unknown cluster of rocks in the Pacific Ocean, he was 42 years old and had been going to see for at least 20 years, perhaps longer. Some years following his retirement to his home in Barnstable, he died there, age sixty-seven.

INSERT ADDITION: I, p 78 (PC Vol II, p 79)
145(10)7. *Persis L Crocker born 4-19-1841, died 1920, married 1st
  33.   David Joy Coleman born 1840, died 1896, son of Mehitable
      (Isham) & Abraham Coleman

INSERT ADDITION: I, p 78 (FF)
Children of Bathsheba (Crocker) Fish (145(10)8.1.)
  & Franklin Fish:

145(108. *Edward Nye Fish born Barnstable MA 8-27-1827, died
  11.   Tucson 12-18-1914, married Tucson 3-12-1874 Maria
      Matilda Wakefield, born Bombay NY 2-9-1845, died
      Tucson AZ 9-23-1909, daughter of Clarinda Adelade
      (Brown) & James Madison Wakefield

INSERT ADDITION: I, p 80 (JRC)
Children of Ezra Crocker (15841.4.)
  & Temperance (Crocker) 145(10)9.) Crocker:

15841. David Crocker Capt born Cotuit MA 1-24-1805, died there
  41.   5-20-1875, married 1st Julia Scudder born 1810; married
      2nd Elizabeth Childs (15841.13.)

15861.42. Arthur Crocker

15861.43. Herman Crocker

15861.44. Betsey Crocker

CORRECTION: I, p 83 (PB)
16324.31. John Gage Chipman Crocker born 8-9-1811, died 1883, married
       1-29-1836 Mary Augusta Alexander born 1810, died 1902

INSERT ADDITION: I, p 85 (BWS, Obit, Martha (Wright) Starbuck)
Children of Sarah (Crocker) Wright (16324.2.)
 & Capt Benjamin Wright: (order uncertain - fourteen children)

16324.21. Benjamin Wright II Capt born Marstons Mills MA 1804, lost at
       sea 1847, married Eunice Crocker (16344.32.) born Osterville
       MA Apr 1809, died 11-20-1889, daughter of Eunice (Chadwick)
       & Benjamin Fuller Crocker.

16324.22. daughter born ____, died Nantucket MA, married Geo C Hussey

16324.23. Asa Wright Capt of Hyannis

16324.24. William Wright, a survivor of the ship ESSEX, which was
       wrecked in the Pacific Ocean by an angry whale.
     (See The Loss of the Ship "ESSEX" Sunk by a Whale, p 61.-- by
     Thomas Nickerson; pub. by Nantucket Historical Society, 1984)

16324.25. *Betsey Crocker Wright born Marstons Mills MA 5-22-1811,
       died there 2-22-1895, married there 1st ____ Bearse;
       married 2d as his 3rd wife Wilson Crocker (16344.21) born
       Marstons Mills Ma 4-28-1808, died there 12-12-1885

16324.26. Martha Wright born Marstons Mills 5-25-1813, died there
       4-18-1903, married 1st Capt William Crocker born 1814, lost
       at sea 1837, had daughter Ellen born 1837, died 1838/9.
       Martha married 2nd her brother-in-law, George C Hussey of
       Nantucket; she married 3d Capt Obed Starbuck of Nantucket

Benjamin Wright I born Plympton MA 7-11-1774, died Barnstable MA 9-2-1842, married Sarah Crocker (16324.2.). His son Benjamin II married at Osterville MA 1832 Eunice Crocker, (16344.32.) born Apr 1809, died 11-20-1889, daughter of Eunice (Chadwick) & Benjamin Fuller Crocker. Benjamin Wright II's grandfather, Adam born Plympton MA 9-27-1724, died there Feb 1776, married there 6-1-1773 Widow of Ephraim Tinkham, Sarah (Standish) born 4-26-1736, daughter of Rachael (Cobb) & Moses Standish, descendant of Myles Standish.

Adam Wright's father, John, born 1-3-1680, married 5-20-1708 Mary Lucas. John Wright's father, Adam, born 1640, married Oct 1679 Sarah Soule (MAYFLOWER).

OBIT-1885--Marstons Mills--Mr Wilson Crocker died on Sunday morning - the 20th inst, one of the oldest residents of this section having been born April 28 1808. His disease, erysipelas, progressed rapidly to its fatal termination, it being but one week from the time he was taken ill to the day of his death.

Mr Crocker had lived for the greater part of his life at the home where he died. He was, however, employed as carpenter for a brief time on a plantation in South Carolina. He had also worked in Provincetown and Hingham in the earlier part of his life.

He was a man of strong temperance principles, a kind neighbor, and thoroughly honest in dealings with his fellowmen. He leaves a widow and three sons; one of the latter, Nelson W, is engaged in farming; another, Charles W served three years in the War of the Rebellion as a member of the 40th Mass. Volunteers Regiment. He is now general agent for the Illinois Mutual Insurance Co and lives at Chicago. His youngest son, Henry Ellis, has been a teacher for many years and is now Supt of Schools at Dedham Mass.

Funeral services held at the house on Tueday last were conducted by Rev A H Somes. (BWS)

OBIT-<u>Mrs Betsey Crocker</u> widow of the late Mr Wilson Crocker, an exemplary Christian, departed this life on the 22nd ult at the advanced age of 83 years, funeral services were conducted at her late residence Sunday morning, Rev Samuel Clarke officiating. Selected pieces were beautifully rendered on the occasion by Miss Bessie J Crocker, Miss Elizabeth O Jenkins, Messrs William F Jenkins, and Edward Howland. The deceased leaves three sons, one sister, and a large concourse of friends who will hold her in sweet remembrance.

OBIT-Feb 22 1895-In West Barnstable, 22nd ult, at the residence of her son, Mr Nelson W Crocker <u>Mrs Betsey C Crocker</u>, widow of the late Mr. Wilson Crocker, age 84 years 9 months.

NOTE-Mr & Mrs Peter Hickman [Marion (Thomas) (16344.2114.) Hickman, and Mrs Hans Vos (Joan Moseley (Thomas) (16344.2113.) Vos supply specifics of Crockers in their lines of the family. The Homestead of their grandfather, Charles Wilson Crocker (16344.211.), in Marstons Mills, Mass., remains in their family.

NOTE-Another descendant, <u>the late Harold Duncan Shaw Jr</u> (16344.21423.2,) and his wife, Barbara (Wissing) Shaw, have also researched Wilson Crocker and learned that he married at least twice and had children by both wives Tabitha (Freeman) and the widow Betsey Crocker (Wright) Bearse.

INSERT ADDITION: I, p 85 (JMTV, MTH)
Children of Shubael Hamblin Crocker (16344.2.)
  & Abigail (Crocker) Crocker (16323.4):

16344. *Wilson Crocker born West Barnstable MA 4-28-1808, died there
21.   12-18-1885 (or 2-22-1895 g.s.), married 1st 2-20-1834 Almira Hinckley who died soon after marriage, of consumption; no children. He married 2nd Sandwich MA 11-4-1841 Tabitha (Betsy) Freeman, born East Sandwich MA 7-24-1809 (or 5-22-1810 g.s., or 7-7-1807, Bunnell,) died West Barnstable MA 5-14-1845 (Bunnell), daughter of Betsy (Fish) & Thomas Freeman. (Betsey Fish's father was Edmond Fish.)

Thomas Freeman born East Sandwich MA 4-6-1767, died 7-20-1841,
married 3-11-1802 Betsy Fish; he was son of Tabitha (Chase)
& Edmond Freeman born East Sandwich 10-10-1743, died Oct 1779,
married 3-14-1765; he was son of Thomas Freeman, son of Edmond
Freeman III, son of Edmond Freeman II, son of Edmond Freeman Sr.

*Wilson Crocker married 3d Widow Betsey Crocker (Wright) Bearse
born 5-22-1811, died 2-22-1895, daughter of Sarah (Crocker)
(16324.2.) & Benjamin Wright. Sarah born 1779, died Barnstable
12-3-1840, was daughter of Martha (Crocker) (17143.) & Abner
Crocker (16324.). Betsey (16324.25) had thirteen siblings.

(See II, p B-19, for article by Henry Ellis Crocker published in
The Barnstable Patriot soon after the death of his mother's
sister, Martha (Wright) Crocker-Hussey-Starbuck.)

INSERT ADDITION: I, p 85 (FF)
16344. *Temperance Hathaway Crocker born 2-23-1807, died 3-20-1900,
  31.   married 2-7-1828 Capt James Parker II born 12-08-1789, died
        3-4-1871, son of Sarah (Nye) & Capt James Parker I

James Parker I born 7-28-1747, died 11-6-1802, son of Mercy
(Crocker) & David Parker, married Sandwich MA 6-15-1779 Sarah
Nye, daughter of Mary (Nye) Nye of Sandwich. Parker family tradi-
tion includes the story that during the Revolution the British
sent out foraging parties along Cape Cod's undefended south shore
for chickens, garden greens, piglets, and lambs to feed the crews
aboard their vessels which were harrassing the colonists' ships.
At the same time the foraging parties picked up men and boys and
transported them to Long Island NY for labor. Among those taken
was young James Parker of Osterville.

Some years later a rescue party, led by Lt Col Return Jonathan
Meiggs of Sandwich, freed Parker along with about 100 others. The
rescue party of whale boats crossed Long Island Sound from Connecticut and brought the young people back from Montauk Point to
Hartford CT where James' nephew, Nehemiah Parker, had taken up
land that Daniel Parker Esq had inherited from Judge Daniel
Parker when he was a member of the Massachusetts legislature.

64

<u>NOTE</u>: Col Meiggs was related to the Parkers through Mercy Meiggs of
Sandwich who had married, as his 2d wife, Ansel Crocker. James
Parker, while making his way back to his Osterville home, stopped
at Edmund Nye's tavern in Sandwich. There he met Sarah, the
tavern keeper's daughter, married her, and brought his bride home
with him to Osterville.

<u>Ethel (Parker) Riedell</u> (16344.3111.1.), descendant of Sarah (Nye)
& James Parker I, has a great granddaughter named Sarah Parker
Levinson; Sarah's younger brother is Daniel. See Vol I, p 187.
Mrs Riedell is credited with the above anedote about the
courtship of Sarah (Nye) & James Parker.

<u>INSERT CORRECTION</u>: I, p 85, (BWS)
16344.*Eunice Crocker born Osterville MA April 1809, died 11-20-1889,
   32. married 1832 Capt Benjamin Wright of West Barnstable, born
       1804, died 1847, lost at sea, son of Sarah (<u>Crocker</u>) <u>(16324.2.)</u>
       & Benjamin Wright, brother of Wilson Crocker's 3rd wife, Betsey

<u>INSERT ADDITION</u>: I, p 88 (CS)
Children of Tillotson/Tilson Ewers (P-16352.2.)
   & Hannah (_____) Ewers:

P-16352. *Joseph Crocker Ewers born Scipio Twp Cayuga Co NY 11-25-1818
   21.   died Bunker Hill Twp, Ingham Co MI 10-20-1895, married 1st
          Iosco Twp, Livingston Co MI 1-12-1863 Eunice Livermore born
          NY 1-16-1825, died Bunker Hill Twp, Ingham Co, MI 3-2-1862,
          daughter of Susan (Watson) & James Livermore.

          *Joseph married 2d Adelia L Harford, born Lima, Washtenaw Co
          MI 2-6-1832, died Bunker Hill Twp, Ingham Co, MI 6-15-1894,
          daughter of Pamelia (Nippin?) & William Harford.

P-16352.22. Seneca Ewers born Scipio Twp, Cayuga Co NY

P-16352. Silvia Ewers born Scipio Twp, Cayuga Co NY 12-7-1822, died
   23.   Unadilla Twp, Livingston Co MI, married Lima, Washtenaw Co
          MI 2-8-1872 Lyman A Babcock

INSERT ADDITION: I, p 89 (SCR)
Children of Francis Crocker (16723.4.)
& Anna (Woodworth) Crocker:

16723.   Jonathan Dorr Crocker born 4-24-1813, died 9-24-1880, married
41.   Sarah Staples born 1812, died 1875

16723.   Lott Woodworth Crocker born 12-21-1815, died 6-28-1875,
42.   married Ellen Henderson

16723.   Francis Platt Crocker born 2-5-1818, died 2-26-1873, married
43.   Louisa Taylor

16723.   John Simpson Crocker born 3-8-1820, died 9-14-1890, married
44.   Harriette Sipperly; had a son, Irving M Crocker

16723.45.   Anna Maria Crocker born 5-27-1822

16723.   Asenath Elizabeth Crocker born 9-1-1824, died 12-21-1860,
46.   married Ansom B. Ransom

16723.   Susanna Hinckley Crocker born 6-1-1827, died 1-10-1896,
47.   married Alonzo Storm

16723.   William Calvin Crocker born 3-11-1830, married Hester Ann
48.   Fetzer

16723.49.   Aurilia Richardson Crocker born 11-22-1832

16723.   James Harvey Crocker born 11-20-1834, died 2-5-1881, married
4(10).   Charlotte Garrison

16723.4(11).   Sarah Denton Crocker born 8-15-1837, died 2-22-1875

16723.   *Jane Eliza (Jennie) Crocker born 10-22-1841, d _____,
4(12).   married Owen Augustus Luckenbach born Bethlehem PA
         1-14-1834, died 10-16-1890, son of William Luckenbach
         Jennie probably was born at Schaghticoke NY

Owen Augustus Luckenbach descended from Eva Maria (Speiss) & Adam
Luckenbach who arrived at Philadelphia from Germany 9-30-1740
on the ship SAMUEL & ELIZABETH, Capt William Chilton. Most of
this German line of the family emigrated to the New World in what
is called the second wave of German immigration. These were
called "church" as opposed to "sect" people. The era of peak
arrivals for Reformed Lutherans and Moravians was between 1720
and 1750. Many Moravians appeared to have come from England for
in 1708, while war raged in the Rhine valley, many Palatines fled
to England. Queen Anne arranged for them to go to New York.

The German emigre settlement at Schoharie southwest of Albany NY
soon moved to Berks County, entering Pennsylvania by the north
branch of the Susquehanna River. The European war ended in 1713,
but Palatine migration continued. In 1719 as many as 7,000 Palatines entered the port of Philadelphia. Members of the Moravian
Church arrived in 1735 at Georgia; by 1740 some moved to Pennsylvania. Along the Lehigh River land they purchased became their
major town, Bethlehem. Others came from Europe and established
the new communities of Nazareth and Lititz. By 1750, an estimated
100,000 German-speaking people lived in Pennsylvania.

At times Adam Luckenbach acted as school teacher in Montgomery,
Lancaster, and Northampton Counties, Pennsylvania. Adam's son
John Ludwig, born in Germany in 1738, emigrated with his parents
in 1740. He married four wives and had children by each.

Owen Augustus Luckenbach born Bethlehem PA 1-14-1834, was a son
of William. During the Civil War he was promoted to lieutenant
and then captain. Wounded, his leg was amputated below the knee.
As a result Owen Augustus was discharged 10-20-1862. In the fall
of 1863, he went to Washington DC as a clerk with the Ordinance
Department; while filling this appointment, he met Jane Eliza
Crocker. He and Jennie were married in Washington 9-15-1864.

INSERT ADDITION: I, p 89 (JRC)
Children of Dennis Crocker (1692(12).1)
& Mary (Cook) Crocker:

1692(12). *Nehemiah D Crocker, Capt born   died
11.   married Sophronia Sims, daughter of Robert Sims

INSERT ADDITION: I, p 89 (JRC)
Children of Daniel Crocker (1692(12).2.)
& Ruth (Hilton) Crocker:

1692(12). *Dennis C Crocker married 11-13-1861 Isabel Raymond,
21.   daughter of Richard Raymond

INSERT ADDITION: I, p 89 (JRC) (DL)
Children of Eleazer Crocker (16972.3.)
& Sarah (Gray) Crocker:

16972. *Soloman Whiten Crocker born 1833, died Dexter ME 4-12-1911,
31.   married 1-5-1859 Sarah Keene born Dexter ME 1838, died
         1-8-1925, daughter of Maria (Jennings) & Samuel Keene.

        Both Sarah (Keene) & Soloman W Crocker were school teachers. He
        was also a mason and worked at that trade while living in Minne-
        sota from 1855, when Minneapolis was a village or trading post,
        until returning to Maine several years before he died.

16972. Silenus Greenville Crocker married Amanda Leathers, daughter
32.   of Joana (Elder) & Levi Leathers; she married 2d ____ Holmes

16972.33. Georgia Crocker died 1842

16972. Sarah Maria Crocker died 1842, married Lewis Fish, had
34.   Winifred Fish who married Leo E Bova and had a son Leo E Jr

16972. Mary Crocker married Daniel Crockett, tinsmith of Dexter ME;
35.   their daughter, Estelle Crockett, married Melvin Randall of
         Ripley ME and ran a millinery shop in Bridgewater ME; Mary and
         Daniel had two sons, Alvin and Daniel Crockett.

16972. *Ruth Crocker married 12-22-1855 Granville Mower son of
36.   Deacon Charles Mower.

16972.37. Maria Crocker

INSERT ADDITION: I, p 89 (JRC) (DL)
Children of Lovell Jackson Ransom Crocker (16972.5.)
& Hannah S (Small) Crocker:

16972.51. Helen Crocker married _____ Jackmay

16972.52. George R Crocker died in Civil War; enlisted from Indiana

16972.53. Abel Crocker

16972. *Lovell Ransom Crocker born Lewiston ME 9-20-1852, died
54.   Minneapolis MN 12-1-1920, married Winnebago MN 11-22-1874
       Sarah Catherine Sickler born Oshkosh WI 3-4-1856, died
       Mankato MN 11-9-1914, daughter of Lydia (Lane) & Gilbert
       Sickler; he married 2d Mary Hagadorn

16972. Alvina Crocker married 1st _____Palmer; married 2d
55.   _____ Austin; lived in California

INSERT ADDITION: I, p 89 (DL)
Children of Aurelia Anna (Crocker) Small (16972.7.)
& Josiah Small:

16972.71. Laura Small probably born Dexter or St Albans ME

16972.72. Rosco Small probably born Dexter or St Albans ME

16972.73. Joseph Small probably born St Albans ME

16972.74. George Small probably born Springfield ME

16972.75. Abel Small probably born St Albans ME or in MA

16972. *Louisa Anna Small born Andover MA 5-30-1849, died Revere MA
76.   4-5-1926, bur with husband, married Chelsea MA 5-3-1870
      Solomon David Samuel(s) [also known as Samuel D Samuel], born
      London, England, 2-23-1846, died Chelsea MA 1-22-1894, son of
      Sophia (Phillips) & Samuel Samuel(s) of London, England.
      Bur Civil War Veteran's Section, Woodlawn Cem. Everett MA

16972.77. Rose Small

16972.78. Luetta Small

INSERT ADDITION: I, p 89 (DL)
Children of Deborah A (Crocker) Denning (16972.(13).
& Alonzo Denning:

16792.(13)1. Lovisa Denning born 1841, died 1856

16972.(13)2. Anna Denning born 1844, died 1863

16972.(13)3. Evalina Denning born 1882, died 1900

16972.(13)4. Florence Denning married _____ Snell

16972.(13)5. Florilla (Horilla?) at one time lived in Kansas City

16972.   Addie Denning married Charles Grant; had two children,
(13)6.   Florence who died young, and Wilmot Bates Grant who had
         three daughters, Beatrice, Thelma, & Gwendolyn Grant.

16972.   Ella Denning died young; married Henry Butler and had a son
(13)7.   Harry Butler of Los Angeles CA, a plumber. Harry graduated
         from a college in Poughkeepsie NY. He married in Guilford ?

16972.   Edith Denning married 1st J Robert Munn; married 2d Samuel
(13)8.   W Herrick of Harmony ME. She died soon after her 2d marriage
         and is buried in Crocker Cem. St Albans ME in the Denning lot

INSERT ADDITIONS: I, p 91 (JG)
17181. *Luther C Crocker born Barnstable 11-14-1802, died 8-18-1883,
15.   married Nantucket MA Chloe Hodges (14326.16.) born Nantucket
5-7-1805, daughter of Capt Isaac Hodges

CORRECTIONS: I, p 91: Change numbers 17181.19., .1(10.), & .1(11) to:
.18., .19., and .1(10)

INSERT ADDITIONS: I, p 91 (JRC)
17181. Mary Crocker born 1-27-1804, died 1-29-1841, married 1st
33.   Capt Elkanah Winslow born Brewster 12-11-1802, died Mexico
7-3-1851, son of Joseph & Abigail (Snow) Winslow. He married
2nd Mary's sister, Susan (Crocker) Baker (17181.39.)

CORRECTIONS: I, p 93 & 94 (CFC)
Children of Ezekiel Crocker (17181.6.)
& Deborah (Jones) Crocker (16333.2):

17181. *Stephen Crocker born 2-3-1816, died 3-5-1891, married Eliza
62.   Jones born Newtown 7-8-1816 died 4-27-1902

17181. Cyrus Crocker born 4-17-1824, died 11-11-1845 of typhoid
67.   fever; unm

17181.68. Mary Emily Crocker born 9-10-1826

INSERT ADDITION: I, p 99 (PV Vol II p 146)
Children of Abigail (Lovell) Hallett (17511.2.)
& Benjamin Hallett:

17511. *Temperance Hallett born Osterville 1783, died 2-211839,
21.   married 1804 Osterville Braddock Crocker (15843.3.) born 1783,
died 1841, son of Mary (Bourne) & Ebenezer Crocker. See I, 81.

17511. *Mercy Hallett born Osterville 1784, died 1850, married Oster-
22.   ville 1804 Samuel Dewey born 1779, died 1813, son of Sabra
(Worthington) & Benoni Dewey

17511.   *Abigail Hallett born Osterville 3-27-1786, died Philadelphia
23.   3-27-1877, married Osterville 1809 Rev Barnabas Bates born
         Edmonton, England 1785, died Boston 10-11-1853; both buried
         Mt Auburn Cemetery NY. He was father "cheap postal service"
         in this country. They had three daughters.

17511.   *Persis Hallett born Osterville 3-5-1789, died Osterville
24.   12-11-1868, married December 1809 Samuel Waitt who died at
         Osterville in December 1847. (SC/MC)

17511.   *Christina Hallett born Osterville MA 1790, died Hyannis MA
25.   12-13-1848, married Osterville 1818 Rev Daniel Chessman born
         1789, died Hyannis 5-21-1839, an 1808 graduate of Brown
         University, Providence RI. He became Baptist minister at
         Hyannis in 1834. Both buried Baptist Cemetery, Hyannis MA.

17511.   Penelope Hallett born Osterville 4-7-1792, died Providence RI
26.   3-10-1825, married Osterville 1816 Isaac Percival.

17511.   Henrietta Hallett born Osterville 1794, died there 2-16-1875,
27.   married 1st Osterville 1825 Lot Hallett; married 2d 1831
         Thomas Delap Scudder who died at North Belgrade ME 7-17-1853

17511.   *Benjamin Franklin Hallett Esq born Osterville 12-2-1797, died
28.   9-30-1862 at Boston MA, married at Providence RI 6-25-1822
         Laura Larned born Providence RI 1799, died Boston MA May
         1860. Both buried Mt Auburn Cemetery, Cambridge MA.

17511.   *Adeline de la Motte Hallett born Osterville 1799, died there
29.   1890, married Osterville 1830 Capt George Lovell born Oster-
         ville MA 7-17-1787, died 11-28-1861, son of Anna (Lumbert) &
         Cornelius Lovell, his 2d wife. George Lovell had six children
         by his first wife, Mary Hilliard, 1791-1828.

17511.2(10).   Eliza Hallett born Osterville 1801, died there 1808.

17511.   *Julia A Hallett born Osterville 1803, died Philadelphia PA
2(11).   1-17-1889. married Osterville 1824 Bradford B Williams born
         Centerville MA 1799, died New York 5-7-1873.

17511.2(12). Martha Hallett born 1805, died 1894, unmarried

17511.2(13). Eliza Hallett born 1810, died 1810

INSERT ADDITION: I, p 100, (PC Vol II, p 291)
Children of James Lovell III (17511.5.)
 & Abigail (Lovell) Lovell:

17511.   James Newton Lovell born Osterville MA 1804, died there 1865
51.   married Osterville 1834 Lucinda Hinckley born Osterville 1805,
       died there 4-9-1896, daughter of Eunice (Marchant) & Marshall
       Hinckley Sr; had son James Allen Lovell.

17511.52. Asa Lovell born 1806, died 1807

17511.   Daniel Lovell born 1810, died 1-13-1888, married in 1832
53.   Eliza E Cammett born 1811, died 9-6-1892; had issue.

17511.54. Shubael Lovell born 1814, died 1814

INSERT ADDITION: I, p 100 (EMcN)
Children of Dr Sturgis Phinney (17552.1.)
 & Alice (Tobey) Phinney:

17552.11. *Franklin S Phinney born 1827, died 1876, married 10-13-1857
           Margaret S Macy born 1836, died 1892, daughter of Sarah L
           (Corlies) & Charles Macy.

Eighth Generation

INSERT ADDITION: I, p 101 (RJG)
Children of Job Childs (11131.13.)
& Jane (Claghorn) Childs:

11131. *Jacob Childs born 1794, died 1864, married Clarissa Fish born
131. 1802, died 1878, daughter of Hannah (Coombs) & Stephen Fish Jr

INSERT ADDITION: I, p 101 (GA)
Children of Lucy (Patterson) Day (11272.11.)
& Jonathan Day:

11272. *Francis Henry Day born Union, Broome Cty NY 10-26-1809, died
111. Dubuque IA 3-16-1865, married 4-28-1831 Sarah Ann Bunting born
Union, Broome Cty NY 3-17-1812, died 2-27-1885, bur Longmont
CO, daughter of Elizabeth (Cafferty) & Samuel Bunting
(of Broome Cty NY, 1821 census)

INSERT ADDITION: I, p 102 (LGW)
Children of Hannah Gates (Percival) Allen (14211.18.)
& Marsena Allen:

14211. *Samuel Percival Allen born Smyrna NY 10-21-1814, died
181. 10-20-1881, married 1838 Harriet C Stanly died Geneseo NY
9-24-1890, daughter of Luman Stanly of Mt Morris NY

Samuel Percival Allen in 1830 went to Geneseo, Livingston Cty, NY
as an apprentice to his uncle James Percival, publisher of a news
paper there. He joined, in April 1831, the Presbyterian Church of
Geneseo. In 1832 Samuel returned to Chenango Cty and worked on a
farm for three years while attending school during the winters.
The winter of 1834/5 he taught school at "Old Four Corners,"
and in 1835 returned to Livingston Cty where, in 1837 he established the newspaper Livingston Republican. A year later he and
Harriet Stanly of Mt Morris NY were married. She was eighth in
descent from John Stanly who came from England in 1644 (or 1684).
(History of Chenango & Madison Counties, James H. Smith, 1880.)

Samuel sold the Livingston Republican in 1846 to purchase an interest in the Rochester Democrat. Two years later, in 1848, he became editor-in-chief of that newspaper.

During the Civil War President Abraham Lincoln appointed Samuel District Collector of Internal Revenue for Monroe & Orleans counties; shortly thereafter he entered a partnership with the Hon B G Berry, publishing the Chenango Telegraph. Five years later in the fall of 1874, at the age of 60 years, Samuel returned to Geneseo to re-purchase the Livingston Republican.

Throughout his adult life Samuel was active in politics as befitted a publisher of newspapers and who, presumably, influenced political activities of upper New York State. In 1840 he was elected clerk of Livingston County, in 1856 and 1858 he won election to clerk of the state Senate, and from 1872 through 1879 he served as assistant clerk of the Assembly.

At the time of his death 10-20-1881, it was said of Samuel Allen "He was a man of pure domestic nature, of a generous sympathetic spirit, firm impulses, sterling integrity, and genial humor. Few of the sons of Sherburne and Smyrna have filled a larger place among men with honor, and few are so kindly remembered among their fellowmen as Samuel P. Allen."

14211. *Ruth Gardiner Allen born Smyrna NY married Robert E Weeks.
  182. After their son Willard Weeks was born in Smyrna NY, the family moved to Mt Morris NY. Their younger son, Rev Frank Weeks, was pastor of a church at North St Paul MN.

14211.183. Sarah F Allen born Smyrna NY married John F Gorman

14211. James Harvey Allen born Smyrna NY 5-13-1820, died Florida
  184. 11-24-1892, married Electa Bixby of Castile NY. They had seven children, among them: Raymond Allen, John Percival Allen, Jennie Allen who married Rev Frank White, and Frank Clarence Allen born 1853 who married Cordelia M Matchetie

James Harvey Allen baptized Sherburne West Hill Church on 2nd
Sunday of June 1820. As an adult he moved to Eau Claire WI. His
daughter Jennie married Rev. Frank White; they were missionaries
in Japan.

14211. *Orsen Parda Allen Rev born Smyrna NY 11-6-1827, died
185. Constantinople Turkey 6-21-1918, married 9-5-1855 Caroline
Reddington Wheeler born Hampden ME 11-2-1828, died Auburndale
MA 11-25-1898, daughter of Sybil (Crosby) & Joel Wheeler and
sister of Rev Crosby H Wheeler

The Rev Orsen Parda Allen, youngest son of Deacon Marsena Allen,
studied for the ministry and was stationed as Missionary in
Turkey for 37 years, most of the time at Harpoot. His earliest
memories are best told in his own words extracted from a letter:

"I have very distinct remembrances of living in two different
places in Sherburne; one at Hatch's Hill, then owned by Mr. Wells
Hatch, and the other at Paddleford's Mill, at each of which
places my father was a miller. Especially the first place is
distinct to me, and my first recollections are connected with the
house where we lived near Hatch's Hill. There I should have lost
my life when four years old had not Mr Hatch snatched me from the
water just as I was being drawn in by the current toward the
water wheel. It is a singular coincidence that Gen J Watts
Depeyster came near being drowned by falling into the same mill
pond a few years later, when a boy, as he recently informed me.

"When I was about five years old, father moved to Smyrna, and
from there to Mt Morris. I left Mt Morris for Amherst College in
1848, was at Bangor and Andover Seminaries, and came to Turkey in
1855. I lived in Constantinople for six months, then a year at
Trebizond, and in 1857 came to this place with my brother-in-law,
Mr Wheeler. Here I have remained since, with the exception of two
visits to America."

Rev Orsen P Allen and his bride sailed from Boston to Turkey
10-27-1855 and arrived there 12-9-1855. Six months later they
were transferred to Trebizond. A year later they were trans-

ferred to Harpoot and reached there in company with Rev and
Mrs Crosby H Wheeler in July 1857. Crosby Wheeler, although five
years older than his sister, went out to Turkey two years later
than the Allens, and the two couples were sent to Harpoot in
1857. The association of brother and sister continued for nearly
forty years in most fruitful and blessed results.

Mrs Allen's health had never been very firm, and finally broke
with the terrible experiences of the massacres of Armenians, a
shattering blow to their special Armenian constituency. Mrs
Allen's life in the mission field was marked by intense
earnestness, activity and zeal, always sustained by a firm faith
that all efforts were ultimately to be crowned with success.
They had the joy of having their son Herbert and their daughter
Annie join them as missionaries in the Eastern Mission, but
three of their children were buried within two years at Harpoot,
Katie, Mary, and Hattie.

Mr Allen toured the field, had his share in the local preaching
and evangelistic work, taught in the theological seminary using
the Armenian language. In a statement dated 1872, he lists
machinery he had imported to Turkey, including "53 flax wheels,
two hand spinning machines, six spindles, one hand loom, two hand
threshing machines, two circular sawing machines, two knitting
machines, one grain mill, one cotton gin, and one plow."

Through trials and blessings, in the midst of famine, pestilence
and violence, as well as through revivals of spiritual life, Mr
Allen was very close to the people and deeply appreciated. In
1890-91 the Allens spent the winter in Van helping out in special
need. They went through the terrible sufferings of the massacres
of 1895/6 and at length were so worn that Mrs Allen's health
failed and the Allens returned to America in the summer of 1896.

Mrs Allen died in Auburndale MA in November 1898. Mr Allen resigned his commission and remained several years in America, but
in the summer of 1903 he returned to Turkey to live with his son
and daughter, Mr & Mrs H N Allen, first at Bardizag and later in
Constantinople, for five years.

After his son's death, he went with his daughter Annie in 1912 to Brousa where she cared tenderly for him until the pressure of the Great War compelled them to withdraw to Constantinople where he died 6-21-1918, the last of that group of pioneers which had made Harpoot Station such a power.

14211.186. Delia Allen died Mobile AL, married Willis G Clark

14211.187. Louisa Content Allen died Mt Morris NY 9-9-1870 age 55

INSERT ADDITION: I, p 104 (PC Vol II, p 193)
Children of Isaac Hodges Jr (14326.12.)
& Hannah (Parker) Hodges:

14326. *Frances Hodges born 1821, died 12-27-1880, married 1840 Capt
121. Henry S Linnell born Centerville MA 1816, died East Boston MA 3-28-1886, son of Esther (Chase) & Abner Linnell. Their first five children died young; daughter Janet born 1858, died 1937; son, William born 1860, died 1928.

Henry S Linnell was a sea captain and resided at East Boston MA. After Frances died, he married 2d her niece, Lucy (Wiley) Lovell, (14326.133.) born 1829, died 7-2-1896, widow of Freeman Lovell Jr and daughter of Sarah Lucy (Hodges) & Capt Samuel Wiley. She had a son, Clifford Lovell, by her 1st marriage.

14326.122. Joseph Hodges 1823-1825

14326. *Joseph Hodges born 1825, died 1853, married 1848 Jane Parker
123. born 1826, daughter of Maria (Phinney) & Jonathan Parker of Osterville MA

14326. *Jehiel P Hodges born 1827, died 1906, married 1850 Elizabeth
124. Scudder born 1829, died 1911, daughter of Elizabeth (Hinckley) & Freeman Scudder, all of Osterville MA

14326.125. Isaac S Hodges born 1830, died 1834

14326.126. Sarah Hodges born 1832, died ?, married ____ Holmes

14326.   Isaac Hodges III born 1835, died 1861, married Medora Robbins,
127.   her 1st husband. He was Osterville Postmaster.

14326.128.   Frederick Hodges born 1837, died 1839

14326.129.   Hannah Hodges born 1839, married Theophilus Gifford

14326.12(10).   Frederick Hodges born 1841, died 1848

INSERT ADDITION: I, p 104 (PC, Vol II, p 382)
Children of Lucy (Hodges) Wiley (14326.13.)
   & Samuel A Wiley:

14326.   *Lydia Wiley, born 1825, died 5-3-1913, married Richard
131.   Baxter born 1826, died Leghorn, Italy, 1-5-1859, son of Eliza
          (Swain) & Shubael Baxter. Their two cildren died young.

14326.   *Samuel S Wiley born 1827, died 1856, married 1850 Penelope
132.   Waitt (17511.24(10.) born 1827, d 1907, daughter of Persis
          (Hallett) & Samuel Waitt

14326.   *Lucy Wiley born Osterville MA 1829, died 7-2-1896, married 1st
133.   Freeman Lovell Jr, his 2d wife. They had Clifford Lovell born
          1858, died 1932, married 1891 Annie L Potter. They had a son
          Stanley Lovell born 1882, died 1969. Lucy married 2d Capt
          Henry S Linnell, widower of her aunt Frances (Hodges) Linnell.
          Their East Bay, Osterville home stood opposite East Bay Lodge.

14326.   Hannah Wiley born 1833, died 1897, married Robert H Lovell
134.   born 1831, died 1882, son Jerusha (Bartlett) & Robert Lovell

14326.135.   David Wiley born 1835, died 1836

14326.   Chloe Wiley born 1837, died 1888, married 1862 William Jenkins
136.   born 1833, died 1884. Their only child, Nellie Jenkins, born
          1870, died 1946, lived in the Jenkins Homestead, W Barnstable.

14326.137.   David Wiley born 1839, died 1840

INSERT ADDITION: I, p 105 (PC Vol II, p 79)
Children of Persis L (Crocker) Coleman (145(10)7.33.)
  & David Joy Coleman:

145(10)7.   Josephine Coleman born 1861, died ?, married in 1880
331.   Wiliam A Fuller

145(10)7.   Jennie Coleman born 1865, died 1955, married Edwin Fuller
332.
145(10)7.   Gilbert Coleman born ?, died ?, married 1888 Mabel Bearse
333.

INSERT ADDITION: I, p 105 (FWF)
Children of Edward Nye Fish (145(10)8.11.)
  & Maria Matilda (Wakefield) Fish:

145(10)8. *Franklin Wakefield Fish Sr born Tucson AZ 1-10-1875, died
111.   San Diego CA 11-24-1964, married Chicago IL 9-19-1907
       Annie May Ashworth born Plymouth England 5-28-1878, died
       San Diego CA 11-19-1962, daughter of Emma (Gregson) &
       Rev John Wigney Ashworth

145(10)8. Clara Cramond Fish born Tucson AZ 9-3-1876, died Sherman TX
112.   (bur Tucson) 10-27-1965, married 6-12-1905 Fredrick
       Carlyle Roberts Sr

145(10)8. Florence Maria Fish born Tucson AZ 10-22-1883, died
113.   Los Angeles CA 3-7-1962, married Tucson AZ 10-4-1909
       John Bayard Taylor Campbell Sr

INSERT ADDITION: I, p 107-B (PH, BWS)
Children of Wilson Crocker (16344.21.)
  & Tabitha (Freeman) Crocker:

16344. *Charles Wilson Crocker born West Barnstable MA 9-16-1842,
211.   died Chicago IL 9-26-1913, married 2d Union City MI 6-18-1871
      Mary Whiting Moseley born Union City MI 8-24-1849, died St
      Augustine FL 3-6-1889; he married 3d 3-19-1890 Arabel Moseley
      born Norwich CT 5-24-1857, died New Brunswick NJ 7-31 1930

Charles Wilson Crocker left the Cape at the age of 17 years to find employment in Boston. Shortly after the Civil War began he volunteered in the Union Army. See excerpts from his diary, kept from 1861 to 1866, at the end of this book.

Charles Wilson Crocker was 2-1/2 years old when his mother died. He grew up in the home of his father and step-mother, Betsy C (Wright) Bearse Crocker, at the Homestead located on Round Pond in Marstons Mills; he attended local schools and at age 18 years was working in Boston at the dry goods and apparel store of Haughton Sawyer & Co. (HS&Co.)

In August 1862, Crocker volunteered in the Mass. 40th Reg't. Union forces, and served for three years in the Civil War. He kept a diary from January 1861 through December 1866, a copy of which is in the Osterville Historical Society archives, a gift in 1987 of his granddaughter, Joan (Thomas) Vos.

After the close of the war, Charles worked one year at HS&Co, his former employer; then another year in Centerville for F.G. Kelley before going west to seek his fortune. He married 1st in Michigan but his first wife died young; he married 2d Mary W Moseley, and 3rd, Mary's first cousin, Arabel. Their fathers, William A and Edwin W Moseley, were brothers.

INSERT ADDITION: I, p 107-B (BWS, PC Vol II, p 185, p 270)
Children of Wilson Crocker (16344.21.)
 & Betsey Crocker (Wright) (16324.21) Bearse Crocker:

16344. Nelson W Crocker born Marstons Mills MA, married
  212. L Annette Phelps, daughter of Henry Phelps of Wilbraham MA
       On her maternal side Annette was connected with the Moseley
       family, prominent in western MA. They had a son, Allen H
       Crocker and a daughter, Cora P Crocker.

16344. Alexander Holway Crocker born Marstons Mills MA 1842
  213. died there 3-5-1880, unmarried

16344. *Henry Ellis Crocker born Barnstable MA 6-13-1848, died
214.   2-11-1918, married Osterville MA 7-28-1870 Helen Howard
        Scudder born Osterville MA 1-8-1850, died 12-31-1936,
        daughter of Augusta (Hinckley) (blank.62.) & Josiah Scudder
        Jr. Both are buried Hillside Cemetery, Osterville MA.

Henry Ellis Crocker in 1898 received from Bates College,
Lewiston, Maine, the honorary degree of Master of Arts for his
services in the cause of education. He was for several years a
member of the faculty of Wesleyan Academy, Wibraham MA and later,
beginning in 1885, served twelve years as Superintendent of
Public Schools in Dedham Ma.

Like earlier generations of Crockers, five of his uncles having
been shipmasters in either merchantmen or whalers, in his youth
Henry followed the sea. One of his uncles, for whom he was named,
was killed in an encounter with a whale. At the age of 16, Henry
Crocker was captain of a barge on the Hudson River, and in 1865
served on a vessel chartered by government service in the South.

Subsequently Henry E Crocker became a student in the Providence
Conference Seminary at East Greenwich RI. Later he and his family
moved to New York where he accepted a position with textbook pub-
lishers, Ginn & Company; Later they moved to New Jersey. While
making his home in Haworth, Bergen County, NJ, Henry ran for and
was elected mayor of the borough of Haworth NJ.

One of his Proclamations follows:

BOROUGH OF HAWORTH

PROCLAMATION

    I, Henry E. Crocker, Mayor of the Borough of
Haworth, in the County of Bergen, N.J., pursuant to
the authority vested in me by an Act of the Legislature of the State of New Jersey, entitled "An Act for
Protection against Mad Dogs," approved March 28, 1862,
and the acts amendatory thereof and supplemental
thereto, by and with the advice and consent of the
Council of the said Borough, believing that the public
safety requires the same, do hereby authorize the des-
truction of all dogs found running at large within the
limits of the Borough, except such as shall be properly
muzzled with a muzzle about the nose and the same
securely fastened, provided that nothing in this
proclamation shall apply to a dog or dogs of a
non-resident passing through the Borough accompanied
by the owner of such dog or dogs. Given under my hand
and seal this thirty-first day of May, 1910.

Henry E. Crocker
Mayor

Attest:
Everett A Bell
Borough Clerk

Helen Howard Scudder, Henry's wife, descended from prominent Osterville families. Helen's mother, Augusta (Hinckley) Scudder, born Osterville 9-8-1819, died there 2-17-1909, daughter of Louisa (Crocker) & shipbuilder Oliver Hinckley of Osterville MA. (See I, p 51 and Vol II, blank 1.), was Josiah Scudder Jr's 2d wife; Josiah Jr born 2-12-1802, died 12-29-1877, married 1st 2-16-1823 Sophronia Hawes born 8-12-1802, died 7-25-1847, by whom he had 12 children; he and Augusta had five children.

[For family of Augusta (Hinckley) Scudder's uncle, Ignatius Crocker please see blank.6., blank.61., & blank.611.]

Of Josiah Scudder Jr's twelve children by his 1st wife, seven lived to maturity; son Joseph W born 2-11-1839, died 5-3-1864, five days after discharge from service in the Civil War. Among five children of Josiah's 2d marriage three survived to adulthood but his youngest son, Charles N born 1-8-1858, died 3-7-1886 at 28 years. Named for his uncle, Methodist minister Rev Charles Noble Hinckley, he married Rosa P Nickerson of Cotuit.

In February 1833 Josiah Scudder Jr received his appointment as Osterville Postmaster, an office he filled for some years. Josiah Jr was named executor of his father's will, a document which left to each of his children and grandchildren specific bequests, showing Josiah Sr's particular concerns for his heirs. Josiah Jr's own estate, valued at the time of his death in 1877, amounted to $18,472. His widow, Augusta, died in Osterville February 22, 1909, having survived him by more than 30 years.

16344.215. Sarah Abby Crocker born 1850, died 6-12-1850

CORRECTIONS: I, p 111 (CFC)
Children of James Harvey Crocker (16346.66.)
 & Cora F (Crocker) Crocker (17181.621.)

16346. *Chester Arthur Crocker born 7-4-1881, died Marstons Mills MA
661.   1962, married Cotuit MA 6-10-1903 Alice Savery born Cotuit
       3-20-1889, died Marstons Mills 1968

16346.662.)
         : Unchanged, See I p 111 (CFC)
16346.663.)

16346.   *Mary Eliza Crocker born 12-20-1889, died Osterville MA
664.   12-26-1937, married 11-27-1920 Raymond Spencer Sinnett
        born Boston MA August 1882, died Marstons Mills MA 1957

INSERT ADDITION: I, p 111 (CFC)
Children of Marcia Abigail (Crocker) Kelley (16346.68.)
   & Herbert Kelley:

16346.   *Una Jennie Kelley married Portland ME 9-4-1910 Ralph Eugene
681.   Rowe

INSERT ADDITION: I, p 111 (CS)
Children of Joseph Crocker Ewers (P-16352.21.)
   & Eunice (Livermore) Ewers:

P-16352. Franklin Ewers born Bunker Hill Twp, Ingam Co MI 10-16-1845
211.   died Denver CO 6-1-1921, buried Bunker Hill Cem; married
        Leslie MI 11-21-1875 Laura Hicks

P-16352. Samuel Ewers born Bunker Hill Twp, Ingham Co MI 4-9-1848,
212.   died there 9-16-1850

P-16352. Seneca Ewers born Bunker Hill Twp, Ingham Co MI 4-18-1850,
213.   died there 9-8-1851

P-16352. Eliza Jane Ewers born Bunker Hill Twp, Ingham Co MI 9-5-1852
214.   died Columbia MO 9-29-1889, married Williamston MI 1-1-1872
        Charles Vernon Havens

P-16352. James Livermore Ewers born Bunker Hill Twp, Ingham Co, MI
215.   10-2-1854, died Divide Creek CO 3-7-1940, married Glenwood
        Springs CO 5-10-1891 Belle Cozad

P-16352. Joseph Emmett Ewers born Bunker Hill Twp, Ingham Co, MI
216.   12-31-1856, died there 3-16-1874

P-16352.217. William Ewers born @ 1859, died before 1870

Children of Joseph Crocker Ewers (P-16352.21.)
  & Adelia L (Harford) Ewers:

P-16352.   Annetta Ewers born Bunker Hill Twp, Ingham Co, MI 10-26-1863
218.   died Ingham Co MI 4-20-1898, married David Carl

P-16352.   Edwin Freeman Ewers born Bunker Hill Twp, Ingham Co, MI
219.   1-29-1866, died Ingham Co MI 1950, married @ 1890 Ella Shaw,
           daughter of Lucy & Orrin Shaw. Edwin bought the Homestead
           after his father's estate was probated.

P-16352.   Eva Ewers born Bunker Hill Twp, Ingham Co, MI 9-18-1869,
21(10).   died 3-13-1917 married 10-20-1889 Charles Shaw, son of Lucy
           & Orrin Shaw

P-16352.   *Ervin Roscoe Ewers born Bunker Hill Twp, Ingham Co, MI
21(11).   9-18-1874, died Fitchburg MI 1-5-1946, married 9-25-1901
           Agnes Heeney born Bunker Hill Twp 11-18-1878, died Jackson
           MI 10-22-1962 daughter of Jane (Fay) & Phillip Heeney

INSERT ADDITION: I, p 111 (PC, Vol II, p 270)
Children of Mercy A (Crocker) (Blank.61) Lovell
  & Isaac Lovell:

Blank.   Hattie D Lovell born Osterville MA 1-10-1864, died there
611.   10-29-1888

Blank.612. Mary Lovell born Osterville MA 1867, died there 1908

Blank.   *Harrison/Harry Crocker Lovell born Osterville MA, died there
613.   1940, married Louise (____); they had one son, Robert Winsor
          Lovell, born Osterville MA 11-30-1910, died 1934, unmarried

INSERT ADDITION: I, p 112 (SCR)
Children of Jane Eliza (Crocker) Luckenbach (16723.4(12).)
  & Owen Augustus Luckenbach:

16723.4(12)1. Gertude Luckenbach became a school teacher

16723.   *Owen Francis Luckenbach born Bethlehem PA 10-8-1871, died
4(12)2.   there PA 2-9-1946, graduated 1898 Lehigh University with a
    degree in Mechanical Engineering. He married 1900 Helen
    Calista Lines born Great Bend PA 7-3-1871, died 12-26-1954,
    buried Bethlehem PA, daughter of Susan Eleanor (Lines) &
    Orrin Asa Lines, descendant of the Lines family that emi-
    grated from England in 1637 to Hartford CT and settled in
    Quinnepac (later New Haven).

Orrin Asa Lines born Montrose PA 4-4-1843 resided there and at
Oil City PA most of his life. At age 17 he enlisted in the Penn-
sylvania Volunteers, served throughout Civil War, fighting at
Wilderness, Cold Harbor, & Petersburg. Mustered out 7-3-1865.

As his granddaughter Jane recalled, Orrin Asa was "Pamp" to his
grandchildren. In his later years he grew a white moustache, wore
a black fedora, and walked uptown every day. He was quite a
character, a big drinker, but also loved to read. His daughter
Helen was always against drinking because he drank so much when
she was young. He lost an eye in the war and carried a bullet in
him. In the Civil War Orrin was a private. A fellow-soldier, an
Indian, followed him around saying, "Who you no like, I go kill."

Orrin and Susan Lines had three daughters; Helen Calista Lines
married Owen Francis Luckenbach; Sarah (Sally) became a nurse;
and Harriet, who worked for Northampton County as secretary of
the Mothers' Assistance Fund. It is said Harriet did not have
suitors because she was so positive (read bossy). Their one son,
Fred, was a successful insurance salesman.

16723.4(12)3. Joseph Luckenbach, died of yellow fever, buried at sea

16723.4(12)4. Jennie Luckenbach married Will Leibert.

INSERT ADDITION: I, p 112 (TC)
Children of Edward Day Crocker (16928.72)
 & Mary Jane (Knight) Crocker:

16928. Edward E Crocker had sons Clifford and Walter Crocker; who had
721.   a daughter, Bertha born 1913, married John Gulliver. They had
       son John Gulliver born 1952, who married Jean Karter; 4 chn.

16928.722. Alice Gertrude Crocker born 1871, died 1971

16928.723. Lizzie Velma Crocker born 1868, died 1970

16928. *Gilbert Knight Crocker born Cape Elizabeth ME 1-4-1875, died
724.   Portland ME 5-16-1931, married 12-1-1903 Emma Louise Towle
       born 1875, died 12-12-1962, daughter of ___ (McKinney) &
       Thomas Towle of Portland ME.

INSERT ADDITION: I, p 112 (JRC)
Children of Capt Nehemiah D Crocker (1692(12).11.)
 & Sophronia (Sims) Crocker:

1692(12).111. Walton Crocker

1692(12).112. Wildred (Mildred?) Crocker

1692(12).113. Mary Crocker

1692(12).114. Louisa Crocker married 9-4-1900 Frederick E Sawyer of
               Cambridge MA

1692(12).115. Charles Crocker

1692(12).116. Robert Crocker

INSERT ADDITION: I, p 112 (JRC)
Children of Dennis C Crocker (1692(12).21.)
 & Isabel (Raymond) Crocker:

1692(12).211. Alice May Crocker born 2-24-1863, died 10-7-1868

1692(12).212. Frank Willis Crocker born 6-15-1865, died 8-15-1866

1692(12).213. Charles Melvin Crocker born 10-19-1867

1692(12).214. Edgar Crocker born 5-14-1870, married 4-30-1895
Ida L Denton of Somerville MA

1692(12).215. Agnes May Crocker born 4-25-1872 married 2-18-1897
William A Pinkney

1692(12).216. Arthur Raymond Crocker born 9-21-1874, died 10-15-1883

1692(12).217. Laura Ethel Crocker born 10-22-1881

INSERT ADDITION: I, p 113 (DL)
Children of Soloman Whiten Crocker 16972.31.)
& Sarah (Keene) Crocker:

16972. *Eleazer G Crocker, a farmer residing at East St Albans ME,
311. married Christina Cole died 1914, daughter Melissa (Boston)
& Dow Cole.

16972. *Joseph E Crocker, a graduate of Harvard College, taught school
312. for several years in Portland OR. He married Edna Leavitt of
Corinna ME, the daughter of Lillian (Young) & Alonzo Leavitt.

INSERT ADDITION: I, p 113 (DL)
Children of Ruth (Crocker) Mower (16972.36.)
& Granville Mower:

16972. *Edwin Mower, a school teacher, married Nettie Robertson,
361. daughter of Juliette (Fuller) & Rufus Robertson of St Albans

16972.362. Mabel Mower married _____ Frost and lived in Templeton MA.

16972.363. Sydney Mower married Chrystal Philbrick of St Albans ME

16972.364. Edwina Mower, unmarried.

16972.365. Eleanor Mower married Scott Hanford of Boston.

16972.366. *Philip Mower married Marjory Heath, a nurse in WWI, and
            lived in St Albans ME

INSERT ADDITION: I, p 113 (JRC) (DL)
Children of Lovell Ransom Crocker (16972.54.)
  & Sarah Catherine (Sickler) Crocker:

16972. Lillian Crocker born Fairmont MN 9-4-1875, died Truman MN
541.   4-19-1914, married Mankato MN 3-4-1892 James Edwin West

16972. Ethel Crocker born Fairmont MN 3-12-1877, died Mankato MN
542.   4-17-1956, married there 3-15-1895 John Henry Hynson

16972. Elva Crocker born Fairmont MN 12-3-1878, died St Paul MN
543.   8-31-1957, married Mankato MN 8-20-1900 Guy Warren Haff

16972.544. George (William) Crocker born Fairmont MN 9-13-1880

16972.545. Ernest R Crocker born Fairmont MN 8-13-1882

16972.546. LeRoy (Roy) Crocker born Fairmont MN 8-16-1887

Children of Lovell Ransom Crocker (16972.54.)
  & Mary (Hagadorn) Crocker:

16972. Alvin (Ransom) Crocker born Mankato (Blue Earth Cty) MN
547.   2-12-1893

INSERT ADDITION: I, p 113 (DL)
Children of Louisa Anna (Small) Samuels (16972.76.)
  & Solomon Samuels:

16972.761. Alfred Samuels born Chelsea MA 2-16-1871

16972. *Joseph Kaufman Samuels born Cambridge MA 1-5-1875, died
762.   8-16-1950, bur. Woodlawn Cem, Everett MA, married Grace
        Frances Bower born Shelbourne Cty N.S. CAN. 10-24-1877,

died Nashua NH 3-14-1960, daughter of Grace Frances (Pearson)
& Adam Henry Bower of Lowell MA and Shelbourne Cty, N.S. CAN.
She is buried Fairview Cem, Hyde Park MA with her daughter
Iola Louise (Samuels) Leary, Lot #68, R.1, Olive Grove Sect.

16972.763. Louisa Rachel Samuels born Cambridgeport MA 7-26-1876

16972.764. Mariette E Samuels born Boston MA 12-24-1878

16972.765. Harry Elsworth Samuels born Cambridge MA 10-12-1880

16972.766. Eleanor S Samuels born Cambridge MA 3-9-1883

16972.767. Aurelia Anna Samuels born Boston MA 6-18-1885

INSERT ADDITION: I, p 114 (TAC) (NYE) (WAW)
Children of Luther Crocker (17181.15.)
  & Chloe (Hodges) Crocker:

17181. *Hercules Hodges Crocker, eldest of four children, was born
  151.   Nantucket 3-6-1828, died Chicago IL 11-1-1878, married
          Franklin Cty IN 6-21-1849 Lydia Ann Nye, born Scipio IN
          6-22-1833, died Chicago IL 11-12-1888, daughter of Mary C
          (Moorehead) & Joshua Nye.

17181. George L Crocker born Nantucket MA @ 1830
  152.

CORRECTIONS: I, p 116 (CFC)
Children of Stephen Crocker (17181.62.)
  & Eliza (Jones) Crocker:

17181. *Cora F born 8-30-1858, died Marstons Mills MA 9-9-1911,
  621,   married 1-1-1880 James Harvey Crocker (16346.66.) born
          6-19-1850, died 6-5-1928, son of Temperance (Crocker)
          (16344.4.) & Asa I Crocker. [Cora is also descended from
          Sgt Joseph & Temperance (Bursley) Crocker (17.)]

INSERT ADDITION: I, p 119 (RJG)
Children of Winslow Lewis (17511.11.)
  & Susan (Eldredge) Lewis:

17511. *Maria B Lewis born R.I. 10-2-1829, died 11-18-1868, married
   111.   (2d of three wives) Marshall Hinckley Jr born 12-18-1818, died
          Hyannis MA 4-1-1898, son of Marshall Hinckley Sr, shipwright
          of Osterville. He was in the oil and lumber business in
          Hyannis, as well as oyster fishery.

INSERT ADDITION: I, p 119 (PC Vol II, p 155)
Children of Mercy (Hallett) Dewey (17511.22.)
  & Samuel Dewey:

17511.   Augusta Dewey born 18--, died 1888, married 1st 1824 Frederick
   221.   Thayer; had a son Frederick Thayer Jr who had nine children.
          Augusta married 2d H Richards; had three children.

17511.222. Samuel Dewey Jr

17511.223. Eliza Dewey married ____ Wade in 1837.

17511.224. William Dewey lived in New Orleans

INSERT ADDITION: I, p 119 (PC, Vol II, p 162)
Children of Persis (Hallett) Waitt (17511.24.)
  & Samuel Waitt:

17511.241. Frederick Waitt born Osterville 1810, died young

17511.242. Augustus Waitt born Osterville 1811, died there 1812

17511.243. Edgar Waitt born Osterville 1812, died 1855 in
            Jacksonville FL

17511. *Henry Waitt born Osterville 1814, died 1856, married 1843
   244. Mary H Lovell born 1826, died Osterville 1897, daughter of
         Merinda (Lombard) & Samuel Lovell. Mary married 2d 1865
         Warren Small born 1815, died 1908

17511.   *Persis Waitt born Charlestown MA 4-6-1817, died Osterville
245.   3-8-1905, married Osterville 1837 Joseph Robbins born Harwich
MA 7-8-1807, died 3-2-1888, son of Hannah (Nickerson) & James
Robbins. They had 14 children of whom seven lived to maturity.

17511..   Henrietta Waitt born Osterville 1818, died 1894, married
246.   1843 Frederick Scudder born 1819, died 1862, son of Chalana
(Lumbert) & Oliver Scudder. They had five children.

17511.   Laura Waitt born Osterville 1820, died 4-4-1905, married
247.   1842 Richard Andrews; married 2d Francis Kerbaugh

17511.248.   George Waitt born Osterville 1822

17511.   Robert Waitt (Capt) born Osterville 1824, died at New
249.   Dorchester May 1900, married 1854 Ellen Hinckley, born 1831,
died 1911, daughter of Mary (Cobb) & Matthias Hinckley. They
had one son, Arthur Waitt 1858-1920.

17511.   *Penelope Waitt born Osterville 3-5-1827, died Wilmar, MN
24(10).   1-17-1907, married Samuel S Wiley born 1827, son of Lucy
(Hodges) & Samuel A Wiley

INSERT ADDITION: I, p 119 (PC vol II, p 166)
Children of Christina (Hallett) Chessman (17511.25.)
& Rev Daniel Chessman:

17511.251.   Benjamin Chessman born 1819, died 1819

17511.252.   Samuel Chessman born 1820, died 1820

17511.253.   Daniel Chessman born 1821, buried Forest Hills Cemetery
Suffolk County, MA

17511.254.   William Chessman born 1823

INSERT ADDITION: I, p 119 (PC Vol II, p 166)
Children of Hon Benjamin Franklin Hallett (17511.28.)
  & Laura (Larned) Hallett:

17511.281. Jane Hallett born 1825, married 1846 Francis Sayles

17511. *Henry L Hallett Esq born Providence RI 1826, died December
282.   1892. An 1842 graduate of Harvard University, he married 1858
        his 1st cousin Corinna Thacher Lovell born 1831, died 6-2-1910
        daughter of Adeline (Hallett) & George Lovell of Osterville
        MA. They had two daughters.

INSERT ADDITION: I, p 119 (LL) (PC Vol II, p 249)
Children of Adeline de la Motte (Hallett) Lovell (17511.29.)
  & Capt George Lovell:

17511. Corinna Thacher Lovell born Osterville MA 3-22-1831, died
291.   6-2-1919, married her 1st cousin, Henry L Hallett Esq
        (17511.282.) born Providence RI 1826, died Boston December
        1892. They had two daughters.

17511. George Thacher Lovell born Osterville 1833, died Mt Vernon NY
292.   11-9-1900, married Ann Marie Kelly.

17511. Gustavus Crocker Lovell born Osterville 1834, died Mt Vernon
293.   NY 11-9-1900, married 1st Ellen A Ewer, daughter of Elizabeth
        (Dottridge) & James Ewer.

17511. *Franklin Hallett Lovell Sr born Osterville 12-26 1836, died
294.   Kingston NY 10-17-1914, married at Brooklyn NY 12-20-1862
        Mary Louise Lewis born NYC 11-30-1846, died Rome, Italy, 1-21-
        1927, daughter of Mary Ann (Caldecutt) & Arnold Angel Lewis.

INSERT ADDITION: I, p 119 (PC Vol II, p 172)
Children of Julia A (Hallett) Williams (17511.2(11).)
  & Bradford B Williams:

17511.   Sarah A Williams born Osterville 1826, died Philadelphia PA
2(11)1. 2-3-1907, married Osterville Dr William Arnold of New York.

17511.2(11)2. Clarence Williams born Boston MA 1831

17511.2(11)3. Attaresta Williams born Boston MA 1833, married DeSilver

17511.2(11)4. Caledonia Williams born Cotuit Port MA 1835, married
        Byron Wood

INSERT ADDITON: I, p 119 (PC Vol II, p 293)
Children of James Newton Lovell (17511.51.)
& Lucinda (Hinckley) Lovell:

17511.511. Lucinda Lovell born 1836, died 1847

17511.512. Eugenia Lovell born 2-9-1847, died 7-12-1906, unmarried

17511. James Allen Lovell born 1857, died 1935, married Ella Scudder
513. born 1857, died 1935, adopted daughter Eliza & Alfred Scudder

INSERT ADDITION: I, p 119 (EMcN)
Children of Franklin S Phinney (17552.11.)
& Margaret S (Macy) Phinney:

17552. *Charles Sturgis Phinney born 1857, died 1940, married Augusta
111. Macy born 1-11-1868, died 1961, daughter of Josiah Henry Macy
[Josiah Henry Macy was born 8-10-1840 and married 11-29-1857.
Augusta's mother's name and parentage are unknown.]

Ninth Generation

INSERT ADDITION: I, p 121 (RJG)
Children of Jacob Childs (11131.131.)
& Clarissa (Fish) Childs:

11131. *Augustus F Childs born 1827, died 1910, married Mary C Fish
1311. born 1838, daughter of Rhoda Braley (Allen) born 1806, died
1845, & Orsmond Fish born 1799, died 1882, Rhoda Braley Allen
was the daughter of Margaret (Braley) born 1795, died 1842, &
Eliashub Allen born ___, died 1814 in the Battle of Sackett's
Harbor. Orsmond Fish was son of Hannah (Coombs) & Stephen
Fish Jr. He was brother of Clarissa Fish, Augustus' mother,
making Augustus and Mary C (Fish) Childs first cousins.

INSERT ADDITION: I, p 121 (GA)
Children of Francis Henry Day (11272.111.)
* Sarah Ann (Bunting) Day:

11272. *Lucy Elizabeth Day born Keating, McKeen Cty PA 12-13-1841,
1111. died Palmyra, Otoc Cty NE 8-24-1916, married 2-11-1860 Thomas
Seabridge Caddy, born Staffordshire England, died Wheeler Cty
NE, winter of 1883

11324. Henry Crocker Fuller born Osterville MA @ 1909, died
1122. Centerville MA 11-15-1995, age 86.

Obituary, Barnstable Patriot 11-17-1995: I, p 121
Henry Crocker Fuller, a MAYFLOWER descendant, was also a member
of the Fuller Historical Society. He served in the Coast Guard
during WWII, was an interior designer in New York City and in
Boston. Sisters Virginia Fuller and Marjorie (Fuller) Bronsdon,
a brother Gordon David Fuller, and many nieces and nephews
survived him. Buried Hillside Cemetery, Osterville MA.

INSERT ADDITION: I, p 122 (LGW)
Children of Samuel Percival Allen (14211.181.)
  & Harriet C (Stanley) Allen:

14211. *Cornelia Stanley Allen married Rochester NY 8-19-1862
1811. Alfred Smith; they moved to Philadelphia PA. She published a
history of the Percival family.

14211.1812. Kate Allen born NY married Joseph Farley Jr

14211. Frederick Percival Allen born 2-26-1853 married Carrie Clark
1813. daughter of Freeman Clark, U S Congressman; their children
were: Henrietta Ward Allen and Mary Percival Allen. Frederick
was cashier at the German-American Bank of Rochester NY

INSERT ADDITION: I, p 122 (LGW)
Children of Ruth Gardiner (Allen) Weeks (14211.182.)
  & Robert E Weeks:

14211.1821. Willard Weeks born Smyrna NY, res Mt Morris NY

14211.1821. Frank G Weeks Rev, pastor of church at North St Paul

INSERT ADDITION: I, p 122 (LGW)
Children of Rev Orsen Parda Allen (14211.185.)
  & Caroline R (Wheeler) Allen:

14211. *Edward Percival Allen born Harpoot Turkey 10-10-1857, died
1851. Westhampton Beach NY 8-26-1947, married Limington ME 7-8-1885
Celia Jane Gates born Washington IA 10-5-1859, died Barre MA
6-14-1936, daughter of Mary (Hobbs) & Charles H Gates. Edward
graduated from Amherst College 1880 and Andover Seminary. He
was pastor at Staceyville IA when his son Harold was born in
1890. Celia taught primary school at Port Washington NY 1884

14211. *Herbert Marsena Allen Rev born Harpoot Turkey 3-8-1865, died
1852. Constantinople Turkey 1-25-1911, married Bangor ME 6-10-1893
Ellen Ropes Ladd, born Upper Clapton, London, England
9-19-1865, died Mt Vernon NY 5-27-1942

Rev Herbert Marsena Allen, a graduate of Williams College, North
Adams MA, decided to pursue journalism in America, but went out
to visit his parents in Van and Harpoot; he also travelled into
Kurdistan with Rev Dr James L Barton of Harpoot. As a result
Herbert became convinced his most promising field of usefulness
lay in Asia Minor. He returned to America, graduated from Bangor
Seminary in 1890, and was ordained. Two days later he married
Ellen R Ladd who had already been a missionary in Van for three
years. They went out to Van where Herbert, acquainted from
boyhood with the Armenian language and with the thoughts,
customs, and needs of the people, began his work immediately.

He sympathized deeply with the Armenians as a race and with their
sufferings and aspirations. He secured to a remarkable degree the
confidence and friendship of the people. As principal of the
Boys' School at Van, and in his preaching and touring in city and
village, he had great influence and was very useful. After the
massacres of 1896, he was sent to Persia by a relief committee to
purchase oxen for the surviving peasants; through this aid and
the seed given them, they were able to escape starvation.

In 1898 family conditions led them to return to America where he
resigned his connection the Board of Missions and was for a
while engaged in Cuban relief, later taking charge, under the
Massachusetts Home Missionary Society, of the religious work
among the Armenians.

He published with much success the Armenian paper "Gotchnag,"
which was later removed to New York and enlarged. In 1903 he
accepted the invitation to return to Turkey to become the editor
of the Avedapar; at the same time he took over the principalship
of the Bithynia High School at Bardizag for two years in the
absence of Dr Robert Chambers.

In 1905 he went to Constantinople, and after making a preliminary
trip through the country to get in touch with the constituency,
he took charge in 1907 of the Armenian Avedaper. He made a great
success of this and subscribers rapidly increased.

In 1910 Herbert also undertook to publish a small sheet in English, Bosphorus News, and later The Orient, to keep English-reading friends in touch with the progress of mission work in Turkey. An able writer with rare gifts as a preacher, Herbert was always ready to work up to and beyond the limits of his strength.

The Board of Missions stated they have had no missionary with a more thorough acquaintance with Armenian history or with a deeper love for the people. He was suddenly struck down with pneumonia and died 1-25-1911. His widow and six children returned shortly thereafter to America. At his funeral in Pera, besides American and English speakers, the vicar of the Gregorian Patriarch made an address, the first time any Gregorian clergyman had stood in a Protestant pulpit. At the memorial service in Van an Armenian Bishop also made a eulogy, and the Armenian Bishop of Ankara wrote the Avedaper of what Herbert Allen had done for his people.

14211.   Annie Theresa Allen born Harpoot Turkey 12-21-1868, died
  1853.   Sivas Turkey 2-2-1922, missionary

Annie Theresa Allen, a graduate of Dana Hall in Wellesley MA, Bible Normal in Springfield MA, and Mt Holyoke College, South Hadley MA 1890, went out from Boston on 8-16-1890, to help her parents in Harpoot. She spent her first winter in Van.

In 1903 she received full appointment from the American Board of Missions and sailed from Boston on 8-8-1903, arriving Brousa Sept, 1903. Annie remained in Turkey till 8-25-1909, returned to America and stayed until 8-8-1912, then returned to Brousa in September of that year, remaining in Turkey until her death.

Throughout WW I Annie was tireless in her relief work among the refugees and other sufferers until conditions made it necessary for her and her aged father to go to Constantinople where he died June 1918. After the war she refused her well-earned furlough, but stayed on in charge of Near East Relief, first in Brousa, then in Angora where she was asked in 1921 to become the representative of the work before the Komalist Government.

She travelled extensively and fearlessly in the interests of the relief work; and few missionaries ever left such an impress on the hearts and lives of such a variety of the inhabitants of Turkey. She was all things to all men, and her soul was apparently absolutely free from all thoughts of self.

During her travels she had a fall from a carriage on 1-18-1922, near Harpoot, which seriously affected her. She became ill on the way to Sivas where her trouble was diagnosed as typhus. Despite the best of American care, she died 2-22-1922 and was buried with military honors, representatives of all the official bodies and a guard of honor accompanying the body to the grave. Persona grata to the Turks, although they fully knew her sympathies with the Armenians, she commanded the respect and admiration of officials wherever she met them. Rear-Admiral Mark L Bristol, the American High Commissioner, sent at her death an official cable to Washington as follows:

"I cannot pay too high a tribute to noble character ALLEN. During three years I have marveled at courage and endurance she showed in travelling all over Anatolia in all seasons of the year in service to humanity. She was known throughout the country from the highest official to the lowest peasant. She travelled without fear because unknowing what fear was. Noble character ALLEN recognized, honored, by all who knew her, was one rarely met in this world. She was broadminded but strong in her convictions, fearless in doing right. It was a privilege to associate with her because of her spirit and optimism born of ideals practically applied. I feel deep personal loss, loss which is still greater to Near East Relief, to her Missionary Society, and to American interests. One best friend of all people of Asia Minor has passed to the great beyond."

14211.1854. Katie Allen died young, buried Harpoot Turkey

14211.1855. Mary Allen died young, buried Harpoot Turkey

14211.1856. Hattie Allen died young, buried Harpoot Turkey

INSERT ADDITION: I, p 122 (PC Vol II, p 228)
Children of Frances (Hodges) Linnell (14326.121.)
& Henry Simpson Linnell Sr:

14326.1211. Henry S Linnell Jr born 1844, died 1846

14326.1212. Esther Linnell born 1844, died 1871

14326.1213. Joseph Linnell born 1846, died 1861

14326.1214. Arabella Linnell born 1848, died 1849

14326.1215. Herbert Linnell born 1854, died 1855

14326.1216. Janet Linnell born 1858, died 1937

14326.1217. William Linnell born 1860, died 1928

INSERT ADDITION: I, p 122 (PC Vol II, p 194)
Children of Joseph Hodges (14326.123.)
& Jane (Parker) Hodges:

14326.1231. Herbert Hodges born 1848, died 1849

14326. *Frank W Hodges born Osterville MA 1852, died there 1915,
1232. married 1876 Annie West born Osterville 4-9-1860, died
7-4-1950, daughter of Sarah (Lewis) & Nathan E West Sr

INSERT ADDITION: I, p 122 (PC Vol II, p 196)
Children of Jehiel Hodges (14326.124.)
& Elizabeth (Scudder) Hodges:

14326. Freeman Hodges born 1851, died 1921, married Cotuit MA 1883
1241. Susan M Chatfield, daughter of Florentine & Thomas Chatfield

14326. Henry Hodges born 1852, died 1926, married Nora Nickerson
1242.
14326. *Lillie Hodges born 1857, died 1934, married 1876 Edgar DeWitt
1243. born Nova Scotia 1847, died 1884

INSERT ADDITION: I, p 122 (PC Vol II, p 383)
Children of Samuel S Wiley (14326.132.)
& Penelope (Waitt) (17511.24(10.) Wiley:

14326.1321. Fannie Wiley, born 1851, died 1855

14326.1322. Ellen Wiley, born 1853, died 1941, married Albert Scudder
born Centerville MA 1846, died Atchison KA 11-28-1907;
they had one son, Orville Scudder of Chicago IL

14326.1323. Percy Wiley, born 1855, died 19__

INSERT ADDITION: I, p 122 (FWF)
Children of Franklin Wakefield Fish Sr (145(10)8.111.)
& Annie May (Ashworth) Fish:

145(10)8.   *Franklin Wakefield Fish Jr Col born Tucson AZ 7-27-1909,
1111.   married Glendale CA 5-25-1935 Mary Elizabeth Dean born
             Carmangay, AL, CAN, 6-13-1912, daughter of Alice Paden
             (Marshall) & Warren Everett Dean

145(10)8.   Edward Gregson Fish Capt born Cananea, Sonora, Mexico
1112.   1-27-1911, died Livermore CA 3-6-1970, bur Colma CA,
             married London England 11-20-1946 Florida Peensalu

145(10)8.   Margaret Louise Fish born Tucson AZ 2-16-1916, married
1113.   Nogales AZ 9-9-1930 Charles Franklkin Blair

145(10)8.   Robert Ashworth Fish born Tucson AZ 5-20-1916, married
1114.   Pomona CA 5-2-1947 Margaret Edith Scott

INSERT ADDITION: I, p 124 (Obituary, Cape Cod Times, 1-29-1997)
14(10)49. John Howland Crocker born Barnstable MA 1914, died
4314.   Barnstable MA 1-22-1997

    John Howland Crocker, 82, a former grocer and long-time resident
    of Barnstable, died Wednesday at the Cape Regency Nursing &
    Rehabilitation Center in Centerville. He was the husband of
    Mary E (Hinckley) Crocker.

OBIT: <u>John Howland Crocker</u> was born in Barnstable and educated in
Barnstable schools. He graduated from Barnstable High School and
attended New England University. He worked for Swift & Co in the
New Bedford and Fall River area for several years. He then owned
and operated J. H. Crocker & Sons Grocery Store in West Barnstable from 1952 to 1963 and worked at Coleman's Package Store
in Hyannis from 1964 until retiring in 1980.

Mr Crocker was a past member of the Barnstable Fire
Department where he served as a call fireman for many years
and worked his way up to become an officer in the rescue squad.
He decorated veterans' graves in the Town of Barnstable with
flowers and flags for many years.

Surviving besides his wife are four sons, William L Crocker
of Marstons Mills, David H Crocker of Mashpee, Alfred Crocker of
Centerville, and Richard S Crocker of South Sandwich, and a
daughter, Constance Jalicki of Yarmouth, twelve grandchildren,
four great grandchildren, and several nieces and nephews.

<u>INSERT ADDITION</u>: I, p 125

<u>Lauchlan McLean Crocker Sr (15848.3525.)</u> A personal memory of Sheriff
Crocker comes to mind as a colorful flashing picture of a meeting of
our two families -- probably 70 years ago. A well-advertized full-
eclipse of the sun to be visible in Chatham, Massachusetts, on a
particular summery afternoon sometime before 1930 drew my parents and
their children to venture forth. Mother packed a lunch of sandwiches
and Father drove a big touring car down-Cape to watch the eclipse.
Each of us was equipped with rectangles of exposed photographic film
to protect our eyes as we witnessed the moon pass between earth and
sun, and plunge us into total darkness. (We didn't know that film was
inadequate protection and that we shouldn't look at the sun through
film or any other way.)

l recall little of the eclipse except disappointment for darkness
wasn't as deep as I had expected. After the sun came out again, and we
had eaten our lunches, we attempted the return trip only to find ourselves locked in the first traffic jam I had ever experienced.

Two solid lanes of traffic wormed westward, each auto jockeying for advantage to escape the crowded highway. Father (not noted for his patience) growled at the delays; Mother spoke soothingly, reminding we need not hurry. Then, unexpectedly, in the other line of cars appeared one similar to ours, similarly laden with several children. "Locky" and Wilhelmina with their family of youngsters hailed Burl and Jess with theirs. Our car and theirs proceeded to inch along, the parents visiting as we went... Our day ended happily, after all!

INSERT ADDITION: I, p 126 (PH)
Children of Charles Wilson Crocker (16344.211.)
& Mary Whiting (Moseley) Crocker:

16344. *Lillian M Crocker born Union City MI 2-17-1872, died Wilmette
2111. IL 2-13-1964, married Wilmette IL 5-16-1900 John Melville
Brown born 3-24-1863, died Wilmette IL 1-20-1948

16344.2112. Frank Wilson Crocker born 3-16-1874, died 10-2-1874

16344. *Charles Henry Crocker born 10-3-1883, married 4-17-1920
2113. Hazel Reck

Children of Charles Wiulson Crocker (16344.211.)
& Arabel (Moseley) Crocker:

16344. *Catherine Crocker born Wilmette IL 10-18-1892, died Barnstable
2114. MA 5-15-1984, married 11-18-1922 Henry Seely Thomas born
Middlebury VT 7-19-1899, died Barnstable MA 12-1-1972

INSERT ADDITION: I, p 126 (BWS)
Children of Henry Ellis Crocker (16344.214.)
& Herlen Howard (Scudder) Crocker:

16344. Helen (Nellie) Brigham Crocker born Marstons Mills 10-6-1871,
2141. died Hyde Park MA 2-6-1895, a graduate of Columbia University

16344. *Henry (Harry) Scudder Crocker born 3-28-1874, died 6-27-1899,
2142. married Wilhelmina (MacDougall)

104

OBIT: Mr Harry S Crocker died on Tuesday at his home in The Plains.
He leaves a wife and three children, father, mother and sister to
mourn his early death. Funeral services in the Methodist Church
on Thursday conducted by Rev Eugene Antrim. Among those present
from out of town were Rev Edward B Hinckley, Provincetown, and
Mrs. J. P. Scudder and sons, Brockton.

16344.2143. Bessie L Crocker born 10-19-1883, died 10-11-1950

CORRECTIONS & ADDITIONS: I, p 129 (CFC)
Children of Chester Arthur Crocker (16346.661.)
& Alice (Savery) Crocker:

16346.   Natalie Martin Crocker born Osterville MA 10-23-1905, died
6611.   Mashpee MA 2-11-1988, married Leonard I Fish born 1901, died
          1973; no children

16346.   *Zilpha Brunton Crocker born 10-27-1909, died Hyannis MA
6612.   9-26-1968, married 10-19-1930 James F (Fred) Gordon born
          Groveland MA 1904

INSERT ADDITION: I, p 129 (CFC)
16346.   Eugene Richard Crocker born Hyannis MA 8-9-1924, died
6632. -   Boston MA 9-20-1996

OBIT- Sandwich MA -- Eugene Richard Crocker, age 72, a retired captain
of oil tankers and tug boats, formerly of Centerville and
Hyannis, died Friday at Brigham & Women's Hospital, Boston MA
after a brief illness. He was the husband of Lois Frances
(Duffy) Crocker who died in 1993. Having a lifelong love of the
sea, Mr Crocker took boat-building courses while attending
Barnstable High School and as a teenager worked at Crosby Boat
Yard in Osterville. During WWII he served with the Merchant
Marene, and twice made the Murmansk run.

After the war Mr Crocker became a tugboat captain, starting on
coal-fired tugboats. He worked on the Mississippi River, the
Great Lakes, and along the Atlantic seaboard, and for the last
ten years of his career was captain of the Exxon Baystate.

Upon his retirement Eugene Crocker became active in several volunteer activities in Sandwich and Falmouth, including day health care for the elderly, an Alzheimer's support group in Sandwich, the Penikese Island School in Woods Hole, and a boat-building project in the Falmouth schools.

He lived in Centerville MA for about 25 years before moving to Sandwich ten years ago. Survivors include his two daughters, Lois C Harvey of West Falmouth and Nancy Murawski of Utica NY, a brother, Charles F Crocker of Marstons Mills, a sister, Ernestine C Monroe of Centerville, and six grandchildren.

INSERT ADDITIONS & CORRECTIONS: I, p 129 (CFC)
Children of Mary Eliza (Crocker) Sinnett (16346.664.)
& Raymond Spencer Sinnett:

16346.   *Harvey Francis Sinnett born Marstons Mills MA 9-8-1921,
6641.   married 5-25-1946 Irene Mary Demianof born 12-17-1917

INSERT ADDITION: I, p 130 (CS)
Children of Ervin Roscoe Ewers (P-16352.21(11).
& Agnes (Heeney) Ewers:

P-16352.   Merlyn Phillip Ewers born Bunker Hill Twp, Ingham Co MI
21(11)1.   8-28-1902, died Jackson MI 11-6-1954, married Anna Wilson

P-16352.   Alva James Ewers born Bunker Hill Twp, Ingham Co MI
21(11)2.   died unmarried

P-16352.   Mary Agnes Ewers born Bunker Hill Twp, Ingham Co MI
21(11)3.   3-5-1907, died there 9-22-1920 unmarried

P-16352.   Infant Laughlin (?) Ewers born Bunker Hill Twp, Ingham Co
21(11)4.   MI 2-1-1909, died there 2-10-1909

P-16352. *Alice Frances Ewers born Bunker Hill Twp Ingham Co MI
21(11)5. 1-6-1910, married Myrlan Paul Stanfield born Bunker Hill
Twp, Ingham Co MI 10-14-1906, died Sault St Marie MI
8-12-1994, son of Melissa Adelia (Smalley) & John William
Stanfield. Melissa was a descendant of John Smalley,
another early settler on Cape Cod.

P-16352.21(11)6. Infant, twin, born & died 8-6-1911

P-16352. Joseph Raymond Ewers, twin, born Bunker Hill Twp, Ingham Co
21(11)7. MI 8-6-1911, married Kate ____; no children

P-16352. Leo Edward Ewers born Bunker Hill Twp, Ingham Co MI
21(11)8. 3-28-1913, died 11-16-1966; married Sue___; no children

P-16352. Louis Anthony Ewers born Bunker Hill Twp, Ingham Co MI
21(11)9. 12-19-1914, died Jackson MI 11-13-1986, married Ruth
Kathleen McLear and had five children.

P-16352. Anna Gladys Ewers born Bunker Hill Twp, Ingham Co MI
21(11)(10). born Bunker Hill Twp, Ingham Co MI 8-14-1916, married
Leon Lockwood and had six children

P-16352. Emmet Aloysius Ewers born Bunker Hill Twp, Ingham Co
21(11)(12). 10-22-1918, died 7-20-1959, unmarried

INSERT ADDITION: I, p 130 (SCR)
Children of Owen Francis Luckenbach (16723.4(12)2.)
& Helen Calista (Lines) Luckenbach:

16723. *Owen Augustus Luckenbach born Oil City PA 10-20-1902, died
4(12)21. Delray Beach FL Dec 1971, graduate of University of Penna,
married 10-02-1928 Margaret Spademan

16723. *Susan Farrar Luckenbach born Oil City PA 8-31-1906,
4(12)22. married Whitwell Newton Middleton born Arlington VA
5-12-1907, died Mobile AL 1-4-1977.

16723.   *Jane Crocker Luckenbach born Oil City PA 5-17-1911 married
4(12)23.   at Long Island NY 6-5-1937 Clifford Theodore Unbekant born
           Long Island 1-26-1913, died Schenectady NY 4-17-1976, son
           of Florence (Stutz) & Emil Unbekant.

           While Clifford Unbekant was in the Army in the European Theatre,
           WWII, Jane volunteered with the American Red Cross. Clifford
           participated in the D-Day landing on the beaches of Normandy and
           was awarded a purple heart. Jane Crocker (Luckenbach) & Clifford
           Unbekant had one child, Susan Crocker Unbekant (16723.4(12)231.)

INSERT ADDITION: I, p 130 (TC)
Children of Gilbert Knight Crocker (16928.724.)
 & Emma Louise (Towle) Crocker:

16928.7241. Constance Crocker born 1905, died 1905

16928.7242. Nathan Crocker born 1907, died 1979, married Elinor Gates

16928.   *Thomas Edward Crocker born Portland ME 5-9-1909, died
 7243.   Washington DC 5-31-1971, married Ft Smith AR 2-2-1917
          Mabel Miriam Hedges born Scranton AR 2-5-1971, daughter of
          LaVerne (Blanks) & Harold H Hedges.

16928.7244. John Crocker born 1912, died 1968, married, no children

16928.7245. Gilbert Crocker born 1914, living in 1995

INSERT ADDITION: I, p 130 (ANCH)
Children of Nellie Baker (Crocker) Nickerson (16941.141.)
 & Clarenton S Nickerson:

16941.   Emmie Louise Nickerson born 1898, died 1979, married
 1411.   _____ Fulcher, res Hyannis MA

16941.   Bertram Bayliss Nickerson born 1899, died 1976, married
 1412.   Rebecca E Crocker (17181.52111.) born Osterville MA 1911, died
         there 1-24-1981. Their daughter Ruth, married _____ Scalata

Children of Nellie Baker (Crocker) Nickerson Clarke (16941.141.)
  & William Lowell Clarke Sr:

16941. *Earle Lowell Clarke Sr born Cedarville Ma 11-28-1909, died
  1413. Hyannis MA 5-29-1966, bur Hillside Cemetery, Osterville MA,
         married Osterville MA 3-16-1928 Anna Adenia Hodges
         (14326.12321.1.) born Taunton MA 4-24-1911, died Hyannis MA
         8-29-1975, daughter of Florence (Manning) & William P Hodges

16941. William Lowell Clarke Jr born 2-16-1914, died New Castle DE
  1414. 6-1-1979, married Buzzards Bay MA Phyllis Reynolds. Divorced.

INSERT ADDITION: I, p 130 (JRC) (DL)
Children of Eleazer G Crocker (16972.313.)
  & Christina (Cole) Crocker:

16972.3131. Lucy Crocker, a school teacher, married Frank Davis

16972. Edgar Crocker married 1st Edith Nutter, died 1925, daughter
  3132. of Ella (Cook) & William Nutter of Lyford's Corner ME; he
         married 2d ?, had a daughter Patricia Crocker born in Arizona

16972. *George Cleveland Crocker married Lura Libby, daughter of
  3133. Nellie (Varney) & John Libby.

16972. Grace Crocker married Roy Thomas; they ran a restaurant in
  3134. Dexter ME before moving to a farm in Norridgewock ME.

16972. Marion Crocker, Eleazer's youngest daughter, married Glenn
  3135. Nickerson; they farmed in Norridgewock; had four children.

INSERT ADDITION: I, p 130 (DL)
Children of Joseph Crocker (16972.314.)
  & Edna (Leavitt) Crocker:

16972.3141. Paul Crocker

16972.3142. Harold Crocker

16972.3143. Guy Crocker

INSERT ADDITION: I, p 130 (DL)
Children of Edwin Mower (16972.361.)
  & Nettie (Robertson) Mower:

16972. *Charles E Mower married Ada Libby, descendant of Zebulon
3611. Libby who settled near Five Corners ME. Charles Mower
       ran a saw mill at St Albans ME.

INSERT ADDITION: I, p 130 (DL)
Children of Sydney Mower (16972.363.)
  & Chrystal (Philbrick) Mower:

16972.3631. Blaine Mower

16972.3632. Richard Mower

INSERT ADDITION: I, p 130 (DL)
Children of Philip Mower (16972.366.)
  & Marjory (Heath) Mower:

16972.3661. Priscilla Mower

16972.3662. Edwin Mower

16972.3663. Winifred Mower

INSERT ADDITION: I, p 130 (DL)
Children of Joseph Kaufman Samuels (16972.762.)
  & Grace Frances (Bower) Samuels:

16972.7621. Milton Joseph Samuels born Chelsea MA 1903

16972.7622. Ray Francis Samuels born Chelsea MA 1905

16972. *Iola Louise Samuels born Weymouth MA 1-21-1908, died Santo
7623.   Domingo, Dom. Rep. 1-22-1967, married 1928 William Francis
        Leary born Charlestown MA 11-8-1896, died Boston MA 11-7-1983
        son of Bridget (Dillon) & John Jerimiah Leary Jr. William &
        Iola resided Hyde Park MA, are bur there in Fairview Cemetery

16792.7624.   Joseph Kaufman Samuels II born Malden MA 1913

16792.7625.   Doris Samuels born Chelsea MA born 1915

INSERT ADDITION: I, p 130 (NYE) (TAC) (WAW)
Children of Hercules Hodges Crocker (17181.151.)
  & Lydia Ann (Nye) Crocker:

17181.1511.   Francis I Crocker b 9-9-1850

17181.1512.   Edwin Joshua Crocker b 8-15-1852, d 7-11-1854

17181.1513.   Mary Luximer Crocker b 10-16-1854

17181.1514.   Willie Crocker b 6-21-1856, died same day

17181.   *Harry Hercules Crocker born at Chicago IL 4-11-1860, died
1515.   Cortland NY 6-10-1927, married Berlin Heights, Erie Cty, OH
          6-26-1879 Rosa Bonheur Tuttle born Berlin Heights OH
          1-31-1859, died 12-31-1905, daughter of Emma Dianis (Rood) &
          Hudson Tuttle. Harry Hercules & Rosa Bonheur (Tuttle) Crocker
          were divorced 1-12-1893 Erie Cty, OH

INSERT ADDITION: I, p 132 (RJG) (PB)
Children of Maria B (Lewis) Hinckley (17511.111.)
  & Marshall Hinckley Jr:

17511.   Myron Lewis Hinckley born 5-22-1863, died 12-19-1922, married
1111.   Bessie Frances Childs (see 11131.13111. etc.) Myron Hinckley
         was a chef for Marston restaurants, Boston.

INSERT ADDITION: I, p 132 (PC Vol II, p 163)
Children of Henry Waitt (17511.244.)
& Mary H (Lovell) Waitt:

17511.2441. Joseph Waitt born Osterville 1844, died 1863, lost at sea

17511. Edward Waitt born Osterville 1842, died Brookville MA 1932,
2442. married 1878 Elizabeth Taylor, had daughter Mrs. Albert Timme.

17511. Minetta P Waitt born Osterville 1848, died Attleboro Springs
2443. MA August 1932, married Osterville 5-7-1896 William H Bennett,
his 2d wife. He was born at Foster RI 1832, died 12-29-1918.
He served in the Civil War; was once war correspondent for the
Boston Herald.

17511.2444. Henry Waitt born Osterville 1851, died there 1852

17511. Willis Waitt born Osterville 1855, died Taunton MA 1921,
2445. married Myra M Cobb daughter of Rev R. H. Cobb. They had
three children: Russell E. Waitt, Mrs. Florence A Nerney of
Chicago, and Louise L Waitt of Taunton.

INSERT ADDITION: I, p 132 (PC Vol II, p 338) (SC/MC)
Children of Persis (Waitt) Robbins (17511.245.)
& Joseph Robbins:

17511. *Medora Robbins born Osterville 1837, died there 1924, married
2451. 1st Osterville 1858 Isaac Hodges III (14326.127.) born Osterville 1835, died there 1861; he was Osterville postmaster.
Medora married 2d Horace S Lovell born 1827, died 2-11-1890,
son of Lydia (Scudder) & Joshua Lovell.

17511.2452. Joseph born Osterville 1839, died Osterville 4-21-1841

17511. *Emeline Robbins born Osterville 4-17-1841, died 9-2-1902,
2453. married 186_ John Henry Cammett III born Marstons Mills MA
7-13-1833, died Osterville 4-18-1907, son of Betsy Holmes
(Handy) & John H Cammett II

17511.   Laura A Robbins born Osterville 1834, died Dorchester MA
2454.   1-9-1894, married 1874 Eugene F Blossom born 1847, died
           Dorchester MA 1927

17511.   Everett Robbins born 1845, died 1913, married 1881 Olive
2455.   Clark

17511.2456.   Adeline Robbins born 1846, died 1848

17511.2457.   Attaresta W Robbins born 8-3-1847, died 4-23-1934,
                married 1872 Andrew Johnson born Denmark 1840, died
                Osterville 1924.

After Andrew Johnson's rescue from a shipwreck off Cape Cod, he
lived in Osterville. During the Civil War he served in the navy.
Upon discharge Andrew found employment with Brown & Sharp Mfg Co
in Providence, tool and die manufacturers. Over the 53 years he
worked there, Andrew became an authority on hardening and heat
treatment of metals. He and his wife family lived in Providence
RI and vacationed at Osterville where he retired.

17511.2458.   Persis Robbins born 1850, died 1855

17511.2459.   Abbott Robbins born 1852, died 1926, married 1886 Fannie
                Lovell born 1860, died 1941

17511.245(10).   Sophronia Robbins born 1854, died 1855

17511.   . *Edith M Robbins born Osterville 1856, died there 1947,
245(11).   married 12-18-1877 Charles H Crosby born Osterville MA
              7-15-1854, died there 1936, son of Laura (Bassett) and
              Cornelius Worthington Crosby.

Charles Crosby, one of a family famous for their boats, built,
among others, the Sea Hound, the Sea Wolf and, together with his
brother, Daniel, the Cleopatra. He practiced his trade in Osterville for 57 years.

Around the turn of the century, <u>Edith M (Robbins) Crosby</u>, affectionaely known as "Edie Bob," ran a dry goods store at Mulberry Corners in the center of the village. Later, with her granddaughter, Ruth Horne, she operated an ice cream parlor called "The Horn of Plenty."

<u>INSERT ADDITION</u>: I, p 132 (PC Vol II,p 383)
Children of Penelope (Waitt) Wiley (17511.24(10).)
& Samuel S Wiley (14326.132.):

17511.24(10)1. Fannie Wiley born Osterville 1851, died there 1855

17511.   Ellen Wiley born Osterville 1853, died Osterville 1941,
24(10)2.   married Osterville 1881 Albert Scudder born 1846, died
            Willmar MN 11-28-1907, son of Asenath (Richardson) &
            Albert Scudder. They had a son, Orville, of Chicago.

17511.24(10)3. Percy Wiley born Osterville 1855, died 19__

<u>INSERT ADDITION</u>: I, p 132 (LL) (PC Vol II, p 262)
Children of Franklin Hallett Lovell (17511.294.)
& Louise (Lewis) Lovell:

17511.   Isabel Lovell born at Brooklyn NY 1864, died at Orlando FL
2941.   4-20-1962, married 6-7-1902 Grafton Duval Dorsey

17511.   *Franklyn Hallett Lovell II born Brooklyn NY 5-16-1867, died
2942.   NYC 5-19-1962, married at NYC 3-4-1903 Florence Brown Lane
            born NYC 5-3-1868, died Edgartown MA 10-19-1936, daughter of
            Isabella (Hooper) & Jonas Henry Lane of Walpole NH

<u>INSERT ADDITION</u>: I, p 132 (EMcN)
Children of Charles Sturgis Phinney (17552.111.)
& Augusta (Macy) Phinney:

17552.   *Margaret Phinney born 7-13-1906, married Haywood Hoben
1111.   Coburn born 11-8-1907

Tenth Generation

INSERT ADDITION: I, p 133 (RJG)
Children of Augustus F Childs (11131.1311.)
& Mary C (Fish) Childs:

11131. *Bessie Francis Childs born 1867, died 1938, married Myron L
13111. Hinckley born 1863, died 1922

INSERT ADDITION: I, p 133 (GA)

Children of Lucy Elizabeth (Day) Caddy (11272.1111.)
& Thomas Seabridge Caddy Sr: (GA)

11272.11111. Ella Caddy born Nebraska 1861, died 1870

11272. *Charles Henry Caddy born Dubuque IA 1862, died Fallon,
11112. Churchhill Co, NV 9-15-1939, married Nampa, Canyon Co, ID
1-3-1909 Addie Viola Hembree born Hartsville, Wright Co, MO
12-18-1873, died Boise, Ada Co, ID 1-21-1958, daughter of
Emily Jane (Hubbs) & Hugh Lawson Hembree

11272. Francis Leon Caddy born Dubuque IA 7-5-1864, died Pleasant
11113. Home OR 11-18-1921, married 4-30-1891 Minnie Elizabeth Boorman, daughter of Lucy (Rand) & William Boorman. Both buried
Douglas Cemetery, Troutdale OR

11272. *Thomas S Caddy Jr born Strawberry Point IA 10-31-1867, died
11114. near Loup City NE 11-5-1935, married Lizzette Mae Atwood
daughter of Lucy Arabella (King) & Libe Atwood

Thomas Caddy Jr bought a farm six-and-a-half miles southeast of
Loup City NE in 1904. His daughter, Belle (Lucy Arabella (Caddy)
Garner) tells of her life on the farm when she was a child:

"We had all sod buildings except a small grainery and barn. And
what a barn! The boards didn't overlap, leaving big cracks.
Father got what they call battens, about four inches wide, and
nailed them over all the cracks. Then he put up a floor for a hay
loft. It was a big old barn. They stored hay here for the stock

in the winter when the weather was too bad to bring hay in from where they had stacked it. The chicken and milk houses were sod.

"We had a real good sod house, believe it or not; it was warm in winter and cool in summer. We had a board floor. It was pretty good size, but all in one room. Father bought lumber and divided it into four rooms. The north end only had one window; that was my parent's room. The south end had two windows so he made two rooms, one for the boys and one for the girls. The middle room was kitchen, dining room, and living room. It must have been 15 feet square--maybe larger.

"Before we left Albion, father had a horse-powered threshing machine which he used one year. Then he got a steam engine power threshing machine. We children sure thought this was a big deal, although father nearly worked himself to death with it.

"He loved horses. I've seen him buy out-law horses, then gentle them until us children could ride or drive them. He bought one thoroughbred, registered, with a long list of papers, called Lincoln. A beautiful horse, but someone had ruined him. Father put him in a box stall, told us never to go near him. Father told the boys to open two little doors by the feed boxes and set a bucket of water in one and put corn in the other one. Hay was put down in his manger from the hay loft above.

"This horse would bite, kick, stomp, and fight anything that went near him. Father always talked to his stock. He talked to Lincoln every time he went near him. In a short time he had him so he could lead him out to drink from the water tank. Then Father got a harness on him. From then on, he gentled fast. By fall Father put him on the wagon at corn-husking time. The next summer I drove him on a buggy. We called it a single-horse buggy. A few times, though, to tell the truth, I was a little afraid of Lincoln. As I remember, Father probably had him about three years. Then he was sold to the government for a breeding stallion for cavalry horses. Father paid $75.00 for him, papers and all included, and sold him for $500.00.

"Father always bought rough-looking horses, curried and brushed them and took good care of them. They always responded in a few weeks. Didn't look like the same horses. One thing I never knew is how Father managed to get a bunch of horses to the sale barns at Grand Island. Loup City is about 45 to 50 miles from Grand Island. Father rode a saddle horse, leading a couple. He tied one onto the tail of each of those he was leading. Maybe he tied some to the saddle, too. I never did know just how he tied them. Then he took off for Grand Island. He always got them there, and made pretty good on them. Must have done it three years or more.

"One thing I remember was when we were still in the soddie (sod house) where we lived about four years. Father came home from town with some printed songs. We children were told we should learn to sing. He always whistled at his work. When he hauled grain to town it was quite a trip for a team. On a clear night we could hear him whistling before we could hear the wagon.

"Anyway, after the chores and the dishes were done, we all gathered around the table and Father tried to learn us to sing. Maybe there was lots better singing. I am sure no one could have enjoyed it more than we did -- or tried any harder.

"At this time (1969) I am 76 years old. I've seen so many things come into use. The first washing machine, cream separator, steam threshing machine. Now combines and corn picking machines. I saw my first automobile when I was 14 years old. My husband took me to the State Fair the fall after we were married. There I saw the first airplane. It looked like a box kite. The pilot sat on a seat with no protection of any kind, and flew it once a day when wind and weather permitted. He got it off the ground, circled around a few times and brought it down again. That was 58 years ago this coming fall. I asked my husband if he thought they would ever get the airplane where they would be used much. He said he didn't think so. Now they are getting ready to land a man on the moon. Who knows? They will probably find other planets out there in space. There seems to be nothing men can't do but stay out of wars and keep the peace." -- Lucy A (Belle) Garner - taped 9-14-1969.

11272. Hannah Caddy born IA 1870, married Cyrus Ohler. In 1935 she
11115. was living in Golden City, MO

11272. *Wilbur Caddy born Strawberry Point IA 6-18-1874, died Loup
11116. City NE 10-7-1955, bur Evergreen Cem., married Unadilla NE
        7-30-1896 Florence Belle Wright born 1879, died 1948

11272. Alice Elizabeth Caddy born IA @ 1877 per 1880 census. She
11117. was crippled.

11272. *Joseph Caddy born Strawberry Point IA 7-13-1880, died Loup
11118. City NE 3-29-1952, married Clara (Cougar) Morsen (1896-1967)
        Both buried Evergreen Cemetery, Loup City NE

INSERT ADDITION: I, p 133 (LGW)
Children of Cornelia Stanly (Allen) Smith (14211.1811.)
  & Alfred Smith:

14211.18111. Alfred Percival Smith

14211.18112. Cornelia Stanley Smith

INSERT ADDITION: I, p 133 (LGW)
Children of Frederick Percival Allen (14211.1813.)
  & Carrie (Clark) Allen:

14211.18131. Henrietta Ward Allen born NY

14211.18132. Mary Percival Allen born Rochester NY

INSERT ADDITION: I, p 134 (LGW)
Children of Rev Edward Percival Allen (14211.1851.)
  & Celia Jane (Gates) Allen:

14211. *Percival Roy Allen born Manchester NJ 1-18-1888, died
18511. 4-4-1978, married 6-20-1917 Winifred H Knapp born Bitlis
        Turkey 3-8-1892, died 5-14-1982. Percival taught at Wentworth
        Institute, Boston MA, for many years

14211. *Harold Gates Allen born Staceyville IA 11-19-1890, died Avon
18512. Park Fl 1-10-1973, married Hartland ME 8-23-1921 Madelyn
Gladys Gray born Pittsfield ME 2-20-1903, died Avon Park FL
3-3-1977, daughter of Ida Jane (McCausland) & Sherman Gray

NOTE-Harold Gates Allen, grandson of Orsen Parda & Caroline Allen,
married Madelyn Gray. Her sister Catherline married Steve Israel-
son, son of an Armenian orphan Orsen Allen helped to escape from
Turkey. This coincidence was discovered at Steve & Kay's wedding.

14211. *Frederick Crosby Allen Rev born Sanford ME 10-12-1892, died
18513. Hartford CT 7-5-1970, married Bristol CT 12-28-1920 Ruth
Dorchester born Westfield MA 8-5-1897, died Hartford CT
8-23-1985, daughter of Eleanor (Hardy) & Livorous Hull
Dorchester. Both buried Putnam CT

Rev Frederick Crosby Allen graduated from Amherst College and
served Congregational churches in Middleury, Manchester, Pleasant
Valley CT, and in 1937 a Methodist church at Meridan CT. Also at
Westhampton Beach NY and at Myrtle, Putnam, West Woodstock, and
East Hartford CT. He retired in 1959.

Ruth, a graduate of Wellesley College in 1919, taught school.
Her brother Donald was Fred's roommate at Yale Divinity School.

INSERT ADDITION: I, p 134 (LGW)
Children of Rev Herbert Marsena Allen (14211.1852.)
& Ellen Ropes (Ladd) Allen:

14211. *Edith Rogers Allen born Van Turkey 8-4-1894 married Tiflis,
18521. Russia 1919 John Edward Todd

14211. *Herbert Marsena Allen Jr born Persia (Iran) 4-16-1896, died
18522. Worcester MA 5-25-1980, married Haverhill MA 1928 Mildred E
Page, died Worcester MA Sept 1979. Family resided at
Worcester the last 48 years of his life.

14211. Dorothea Martendale Allen born Van Turkey 2-14-1898,
18523. married Brooklyn NY 1931 Jon Elmer Frazee

14211. *Gladys Marvin Allen born Auburndale MA 12-27-1900, married
18524. Worcester MA 1926 Henry Day Brigham

14211. Winifred Ladd Allen born Auburndale MA 11-15-1902, died
18525. Frankfort KY Sept 1951

14211. *Gwendolyn Allen born Constantinople Turkey 10-26-1908,
18526. married Boston MA 6-22-1929 Carl Gustave Hammar

INSERT ADDITION: I, p 134 (PC Vol II, p 194)
Children of Frank West Hodges (14326.1232.)
  & Annie (West) Hodges:

14326. Warren M Hodges born Osterville MA 1881, died 1954,
12321. married Osterville Esther Chase; had four sons

14326. *William Hodges born Osterville 1883, died there 1950, married
12322. Florence Manning of Taunton MA, born 1884, died 1948

INSERT ADDITION: I, p 134 (PC Vol II, p 400)
Children of Lillie (Hodges) DeWitt (14326.1243.)
  & Edgar DeWitt Sr:

14326.12431. Freeman DeWitt born 1881, died 1896, buried Osterville

14326.12432. Edgar DeWitt Jr born 1883, buried Osterville MA

14326.12433. Earl M DeWitt born 1885, twin, died 1918, married 1913
             Sarah Howes born 1892, died 1973, both buried Osterville

14326.12434. Ernest William DeWitt born 1885, twin, died 1971, married
             Merle (?); had son Ernest W DeWitt Jr born Chicago IL. Sr
             Ernest married 2d Marie (Adams) Scudder born 2-12-1895,
             died 4-28-1995, daughter of Matilde (Motsch) & Freeman
             Adams, widow of Stuart F Scudder of Osterville. Both
             buried Hillside Cemetery, Osterville MA

120

INSERT ADDITION: I, p 134 (FF)
Children of Franklin Wakefield Fish Jr Col (145(10)8.1111.)
& Mary Elizabeth (Dean) Fish:

145(10)8.   Franklin Wakefield Fish III born Washington PA 6-13-1939,
11111.   married Bakersfield CA 3-23-1962 Barbara Baergen

145(10)8.   Robert Dean Fish born Salt Lake City UT 5-5-1843, married
11112.   Pasadena CA 12-28-1969 Melody Huff

145(10)8.   Marjorie Ann Fish born Pomona, L.A. Co, CA 10-20-1947,
11113.   married San Diego CA 7-22-1979 Major Michael John Hanaway

INSERT ADDITION: I, p 137
15848.35251. Lauchlan Crocker. His 2d wife's maiden name: Sheraton.

INSERT ADDITION: I, p 138 (JTV, MTH, PH, Family Tree prepared 1996 by
    James Oliver Brooks Jr)

Children of Lillian M (Crocker) Brown (16344.2111.)
& John Melville Brown:

16344.   *Elizabeth N Brown born Wilmette IL 2-8-1901, died Wilmette IL
21111.   12-21-1994, married 2-2-1929 James Oliver Brooks born Gales-
         ville WI 4-17-1900, died Winnetka IL 10-1-1940

16344.   *Robert M Brown born 5-29-1911, died Beloit WI 7-2-1969,
21112.   married 6-10-1939 Irene Putnam born 11-25-1913

Children of Charles Henry Crocker (16344.2113.)
& Hazel (Recks) Crocker:

16344.21131. Charles K Crocker born 3-8-1922

16344.21132. Donald Wilson Crocker born 4-29-1926

Children of Catherine (Crocker) Thomas (16344.2114.)
& Henry Seely Thomas Jr:

16344.   Sarah E Thomas born Washington DC 11-18-1923, died
21141.   New York City NY 1-26-1986, unmarried

16344.   *Henry Seely Thomas Jr born Washington DC 1-1-1925, died
21142.   Barnstable MA 8-20-1994, married 6-14-1952 Anne Clotilde
         Moreau born Trenton NJ 5-28-1930

16344.   *Joan Moseley Thomas born New Brunswick NJ 7-14-1926, married
21143.   Amsterdam Netherlands 2-16-1959 Hans Vos born Amsterdam
         Netherlands 12-11-1921

16344.   *Marion Martin Thomas born New Brunswick NJ 10-14-1927,
21144.   married New Brunswick NJ 4-24-1954 Peter Hickman born
         London, England 5-31-1924

INSERT ADDITION: I, p 139 (BWS)
Children of Henry (Harry) Scudder Crocker (16344.2142.)
& Wilhelmina (MacDougall) Crocker:

16344.   . Henry Wilson Crocker born 10-28-1895, married Ruth ___; had
21421.   Wilson Crocker, Virginia Crocker, & Neil McKinley Crocker

16344.   *Susan Elizabeth Crocker born Osterville MA 2-18-1897, died
21422.   Toms River NJ 5-11-1981, married New York City NY 4-7-1917
         Harold Duncan Shaw Sr born Roslindale MA 1-9-1892, son of
         Emma B (Lewis) born New Brunswick, CAN, and George Duncan
         Shaw, born New Brunswick, CAN.

16344.21423. John McKinley Crocker born Oct 1898

CORRECTION: I, p 140 (EBH)
16344.31472. Mildred Elizabeth (Herrick) Batts-Palmetier died 5-2-1968

INSERT ADDITION: I, p 141 (CFC)
Children of Zilpha Brunton (Crocker) Gordon (16346.6612.)
  & James F (Fred) Gordon:

16346.   Walter Arthur Gordon born Hyannis MA 9-9-1932, died
  66121. Tewksbury MA 10-22-1993, married Methuen MA 9-26-54 Shirley
          Faith Carmichael born Methuen MA 1-12-1932

INSERT CORRECTION: I, p 141 (CFC)
16346.66311. Anne Lewis Thuermer born <u>Chicago IL</u>

INSERT ADDITION: I, p 141 (CFC)
Children of Harvey Francis Sinnett (16346.6641.)
  & Irene Mary (Demianof) Sinnett:

16346.66411. Judith Ann Sinnett born New York City 8-7-1948

16346.   Barbara Louise Sinnett born 5-20-1954, married 7-19-1980
  66412. Michael Peter Lee

INSERT ADDITION: I, p 142 (CS)
Children of Alice Frances (Ewers) Stanfield (P-16352.21(11)5.)
  & Myrlan Paul Stanfield:

P-16352.   *Eugene Paul Stanfield born Bunker Hill Twp, Ingham Co MI
  21(11)51. 4-29-1928, married Jackson MI 5-8-1954 Betty Lou England
             born Jackson MI 3-28-1930, daughter of Lucinda Louiza
             (Miller) & Joseph Nathan England

P-16352.   Elizabeth Louise Stanfield born Bunker Hill Twp, Ingham
  21(11)52. Co, MI, married 4-4-1959 Theron Stephen Patterson

INSERT ADDITION: I, p 142 (SCR)
Children of Owen Augustus Luckenbach (16723.4(12)21.)
  & Margaret (Spademan) Luckenbach:

16723.   *Carl Luckenbach born Detroit MI 1-22-1935; Carl, an
  4(12)211. architect in Birmingham MI, has one daughter, Elizabeth
             Loren Luckenbach born 6-30-1968. She resides Seattle WA

Children of Susan Farrar (Luckenbach) Middleton (16723.4(12)22.)
& Whitwell Newton Middleton:

16723.   *Whitwell Newton Middleton Jr born New York City 1938,
4(12)221. married Rosalie Row of Carrollton GA. They had three sons,
William Whitwell Middleton born 1966, John Richard Middleton born 1968, and James Fletcher Middleton born 1972.

Children of Jane Crocker (Luckenbach) Unbekant (16712.4(12)23.)
& Clifford Unbekant:

16723.   *Susan Crocker Unbekant born Bethlehem PA 9-22-1943, married
4(12)231. 1st 5-11-1966 John Barker Houle Jr, born Albany NY
9-22-1945, son of Elinor K & John B Houle Sr of Troy NY.
They separated 1978; divorced 5-11-1981. Susan married 2d
8-7-1981 Ralph Henry Rosenthal born Amsterdam, Holland,
4-2-1937, son of Johannah (Glazer) & Fritz Rosenthal. When
she remarried, Susan gained two step-children: Renee Karla
Rosenthal born 4-27-1966 and Daniel George Rosenthal born
5-28-1970.

INSERT ADDITION: I, p 142 (TC)
Children of Thomas Edward Crocker (16928.7243.)
& Mabel Miriam (Hedges) Crocker:

16928.   *Thomas Edward Crocker Jr born Washington DC 6-9-1949 married
72431. Alexandria VA 4-7-1990 Elizabeth Jane born Lexington MO 2-1-
1952, daughter of Jeanne (Robbins) & Paul August Lichte.

124

INSERT ADDITION: I, p 142 (ANCH)
Children of Earle Lowell Clarke (16941.1413.)
& Anna Adenia (Hodges) Clarke (14326.12321.1.)

16941. *Earle Lowell Clarke Jr born Hyannis MA 7-10-1928, married
14131. Yarmouth MA 9-25-1951 Josephine Gladys O'Neil born Hyannis MA
12-11-1935, daughter of Ruth Beatrice (Hatch) & Ira Bernard
O'Neil

16941. *Anne Neckermann Clarke born Hyannis MA 5-20-1933, married
14132. Osterville MA 9-9-51 Robert F Harmon born Northeast Harbor ME
4-25-1930, son of Delores M (Munn) & Theodore S Harmon

INSERT ADDITION: I, p 142 (JRC, DL)
Children of George Cleveland Crocker (16972.3133.)
& Lura (Libby) Crocker:

16972. *Eleazer Carl Crocker of Dexter ME born 3-15-1914, died
31331. 1-25-1995, married Winnifred Rines

Obituary: DEXTER ME -- E Carl Crocker, 80, died January 25, 1995, at
his home on Pleasant Street in Dexter. He was born March 15, 1914
in St Albans, the son of George & Lura (Libby) Crocker. He was a
machinist at the Naval Torpedo Station in Newport R.I. during
WWII and then worked for many years as a machinist for Fay Scott
in Dexter. He owned and operated Crocker Bottled Gas & Appliance
for several years.
    Before his retirement, he worked as operator and assistant
librarian for the state bookmobile. He was an active member of
the First Baptist Church in Dexter and held many offices including deacon. He was a lifelong member of the Dexter Grange; a 65-
year member of Plymouth Lodge IOOF No. 65, where he had served as
noble grand, treasurer, district deputy and grand master.
    He is survived by his wife, Winnifred (Rines) Crocker, a son
and his wife, Barry and Ruth Crocker of Hampden; a daughter and
her husband, Shirley and Bill Grant of Danforth, a brother, Ivan
Crocker of St Albans, two sisters, Nancy Tibbetts of Newport and
Jeane Martin of Brattleboro, VT; also by five grandchildren,

Tropper Matthew Grant of Medway, Kelly Crocker of Hampden, Amy Grant-Thurlow of Newburgh, Cory Crocker of Hampden, and Sara Grant of Gloucester MA; a great-granddaughter, Abigail Grant of Medway, and several nieces and nephews. He was predeceased by two sisters, Muriel Nelson and Thelma Patterson Smith.

16972. Thelma Elizabeth Crocker born 6-4-1917, married 1st Durwood
31332. Patterson; had nine children; married 2d Frederick Smith

16972. Muriel Ruth Crocker born 6-7-1922, married Philip Nelson;
31333. had three children

16972. Ivan George Crocker born 4-21-1926, married Evelyn Dickey,
31334. had four children

16972. Jeane Anne Crocker born 1-21-1934, married George Martin,
31335. had two children

16972. Nancy (Nellie Lou) Crocker born 11-22-8-1935, married Blaine
31336. Tibbetts, had four children

INSERT ADDITION: I, p 142 (JRC) (DL)
Children of Charles E Mower (16972.3611.)
  & Ada (Libby) Mower:

16972.36111. Ruth Mower married Thomas Mills, St Albans postmaster

16972.36112. Meredith Mower married _____ Fisher

INSERT ADDITION: I, p 142 (DL)
Children of Iola Louise (Samuels) Leary (16972.7623.)
  & William Francis Leary:

16972. *Donald Francis Leary born Scituate MA 2-5-1929, died Largo FL
76231. 11-3-1996, married Westover AFB Chapel, Chicopee Falls MA
        10-1-1954 Vivian Pearl Bagwell born Weston W VA 7-13-1935,
        daughter of Mona Mae (Ice) & Arlo Bagwell. They adopted both
        their children.

16972. *Mary Louise Leary born Boston MA 2-8-1932, Married Boston MA
76232. 1949 William Harold Greene died Hyde Park MA in accident
    11-21-1973, son of Ann (?) & Harold Greene of Union Beach NJ,
    buried Fairview Cemetery, Hyde Park MA

INSERT ADDITION: I, p 143 (TAC)
Children of Harry Hercules Crocker (17181.1515.)
& Rosa Bonheur (Tuttle) Crocker:

17181.   Madge Tryphena Crocker born 7-12-1885, died ?   ,
 15151.   married Raymond R Smith of South Bend IN

NOTE-Tracy Ashley Crocker dedicated his genealogy work to his great
aunt Madge, above, and another ancestor, Florence Edna Miller. He
wishes Madge could have known how much he appreciates her extensive work on the Crocker line, and others, back to the MAYFLOWER.
Although her brother, his grandfather, was disinterested, he,
Tracy, is pleased to carry on and add to all the research she
did that made his efforts so much easier. Birth, death, & marriage certificates, and letters and other documents she gathered,
he believes, will enrich family history for generations to come.

17181. *Glyndon Harry Crocker Sr born Berlin Heights OH 7-19-1887,
 15152. died Cortland NY 8-2-1945, married Chicago IL 8-8-1908 Myrl
    Zelpha Brown born Robinson IL 5-8-1888, died Cortland NY
    10-18-1972, daughter of Rose M (Surell) & Charles E Brown

Glyndon Harry Crocker Sr: After a general education in public
schools of Berlin Heights OH Glyndon attended business school in
Norwalk OH. Then after leaving home as a youth he began a career
in Chicago with Marshall Field & Company. Two years later he was
employed by Warner Brothers Co, a corset manufacturer, where he
worked ten years. After moving to Cortland NY in 1915, however,
he joined the Miller Corset Company as vice president and sales
manager and became a prominent figure in the business world.

In 1920, after negotiating with J C Penny Co in NYC a major order
which the Miller Company felt was much too large for them to
handle, Glyndon organized what would become the Crescent Corset

Company, one of the country's largest producers of women's wearing apparel. He served as president and general manager until his death in 1945. As a member of the board of directors of J C Penny Co and the First National Bank of Cortland, he earned the respect of all who knew him. -- Tracy Ashley Crocker.

NOTE-See I, p 143, (Obituary, Cape Cod Times)

17181. Anna (Berube), widow of Chauncey Bearse Crocker, born in Fort
52131 Kent, Maine, died 1-13-1996, age 85 years, the last survivor of a family of sixteen children. She was survived by a son, Carlton B Crocker of Centerville MA, two daughters, Carole B Martin & June B (Mrs Albert) Smith, both of Osterville MA, & five granddaughters, Alison (Smith) Sargent, Karen (Crocker) Balthezard, and Catherine, Wendy & Lynn Crocker. She was predeceased by Karen Buster, daughter of Carole.

NOTE-See I, p 144 (Obituary, Cape Cod Times)

17181. *Elizabeth (Rankin) Pigott, born Osterville MA 1911, died
52143. Centerville MA 9-8-1995. She was the widow of Roy Pigott, who was originally of Coinjock NC, who died in 1980. She was survived by daughter Audrey E (Pigott) Killian of Winchester MA, a brother Robert Rankin and a sister Marjorie Rankin, both of Osterville.

INSERT ADDITION: I, p 146 (SC/MC) (PC Vol II, p 57)
Children of Emeline (Robbins) Cammett (17511.2453.)
& John H Cammett III:

17511. Minnie Isabel Cammett born 5-26-1866, died 1952, married
24531. 1907 Nathan Hastings Allen born 1843, died Osterville 1909, son of Caroline (Hastings) & _____ Allen. No children.

17511. *Henry Delvern Robinson Cammett born Osterville 1868, died
24532. Osterville 10-18-1945, married 1st Annie Stuart Hyland, born 1866 in Scotland, died 1929. No children by his 2d marriage.

17511.   Bessie Cammett born Osterville 1874, died Taunton MA 1935,
24533. married Osterville 8-27-1893 Lucian Willis Leonard
        (16344.3121.) born Osterville 2-15-1856, died 10-15-1902,
        son of Mercy Maria (Parker) & Simeon L Leonard. No children.

INSERT ADDITION: I, p 146 (PC Vol II, p 109 & 407)
Children of Edith (Robbins) Crosby (17511.245(11).
& Charles H Crosby:

17511.   Edna Browning Crosby born Osterville 1879, died there 1915
245(11)1. married there 1903 James Horne born 1880, died there 1946,
        son of Margaret (Hanlon) of Newfoundland & William Horne.
        They had Ruth, born 1904, married Clifford Jones (no chn)
        and Bernard Horne, born 1915, died 1965, unmarried.

INSERT ADDITION: I, p 146 (PC Vol II, p 245)
Children of Medora (Robbins) Hodges-Lovell (17511.2451.)
& Horace Lovell:

17511.   *Blanche Lovell, born Osterville 1876, died there 1945,
24511.   married 1905 Robert Daniel born Boston 1875, died Osterville
        1935, son of Katherine (Morris) & Charles Daniel Sr.

INSERT ADDITION: I, p 146 (LL)
Children of Franklyn Hallett Lovell II (17511.2942.)
& Florence Brown (Lane) Lovell:

17511.   *Elizabeth Lovell born Madison NJ 5-25-1905, died Newport RI
29421. 1996, married Edgartown MA Wallace E Tobin Jr born Ipswich MA
        2-26-1908, died Providence RI 3-31-1987, son of Emma Kate
        (Hussey) & Wallace E Tobin Sr

17511.   *Lane Lovell born Madison NJ 2-18-1908, married at Carmel NY
29422. 4-26-1935 Patricia White born Kenilworth IL 7-24-1907,
        daughter of Lilian M (Bergh) & Burton Friend White

INSERT ADDITION: I, p 146 (EWMcN)
Children of Margaret (Phinney) Coburn (17552.1111.)
  & Haywood Hobden Coburn:

17552. *Carol Macy Coburn born 3-21-1930, married Joseph Eliot Wood-
  11111. bridge PhD born 7-15-1921, son of Helen Josephine (McFarland)
        Woodbridge born 6-21-1892, died 11-30-1971, & Donald Eliot
        Woodbridge. EWMcN is Joseph Eliot Woodbridge's sister.

NOTES

Eleventh Generation

INSERT ADDITION: I, p 147 (RJG)
Children of Bessie Francis (Childs) Hinckley (11131.13111.)
& Myron L Hinckley:

11131.   *Harold Franklin Hinckley born 1894, died 1954, married Ruth
13111.   Eliza Lewis born 1896, died 1934, daughter of Edith May
1.   (Gray) & Sumner Tibbetts Lewis. Rev Robert J Goode Jr says
          Ruth Eliza Lewis descended from Margaret Stephenson of
          Rowley, one of the last Salem "witches" to be executed.

11131.   Florence Southward Hinckley married 1913 Sumner Dole;
13111.2. they had issue.

11131.   Alma Hinckley, late of Centerville MA, married Roscoe
13111.3. Goddard; they had issue.

INSERT ADDITION: I, p 148 (GA)
Children of Thomas S Caddy Jr (11272.11114.)
& Lizzette Mae (Atwood) Caddy:

11272.   Nelson Adelbert Caddy born Loup City NE 5-30-1891, died there
11114.   11-17-1957, married Kearney NE 4-13-1915 Marie Jensen, died
1.   Caspar Wyoming 6-25-1983, both buried Evergreen Cemetery
          Loup City NE

11271.   *Lucy Arabelle Caddy born Loup City NE 5-19-1893, married
11114.2. Fremont NE 7-2-1911 William D Garner

11271.11114.3. son died in infancy

11271.11114.4. Alice Caddy

11271.11114.5. Thomas Caddy III

11271.11114.6. Frank Caddy

INSERT ADDITION: I, p 148 (GA)
Children of Wilbur Caddy (11272.11116.)
& Florence Belle (Wright) Caddy:

11272. Blanche Marie Caddy born Palmyra NE 2-16-1898, died Loup
11116. City NE 11-7-1989, married Loup City NE 2-8-1919 Earl Stamm,
1.   both buried Evergreen Cemetery., Loup City NE

11272.11116.2. Carl Caddy born 12-16-1901, died 6-11-1926 unmarried

11272. Ruth Edith Caddy born Albion NE 4-16-1903, died Loup City NE
11116. 4-30-1966, married Grand Isle NE 10-3-1925 Oscar B Kaiser
3.   born 11-9-1896, died 7-3-1977, son Ida (Erdman) & Karl Kaiser

11272. Myrtle Florence Caddy born Albion NE 4-1-1906, died Folsom LA
11116. 9-16-1992, married Kearney NE 8-22-1929 Ernest Thode born
4.   Loup City NE 8-23-1904, died Folsom LA 10-16-1992, both
        buried Evergreen Cemetery, Loup City NE

11272. Raymond James Caddy born Loup City NE 6-20-1909, died Hood
11116. River OR 8-26-1968, buried Idlewild Cemetery, Hood River OR,
5.   married Merna Negley

11272. Clarence Lee Caddy born Loup City NE 1-19-1916, died Grand
11116. Island NE 1-1-1969, buried Evergreen Cemetery, Loup City NE,
6.   married Michigan 8-9-1941 Mary Ann Eiche

11272. Velma Loree Caddy born Loup City NE 9-10-1919, married 1st
11116. Grand Island NE Alfonso T Stobbe, div., married 2d Matt
7.   Roberts

INSERT ADDITION: I. p 148 (GA)
Children of Charles Henry Caddy Sr (11272.11112.)
& Addie Viola (Hembree) Caddy:

11272.11112.1. Charles Henry Caddy Jr born ____, died Germany
                8-4-1945, served in WWII

11272.   *Idona Dolly Caddy born Nampa, Canyon Co ID 1-15-1913, died
11112.   Turlock, Stanislaus Co CA 11-5-1986, married Washington Co ID
2.   8-16-1930 Clyde John Scholes born Idaho 3-6-1909, died Salt
         Lake City UT 1-13-1964, son of Gertrude Garfield (Fuller) &
         John Frederick Scholes. Both bur Cloverdale Cem., Boise ID

11272.   LeRoy T Caddy born Montour ID 6-29-1916, died Idaho 8-4-1983
11112.3.

11272.   Gurney Caddy Col born Wilder ID 9-2-1918, died OR 10-20-1995,
11112.   buried Willamette National Cemetery, married 1st Hazel
4.   Spires, divorced; married 2d Anita _____.

         Gurney Caddy, a mechanic during WWII, helped establish "mobile"
         hospitals, later called M.A.S.H. After the war he was promoted to
         full colonel. His picture appeared on the cover of LIFE magazine
         for an article on the mobile operating rooms.

INSERT ADDITION: I, p 148 (GA)
Children of Joseph Caddy (11272.11118.)
   & Clara (Cougar) (Morsen) Caddy:

11272.   *William H Caddy born Albion NE 5-2-1907, died Port Heneneme
11118.1. CA 8-15-1981, married Iola Oxford, died 12-27-1975

11272.11118.2. Leah Caddy born @ 1910, married Leonard Berzina

INSERT ADDITION: I, p 148 (LGW)
Children of Percival Roy Allen (14211.18511.)
   & Winifred H (Knapp) Allen:

14211.   *Virginia Allen born 4-19-1918, married 4-14-1945
18511.1. Gifford N Hartwell born 2-17-1920

14211.   *Noel Jeanette Allen born Erie PA 12-23-1919, married
18511.   8-27-1946 Charles Vernon Baston born 11-15-1919. Div
2.   Dec. 1976. Charles served in the navy in WWII.

INSERT ADDITION: I, p 148 (LGW)
Children of Harold Gates Allen (14211.18512.)
& Madelyn Gladys (Gray) Allen:

14211.   *Stuart Edward Allen born Hartland ME 8-27-1923, died
18512.   3-22-1976, married Rockland ME 7-19-1946 Eileen Beach born
1.   6-10-1924, daughter of Janie (Lockhart) & David S Beach.
          Stuart served with the 293rd Engineers in France/Germany
          during WWII, 1945. Eileen married 2d Ray Needham

14211.   *Dorothy Allen born Bar Harbor ME 9-25-1924, married Monroe
18512.   LA 1-29-1944 Andrew Thomas Goettman Sr born Carlstadt NJ
2.   7-9-1921, son Mildred M (Fulton) & Andrew Adolph Goettman.
          An electrical engineer, Andrew Thomas Goettman Sr served in
          the Army Air Corps 1943-1945, WWII

INSERT ADDITION: I, p 148 (LGW)
Children of Frederick Crosby Allen (4211.18513.)
& Ruth (Dorchester) Allen:

14211.   *Robert Dorchester Allen born Hartford CT 6-17-1923
18513.1. married 5-21-1945 Beryl Saunders born Wales 10-31-1925

14211.   *Daniel Dorchester Allen Rev born Hartford CT 8-4-1925,
18513.2. married Lahore Pakistan 4-14-1950 Elizabeth Jane Stuntz,
          born Morristown NJ 3-4-1925, daughter of Florence (Watters)
          & Rev Clyde B Stuntz. Daniel is a missionary India/Pakistan

14211.   *Barbara Jane Allen born Manchester CT 5-17-1930, married
18513.3. Putnam CT 8-23-1952 Rev Edwin A Vonderheide

INSERT ADDITION: I, p 148 (LGW)
Children of Edith Rogers (Allen) Todd (14211.18521.)
& John Edward Todd:

14211.   *Margaret Elizabeth Todd born Bangor ME 8-12-1920, married
18521.1. 1948 Henry Hatch

14211.18521.2. Ellen Bernice Todd born Cedar Rapids IA Feb 1925

134

INSERT ADDITION: I, p 148 (LGW)
Chidren of Herbert Marsena Allen Jr (14211.18522.)
  & Mildred E (Page) Allen:

14211.   *Priscilla Marcia Allen born Haverhill MA Jan 1929, married
18522.1. 1950 Fred Gifford (According to Dorothy Allen Goettman, in
        1981 Priscilla is married to James V Rea and has three
        daughters and three sons.)

INSERT ADDITION: I, p 148 (LGW)
Children of Gladys Marvin (Allen) Brigham (14211.18524.)
  & Henry Day Brigham Sr:

14211.18524.1 Henry Day Brigham Jr born Pittsfield MA Dec 1926

14211.18524.2. Peter Allen Brigham born Pittsfield MA Aug 1939

INSERT ADDITION: I, p 148 (LGW)
Children of Gwendolyn (Allen) Hammar (14211.18526.)
  & Carl Gustave Hammar:

14211.18526.1. Joanne Ladd Hammar born Worcester MA 1-11-1931

14211.   Carl Allen Hammar born Worcester MA 5-28-1932, married
18526.2. 11-3-1956 Cynthia Bliss Phinney

14211.18526.3. Peter Ladd Hammar born Slaterville RI 12-4-1942

INSERT ADDITION: I, p 148 (ANCH)
Children of William Hodges (14326.12322.)
  & Florence (Manning) Hodges:

14326.   *Anna Adenia Hodges born Taunton MA 4-29-1911, died Hyannis MA
12322. 8-31-1975, married Osterville MA 3-16-1928 Earle L Clarke
1.   (16931.1413.) born Cedarville, Plymouth Co MA 11-28-1907, son
       of Nellie Baker (Crocker) Nickerson-Clarke & William Lowell
       Clarke of Falmouth MA [See (16931.1413.)]

INSERT ADDITION: I, p 155 (JTV, MTH, PH, from Family Tree prepared
by James Oliver Brooks Jr - 1996)

Children of Elizabeth N (Brown) Brooks (16344.21111.)
& James Oliver Brooks Sr:

16344.   *James Oliver Brooks Jr born Evanston IL 7-7-1930, married
21111.1. 1st Ann Arbor MI 8-24-1958 Maria Anna Zagorska born Warsaw,
          Poland, 1-11-1933, div; married 2d Villanova PA 10-13-1984
          Maria Flaschberger born Moederndorf, Austria 6-3-1938

16344.   *David Melville Brooks born Evanston IL 2-14-1033, died
21111.2. Wheaton IL 6-1-1986, married 12-12-1953 Margaret Klein
          born 6-31-1932

Children of Robert M Brown (16344.21112.)
& Irene (Putnam) Brown:

16344.21112.1. Barbara M Brown born 12-8-1948, married Thomas Wolf

16344.21112.2. Christopher Brown born 12-15-1950

Children of Henry Seely Thomas Jr (16344.21142.)
& Ann Clotilde (Moreau) Thomas:

16344.   *Catherine Dale Thomas born Newark NJ 12-1-1952, married
21142.1. Flemington NJ 9-24-1977 John Arthur Langley born Hartford
          CT 12-29-1948

16344.   *John Martin Thomas born Flemington NJ 2-21-1955, married
21142.2. there Mary Lou Scuro born Jersey City NJ 2-21-1955

16344.   *Howard M Thomas born Flemington NJ 1-16-1960, married
21142.3. High Bridge NJ 9-3-1988 Linda Susan Monn born Plainfield
          NJ 11-15-53

Children of Joan Moseley (Thomas) Vos (16344.21143.)
& Hans Vos:

16344.   Ralph Henry Vos born New Brunswick NJ 11-28-1960, married
21143.1.   Radford VA 6-1-1996 Rhonwen M Churchill

Children of Marion M (Thomas) Hickman (16344.21144.)
& Peter Hickman:

16344.   *Mark Thomas Hickman born Manhasset LI NY 12-25-1954,
21144.1   married Tolland CT 7-17-1982 Mary Wargo born Stafford CT
5-3-1959

16344.   *Stuart Crocker Hickman born Bryn Mawr PA 7-8-1957,
21144.2.   married Attleboro MA 9-15-1984 Johnna C Avero born there
5-23-1961

16344.   Robert Peter Hickman born Bryn Mawr PA 4-15-1960, married
21144.3.   Shelbyville TN 4-22-1989 Holly Lane born Winchester TN
10-29-1950

INSERT ADDITION: I, p 155 (BWS)
Children of Susan Elizabeth (Crocker) Shaw (16344.21422.)
& Harold Duncan Shaw Sr:

16344.   Jean Shaw born Englewood NJ 7-24-1921, died 7-20-1927
21422.1.   of brain tumor

16344.   *Harold Duncan Shaw Jr born Englewood NJ 5-13-1924, died
21422.   8-25-1980 of cancer, ashes bur at sea, married 7-15-1953
2.   7-15-1953 Barbara Wissing, born Newburgh NY 8-7-1921,
daughter of Rosemary (McManus) & John Lee Wissing

CORRECTIONS: I, p 126, 156, 169: (SCP)
Lt Col Stanton Crocker Parker (16344.31111.2.), before he died
in Decatur TX 1996, sent corrections: (p 126): his grandfather,
Charles F Parker should be Charles F Parker Esg; (p 156): his

2d wife's maiden name was Herford; his 3d wife Lillian (Williams)
Barnard-Parker born 1893, died April 1995; (p 169): the elder of
his twin sons is Hugh Stanton Parker, the younger, Joseph Lee
Parker. Their #s should be reversed.

INSERT ADDITION: I, p 156
16344.   Marjorie (Albert) Leonard, wife of Willis H Leonard,
31232.1. died Osterville MA 3-18-1997

OBIT: Marjorie M (Albert) Leonard, 75, died at her Osterville
home Tuesday, March 18, 1997. The wife of Willis H Leonard, she
was born in Rockville Centre NY and was a graduate of Pratt In-
stitute in Brooklyn and Adelphi University in Garden City, NY. A
registed nurse for many years in Nassau County NY, Mrs Leonard
was also an artist contributing cartoons for various newspapers
on Cape Cod. She also illustrated books for the Osterville
Historical Society and was a former member of the Cape Cod Art
Association. Mrs Leonard was a member of the Friends of the
Osterville Free Library and the Osterville Historical Society.
She was a resident of Osterville for 15 years after having lived
in Wantagh NY. Surviving besides her husband are a son, Jonathan
G Leonard of Richmond VT, a granddaughter, Emma M Leonard, and a
sister, Mrs Donald (Edna Albert) Jackson of Anandale VA.

CORRECTION: I, p 156 (LBL)
16344.   *Philip Leonard born Hyannis MA 1-16-1925, married
31232.   Jersey City NJ 9-25-1946 Leona Buggert born Grantsbury WI
3.   12-31-1922, daughter of John & Lena (Rickers) Buggert.

Philip Leonard graduated from Massachusetts Maritime Academy,
Hyannis, MA, September 22, 1944. Licensed by the U S Coast Guard
as Chief Mate, U S Merchant Marine, he served 1944-1948.
In 1952 he joined Leonard Insurance Agency, Osterville MA, a
business begun by his paternal grandfather, James Milton Leonard;
six years later Philip purchased the agency and operated it until
his retirement in 1992. Mr and Mrs Leonard live in New Ulm MN.

RECOLLECTIONS OF SOME EARLY DAYS IN THE MIDWEST

William Buggert I born Hamburg, Germany, 1825, was a Prussian who
settled in New Ulm MN after immigrating to the United States; he
later moved to Brown Co, WI. When Sigel Township was incorporated
4-28-1862, William Buggert I served as Clerk. His hand-written
record of the meeting was preserved at the local museum until
about ten years ago; it has since disappeared. Only in a book
does a brief mention of William Buggert's "beautifully-written
script" remain. John Buggert told his daughter, Leona, that his
father, William I, had been a music and writing teacher.

William Buggert II, with his wife, Ellen, became the first of the
family to purchase a farm in a woodsy area near Grantsburg, WI.
Soon his two brothers also moved there; Charley, who never
married, and John who married 11-11-1918 Lena Rickers. They
bought small farms nearby. John & Lena's eldest child, son
Leslie, their second, daughter Leona, and their third, son
Willie III, were born while the family farmed near Grantsburg.
In 1923 due to sandy soil and sparse rainfall, John and Lena
abandoned farming and returned with their children to New Ulm MN.

From time to time, the Minnesota Buggerts welcomed visits from
the Wisconsin families, and once, probably in 1940, Leona recalls
taking a train with her younger sister, Adeline, to Pine City MN
where Uncle Willie met them.

During their visit Uncle Willie showed the girls a heap of fresh
water oyster shells on the bank of the St Croix River. He pointed
out holes in the shells, punched by button manufacturers to check
their quality. Sometimes Uncle Willie found pearls in oysters. He
gave a pearl (kept in a watch case) to each of his nieces.

Uncle Willie, a life-long hunter, had a collection of bows and
arrows; he told how many bears, wolves, and deer he had shot.
"Foxes," he said, "I never counted." He trapped beavers and
muskrat, then cured and sold their hides. As we walked with him
on a carpet of pine needles through the forest to get the cows,

chickadees flew down to ride on his shoulders. At times, he admitted, he shot a bear out of season, cut it up, and concealed the pieces of meat under a layer of blueberries to hide it from the game warden's eyes.

Ellen & William II had a son, Raymond, who married Mildred and had two sons, Raymond Jr and Gerald. While working on a highway one day, Raymond Sr, the county surveyer, was struck by a van. He showed me and our daughter, Lauri, a souvenir of the accident, his badly damaged transit. Another time we visited after Raymond had died; his widow, Mildred, drove us down dirt roads in her old car to show us sites that had once belonged to Buggert families. We also visited an excellent Indian museum in that area.

When in his early 20s, my father became friendly with Jack Pike, a half-breed Chippewa Indian whose wife, a full-blooded Chippewa, made for Dad the Indian belt that is framed and hanging on our fireplace in our New Ulm home. She also made moccasins for my brother, Leslie, and me. Mother said she regretted not rescuing them before we wore them out; she never dreamed they would one day be artifacts. Mother told of going with Aunt Ellen, who could speak Chippewa, to visit Mrs Pike.

About six years ago while we visited my brother Les and his wife, Eunice, in West St Paul, two ladies dropped in to see them. One proved to be an adopted daughter of the Pikes. Eager to learn more about them, I encouraged her to talk about her parents. She said the Pikes had had no children of their own, but when relatives lacked food for a child, the Pikes would take the child into their home. After Jack died, Mrs Pike decided she could take no more, but when the tenth child was brought to her, she saw how malnourished he was, and she kept him, too.

I asked about the Pike's source of income. Mrs Pike, she said, set traps for fur-bearing animals and sold the skins. She continued trapping almost until, in her nineties, she died.
                    (As told by Leona Buggert Leonard, 1995)

140

INSERT ADDITION: I, page 159 (CFC)
Children of Walter Arthur Gordon (16346.66121.)
  & Shirley Faith (Carmichael) Gordon:

16346.   *Linda Sue Gordon born 4-19-1955, married Lowell MA
66121.1. 4-26-1982 Scot Serkman

INSERT ADDITION: I, p 160 (CFC)
Children of Barbara Louise (Sinnett) Lee (16346.66412.)
  & Michael Peter Lee:

16346.66412.1. Ian James Lee born London England 12-3-1980

16346.66412.2. Alice Jane Lee born London England

INSERT ADDITION: I, p 160 (CS)
Children of Eugene Paul Stanfield (P-16352.21(11)51.)
  & Betty Lou (England) Stanfield:

P-16352.   *Cheryl Ann Stanfield born Jackson MI 10-21-1954,
21(11)51.1. married 1st Cuyahoga Co, OH 2-2-1985 Lawrence Roy
Deming born Carson City MI 12-04-1958; divorced
Sept 1986; married 2d Lake Odessa MI 4-17-1993
Wilhelmus van Leeuwen born Rotterdam, Netherlands
1-12-1949, son of Maria (van Vugt) & Antonius van
Leeuwen.

INSERT ADDITION: I, p 160 (SCR)
Children of Susan Crocker (Unbekant) Houle-Rosenthal (16723.4(12)231.)
  & John Barker Houle Jr:

16723.4(12)231.1. John David Houle b 2-09-1967

16723.4(12)231.2. Paul Clifford Houle b 9-30-1976

INSERT ADDITION: I, p 160 (TC)
Children of Thomas Edward Crocker Jr (16928.72431.)
& Elizabeth Jane (Lichte) Crocker:

16928.72431.1. Edward Day Hedges Crocker born Washington DC 3-21-1991

16928.72431.2. Thomas Paul August Crocker born Washington DC 6-3-1994

INSERT ADDITION: I, p 161 (ANCH)
Children of Earle Lowell Clarke Jr (16941.14131.)
& Josephine Gladys (O'Neil) Clarke:

16941.   *Wayne W Clarke born Hyannis MA 7-30-1955, married
14131.1. Hyannis MA 1973 June Miller, divorced.

16941.   *Dawn Marie Clarke born Hyannis MA 11-16-1957, married 1977
14131.2. Jack Hayes, divorced.

16941.   *Theresa Jo Clarke born Hyannis MA 10-12-1959, married
14131.3. 9-18-1980 William Patrick O'Keefe, divorced.

16941.14131.4. Cynthia Jean Clarke born Hyannis MA 11-16-1963

INSERT ADDITION: I, p 161 (ANCH)
Children of Anne Neckermann (Clarke) Harmon (16941.14132.)
& Robert F Harmon:

16941.   *Anne Louise Harmon born Hyannis MA 8-19-1952, married 1st
14132. 8-31-1974 Alan Davis, div; married 2d 5-1-1981 William
1.   Hallett, div; married 3d Peacham Vt 6-24-1989 Peter Jordan

16941.   *Sharon Amy Harmon born Hyannis MA 3-14-1955 married
14132.2. Osterville MA 9-6-1975 Frank W Lapham

16941.   *Claire Roberta Harmon born Hyannis MA 6-10-1959, married
14132.3. Osterville MA 6-21-1980 Loring S Hogan III

16941.   *Robert F Harmon Jr born Hyannis MA 11-7-1961, married
14132.4. Sandwich MA 3-25-1995 Leslie Gerhard

142

INSERT ADDITION: I, p   (DL)
Children of Donald Francis Leary (16972.76231.)
& Vivian Pearl (Bagwell) Leary:

16972. *Michael Patrick Leary born Ludwigsburg, W Germany 11-8-1958,
76231. C.L. marriage 1982/83 to 1993 with Jeannine Sheree Duncan
1.   born Flint MI 11-11-1954; married 1st 1-15-1994 Kelli Dawn
        Rhodes

16972. Sheila Kathleen Leary born US Naval Hosp, Portsmouth VA
76231. married Tampa FL 7031-1993 Timothy Mark Oxley, born Tampa FL
2.   6-28-1969, son of Carolyn Sue & Donald Oxley

Children of Mary Louise (Leary) Greene (16972.76232.)
& William Harold Greene:

16972.. *William Joseph Greene born Brookline MA 1-18-1951, married
76232. 1st Debra Ann Minichino; div early 1980s; married 2d
1.   Jayne M Fiasconaro; div.

16972.   *Michael James Greene born Brookline MA 4-9-1953, married
76232.2. in early 1980s Sharon Tyrell of Hillside NJ.

16972.76232.3. Donna Francis Greene born Brookline MA 7-19-1956

INSERT ADDITION: I, p 161 (TAC)
Children of Glyndon Harry Crocker Sr (17181.15152.)
& Myrl Zelpha (Brown) Crocker:

17181. *Glyndon Harry Crocker II born Chicago IL 11-5-1909; married
15152. 1st Cortland NY 6-27-1936 Florence Lucille Ashley born
1.   Cortland NY 12-11-1913, died there 4-27-1963, daughter of
        Florence Edna (Miller) & Tracy Hollis Ashley Sr. They
        divorced Cortland Co NY, 1949. Glyndon II married 2nd
        Buffalo NY 9-4-1953, Jean Lanore Wiggins born 2-23-1913,
        daughter of Luella Mae (Wark) & Percival Thomas Wiggins.

Glyndon Harry Crocker II: "It may be only hearsay, but it has
been hinted that "Happy" Crocker first rode into Amherst on
horseback, and that ever since that memorable day he has advo-
cated turning Walker Hall into a stable or the football field
into a horse show ring. Glyn has three big interests in life and
all three of them are horses." - OLIO, 1935 Amherst University
Year Book, as quoted by his son, Tracy Ashley Crocker.

17181.15152.2. Myrl Rose Crocker born Chicago IL 12-24-1911

17181.   *Robert Lyle Crocker born 1920, died 1982/3, married c. 1944
15152.   Muriel Whitman born 1923. Robert was a pilot and ran Crocker
3.   Farms, milk bottlers. He enjoyed hunting & outdoor sports.

INSERT ADDITION: I, p 162, (GNT)
17181.   *Garfield N Toolas born 2-15-1946, married 6-5-1966 Diane
52153.1.   Sweetser, daughter of Betty S & Stanley R Sweetser

INSERT ADDITION: I, p 163 (VCS)
Children of Blanche (Lovell) Daniel (17511.24511.)
   & Robert Daniel: (VCS)

17511.   *Rachel Lovell Daniel born Osterville MA 8-1-1908, married
24511.   there 4-25-1932 Anthony Campana born Metti Bora, Italy
1.   12-5-1906, died Osterville MA July 1974, son of
          Margharetta & Antonio Campana

INSERT ADDITION: I, p 163 (JMcKC)
Children of Henry D Robinson Cammett (17511.24532.)
   & Annie Stuart (Hyland) Cammett: (SC/MC

17511.   *Stuart Hyland Cammett Sr born Minneapolis MN 7-20-1897,
24532.1.   died Detroit MI 4-18-1967, married June 1925 Minneapolis MN
           Belle Constance MacKay born Minneapolis MN 12-13-1905, died
           Detroit MI 9-9-1987, daughter Nannie (Eels) & Fred MacKay.
           Stuart Cammett Sr was a teacher in Detroit Public Schools.

144

INSERT ADDITION: I, p 163 (LL)
Children of Elizabeth (Lovell) Tobin (17511.29421.)
& Wallace E Tobin Jr:

17511.   Wallace E Tobin III born NYC 7-23-1937, married Charlotts-
29421.1.   ville VA 9-10-1960 Deborah R Gelderd. Res Portland ME

17511.   Florence Lane Tobin born Oak Bluffs MA 8-5-1939, married
29421.2.   Vineyard Haven MA 12-30-1963 Bartlett S Dunbar

17511.   Mary Dorsey Tobin, twin, born Oak Bluffs MA 5-13-1944,
29421.3.   married at Vineyard Haven MA 10-12-1966 Robert M Naylor

17511.   Hallett Lovell Tobin, twin, born Oak Bluffs MA 5-13-1944,
29421.4.   married Osterville MA 3-6-1970 Mary Dorothy Dion

17511.   Matthew O'Flanagan Tobin, born Oak Bluffs MA 3-14-1950,
29421.5.   married at Chilmark MA 9-13-1972 Bridget Burket

INSERT ADDITION: I, p 163 (LL)
Children of Lane Lovell (17511.29422.)
& Patricia (White) Lovell:

17511.   *Linda Lovell born NYC 4-12-1938, married Essex Fells NJ
29422.1.   4-7-1961 Lawther O'Dell Smith, born 4-14-1937, son of
             Philip Chabot Smith.

17511.   Benjamin Hallett Lovell born at NYC 8-12-1941, unmarried
29422.2.

Twelfth Generation

INSERT ADDITION: I, p 165 (RJG)
Children of Harold Franklin Hinckley (11131.13111.1.)
  & Ruth Eliza Gray Lewis Hinckley:

11131. *Maxine Hinckley born 1915, died Honolulu HI 1993, married
13111. Robert Joseph Goode Sr born 1914, died Honolulu HI 1993.
   11. He was son of Annie Victorine (Pecheur) born 1868 & William
        Henry Goode born 1871, died 1953. Annie Victorine Pecheur was
        daughter of Marie (Bastien) & Auguste Antoine Pecheur, both
        born in France; married in 1859. William Henry Goode was son
        of Mary Bridget (O'Brien), born in Ireland, died 1914, &
        Thomas Goode born @ 1844, also in Ireland.

INSERT ADDITION: I, p 165 (GA)
Children of Idona Dolly (Caddy) Scholes (11272.11112.2.)
  & Clyde John Scholes:

11272.   Mary Ann Scholes born Wilder ID 8-19-1931, died Boise, Ada
11112.21. Co ID 10-10-1990 unmarried

11272.   *Idona Rae Scholes born Onterio, Malheur Co, OR 1-14-1939
  11112. married 1st Boise ID 2-18-1956 Alan Roy Pope born Spencer,
  22.   Worcester Co, MA 3-25-1936, son of Laura Marie (Christian/
          Chretien) & Oscar Gothfry Pope. Div 6-3-1960, married 2d
          Boise ID 6-3-1960 Howard D Lambert, died Nov 1986, married
          3d Nevada Oct 1987 Larry Thomas. Lambert adopted Idona's
          two children by her 1st marriage.

INSERT ADDITION: I, p 165 (GA)
Children of Lucy Arabelle (Caddy) Garner (11272.11114.2.)
  & William D Garner:

11272.   Jesse Garner born Loup City NE 1912, died Fremont NE
11114.21. Jan 1986 unmarried

11272.   Eddie Garner born Loup City NE 5-12-1913, married Janet
11114.22. Weaver. He wrote: "The Way It Was," of his early life.

11272.11114.23. Willard "Bat" Garner born @ 1919, died 1985

11272. Robert Garner born @ 1925, died Truth or Consequences
11114.24. NM 1977. He was a teacher and was called "Pop" Garner
by friends and students

INSERT ADDITION: I, p 165 (GA) (REC)
Children of William Henry Caddy (11272.11118.1.)
& Iola (Oxford) Caddy:

11272. *Ronald Eugene Caddy born Angley NE 11-09-1927, married 1st
11118. Dorothy Ruzicka born Sweetwater NE 2-13-1931, daughter of
11. Sophia (Scrabble) & Clarence Ruzicka, div.; married 2d Grand
Island NE 7-8-1949 Gerry Lou (Scheuneman) Miller born Minden
NE 8-22-1935, died Hastings NE 6-25-1996, daughter of William
Scheuneman

INSERT ADDITION: I, p 165 (LGW)
Children of Virginia (Allen) Hartwell (14211.18511.1.)
& Gifford N Hartwell:

14211.18511.11. Joan Maybelle Hartwell born Wareham MA 12-24-1946

14211. *Joyce Winifred Hartwell born 7-20-1950, married
18511.12. 12-11-1971 Larry Pelletier born 1-20-194_.

INSERT ADDITION: I, p 165
Children of Noel Jeanette (Allen) Bastow (14211.18511.2.)
& Charles Vernon Bastow:

14211. *Gerard Allen Bastow born 9-24-1947, married 1-15-1972
18511.21. Cynthia Myers

14211. David Edward Bastow born 10-20-1950, married 12-15-1973
18511.22. Carol Drury

14211.18511.23. Margaret Anne Bastow born 12-9-1956

INSERT ADDITION: I, p 165 (LGW)
Children of Stuart Edward Allen (14211.18512.1.)
  & Eileen (Beach) Allen:

14211.18512.11. Susan Mary Allen born Milford CT 3-25-1948

14211.18512.12. David Edward Allen born Milford CT 1-10-1951

14211.18512.13. Scott Harold Allen born Milford CT 7-12-1953, married
                 Nancy Cantanese

INSERT ADDITION: I, p 165 (LGW)
Children of Dorothy (Allen) Goettman (14211.18512.2.)
  & Andrew Thomas Goettman Sr:

14211.18512.21. Nancy May Goettman born Holden MA 2-23-1945

14211.   *Linda Jeanne Goettman born Holden MA 11-7-1946, married
18512.   Orlando FL 12-19-1970 James Thomas Wilson, born Indianapolis
22.   IN 7-13-1945, son of Katherine Isobel (Egan) & James Franklyn
         Wilson. Divorced Sanford FL Nov 1985. James Thomas Wilson
         graduated June 1967 University of Mississippi and served in
         Viet Nam 1969-1973, USAF. Linda G Wilson graduated August
         1968 University of Mississippi, earned a Masters degree in
         Social Work, Florida State University, June 1979. She served
         with the American Red Cross in Viet Nam, and is now employed
         by the Veteran's Administration in Washington DC.

14211.   Carol Lynn Goettman born Hartford CT 12-14-1950, died
18512.23. Marietta GA 12-26-1994

14211.   *Diane Shirley Goettman born Hartmord CT 6-5-1952, married
18512.   Raleigh NC 5-9-1981 Robert Charles Towe born 10-11-1950, son
24.   Bonnie (?) & Mack Towe. Diane Goettman graduated from East
         Carolina University @ 1973 and is an interior designer. Her
         husband is a realtor. Their children were adopted as infants.

14211. *Andrew Thomas Goettman Jr born Laurel MS 12-24-1962 married
18512. Coats NC 5-12-1984 Melissa Farless; div Roanoke Rapids NC
25.   Feb 1996. Andrew Thomas Goettman Jr graduated from Campbell
        University May 1984 and earned E.C.U. Greenville NC May 1986

INSERT ADDITION: I, p 165 (LGW)
Children of Robert Dorchester Allen (14211.18513.1.)
   & Beryl (Saunders) Allen:

14211.   *Thomas Saunders Allen born 6-4-1947, married 8-25-1968
18513.11. Vicki Ann _____ born 5-20-1947

14211.   Doreen Elizabeth Allen born 4-14-1949, married 3-15-1974
18513.12. Bruce Charette born 6-22-1946

14211.   *Beryl Jean Allen born 4-22-1951, married 7-31-1971 Richard
18513.13. C Anderson born 11-1-1950

14211.   *Robert Cedric Allen born 7-4-1955, married 5-23-1976 Donna
18513.14. _____, born 6-13-1952

14211.   *William Frederick Allen born 2-27-1959, married 3-31-1978
18513.15. Cheryl Ann _____ born 11-8-1961, divorced

14211.   *Rosemary Allen born 5-22-1963, married 11-14-1981 Terry G
18513.16. Gale Booth born 6-23-1955

INSERT ADDITION: I, p 165 (LGW)
Children of Rev Daniel Dorchester Allen (14211.18513.2.)
   & Elizabeth Jane (Stuntz) Allen:

14211.   *Janet Ruth Allen born Mussoorie, India 5-14-1951,
18513.21. married Paul Machula

14211.   Martha Anne Allen born Karachi Pakistan 1-26-1953,
18513.22. married 6-21-1975 Frank H Krautter born 2-16-1953

14211.   Kenneth Stuntz Allen born Bareih India 4-5-1955,
18513.23. married Naugatuck CT 8-17-1979 Peggy Dibble

14211.   Eugene Frederick Allen born Landour, India 8-14-1959,
18513.24. married 8-10-1983 Sandy Edwards

INSERT ADDITION: I, p 165 (LGW)
Children of Barbara Jane (Allen) Vonderheide (14211.18513.3.)
& Rev Edwin A Vonderheide:

14211.18513.31. Mark Vonderheide born 8-10-1953

14211.18513.32. Peter Vonderheide born 3-22-1956

INSERT ADDITION: I, p 165 (LGW)
Children of Margaret Elizabeth (Todd) Hatch (14211.18521.1.)
& Henry Hatch:

14211.18521.11. Elise Hatch born 1949

14211.18521.12. Susan Hatch born 1951

14211.18521.13. Melissa Hatch born 1954

INSERT ADDITION: I, p 165 (LGW)
Children of Priscilla Marcia (Allen) Gifford (14211.18522.1.)
& Fred Gifford:

14211.18522.11. Joanne Allyson Gifford born 1951

14211.18522.12. Diane Elizabeth Gifford born 1954

14211.18522.13. David Earl Gifford born 1956

INSERT ADDITION: I, p 169 (JTV, MTH, JOB, Family Tree Prepared 1996
                    by James Oliver Brooks Jr)

Children of James Oliver Brooks Jr (16344.21111.1.)
& Maria Anna (Zagorska) Brooks:

16344.21111.11. Christopher C Brooks born Norman OK 8-1-1963,
                died Bala Cynwyd PA 7-6-1987

16344.21111.12. James Stanley Brooks born Philadelphia PA 2-12-1970

Children of David Melville Brooks (16344.21111.2.)
  & Margaret (Klein) Brooks:

16344.   *Carol E Brooks born 2-22-1957, married 1st Michael
21111.21. Juza; div.; married 2d 2-28-1975 Kenneth Lynn Warren

16344.   *Paul Arthur Brooks born 4-2-1958, married 8-9-1980
21111.22. Joan Halbert born 3-15-1958

Children of Catherine Dale (Thomas) Langley (16344.21142.1.)
  & John (Jay) Arthur Langley:

16344.21142.11. Thomas G Langley born Flemington NJ 3-3-1980

16344.21142.12. E Dale Langley born Flemington NJ 7-24-1981

Children of John Martin Thomas (16344.21142.2.)
  & Mary Lou (Scuro) Thomas:

16344.21142.21. Kelly Anne Thomas born Flemington NJ 11-24-1989

16344.21142.22. Sarah D Thomas born Flemington NJ 5-19-1992

Children of Howard M Thomas (16344.21142.3.)
  & Linda Susan (Monn) Thomas:

16344.21142.31. Ellen Thomas born Flemington NJ 10-13-1989

16344.21142.32. Lauren Thomas born Flemington NJ 7-30-1991

Children of Mark Thomas Hickman (16344.21144.1.)
  & Mary (Wargo) Hickman:

16344.21144.11. Tyler Hickman born Manchester CT 9-6-1983

16344.21144.12. Kathryn Hickman born Newport RI 12-22-1985

Children of Stuart Crocker Hickman (16344.21144.2.)
& Johnna C (Avero) Hickman:

16344.21144.21.   Christine V Hickman born Worcester MA 10-7-1985

16344.21144.22.   Kara Hickman born Providence RI 6-12-1989

16344.21144.23.   Kendra Hickman born Hyannis MA 4-21-1992

INSERT ADDITION: I, p 169 (BWS)
Children of Harold Duncan Shaw Jr (16344.21422.2.)
& Barbara (Wissing) Shaw:

16344.   *Harold Duncan Shaw III born Englewood NJ 6-4-1954, married
21422.   Cresskill NJ 9-15-1984 Mary Leonore Mattern, born Teaneck
21.   NJ 9-3-1951

16344.   *Sword Crocker Shaw born Englewood NJ 12-14-1956, married
21422.   Alpine NJ 9-11-1982 Delia Feliciatti born Blue Island IL
22.   9-16-1960; div.

16344.   *Ian Lee Shaw born Englewood NJ 1-31-1960, married Little
21422.   Falls NY 11-18-1990 Lisa Florence Favia born Jersey City
23.   NJ 2-2-1965

NOTE: See I, p 170 (AL)
16344.   Judith (Leonard) Van Leeuwen-Staples & Thomas Staples
31232.21. div, Barnstable MA 5-3-1995. No children

INSERT ADDITION: I, p 176 (CFC)
Children of Linda Sue (Gordon) Serkman (16346.66121.1.)
& Scot Serkman:

16346.   Samuel Gordon Serkman born Colorado Springs CO 3-19-1987
66121.11.

INSERT ADDITION: I, p 176 (CS)
Children of Cheryl Ann (Stanfield) Deming (P-16352.21(11)51.1.)
& Lawrence Roy Deming:

P-16352.21(11)51.11. Nicole Lynn Deming born Lansing MI 4-2-1985

INSERT ADDITION: I, p 176 (ANCH)
Children of Wayne W Clarke (16941.14131.1.)
& June (Miller) Clarke:

16941.14131.11. April Lee Clarke born 8-10-1973

16941.14131.12. Donald Earl Clarke born 7-15-1977

16941.14131.13. Diana Lynn Clarke born 12-7-1980

INSERT ADDITION: I, p 176 (ANCH)
Children of Dawn Marie (Clarke) Hayes (16941.14131.2.)
& Jack Hayes:

16941.14131.21. Ryan John Hayes born 6-13-1980

16941.14131.22. Kevin Hayes born 8-9-1984

INSERT ADDITION: I, p 176 (ANCH)
Children of Theresa Jo (Clarke) O'Keefe (16941.14131.3.)
& William Patrick O'Keefe:

16941.14131.31. Jennifer Lee O'Keefe born 12-24-1980

16941.14131.32. Adam Clarke O'Keefe born 2-22-1984

INSERT ADDITION: I, p 176 (ANCH)
Children of Anne Louise (Harmon) Davis (16941.14132.1.)
& Alan Davis:

16941.14132.11. Molly Anna Davis born 11-10-1975

Children of Anne Louise (Harmon) Jordan (16941.14131.1.)
& Peter Jordan:

16941.14132.12. Daniel L Jordan born 8-15-1990

INSERT ADDITION: I, p 176 (ANCH)
Children of Sharon Amy (Harmon) Lapham (16941.14132.2.)
& Frank W Lapham: (all five adopted, 3, 4, & 5 are siblings)

16941.14132.21. Aiya Grace Lapham born India June 24 ____

16941.14132.22. Joshua Curtis Mariano Lapham born El Salvador Feb 21

16941.14132.23. Tina Lapham born October 16 ____

16941.14132.24. David Lapham born January 5 ____

16941.14132.25. Matthew Joseph Lapham born October 12 ____

INSERT ADDITION: I, p 176 (ANCH)
Children of Claire Roberta (Harmon) Hogan (16941.14132.3.)
& Loring S Hogan III:

16941.14132.31. Amy Louise Hogan born Hyannis MA 5-23-1982

16941.14132.32. Alyssa Kate Hogan born Hyannis MA 5-23-1985

16941.14132.33. Robert Loring Hogan born Hyannis MA 12-19-1994

INSERT ADDITION: I, p 176 (ANCH)
Children of Robert F Harmon Jr (16941.14132.4.)
& Leslie (Gerhard) Harmon:

16941.14132.41. Madison Rose Harmon born Hyannis MA 7-26-1995

154

INSERT ADDITION: I, p 176 (DL)
Children of Michael Patrick Leary (16972.76231.1.)
  & Sheree Duncan:

16971.76231.11. Andrea Nicole Leary born St Petersburg FL 5-23-1985

Children of Michael Patrick Leary (16972.76231.1.)
  & Kelli (Rhodes) Leary:

16972.76231.12. Mallory Lauren Leary born St Petersburg FL 8-8-1994

INSERT ADDITION: I, p 176 (DL)
Children of William Joseph Greene (16972.76232.1.)
  & Debra Ann (Minichino) Greene:

16972.76232.11. Kerry Ann Greene born Norwood MA 11-8-1974

Children of William Joseph Green (16972.76232.1.)
  & Jayne M (Fiasconaro) Greene:

16972.76232.12. William Francis Green born Boston MA 9-8-1981

16972.76232.13. Erin Marie Greene born Boston MA 3-13-1984

INSERT ADDITION: I, p 176 (DL)
Children of Michael James Greene (16972.76232.2.)
  & Sharon (Tyrell) Greene:

16972.76232.21. Michael Lee Greene born Santa Barbara CA 9-30-1982

16972.76232.22. Katelyn Greene born New Jersey 7-24-1986

INSERT ADDITION; I, p 177 (TAC)
Children of Glyndon Harry Crocker II (17181.15152.1.)
  & Florence Lucille (Ashley) Crocker:

17181. *Glyndon Harry Crocker III born Cortland NY 2-15-1938
 15152. married Simsbury CT 1-26-1963, Janet Rae Schaefer,
 11.   daughter of Norma (Kenyon) & (?) Schaefer.

17181. *Tracy Ashley Crocker born Cortland NY 3-6-1945, married 1st
15152. Ithaca NY 2-4-1967 Patricia Amy Mangold, born Queens Co NY
12.   3-12-1944, daughter of Eleanor Magdalene (Bandini) & Joseph
Francis Mangold; div. St Louis MO 10-5-1981; he married 2d
Reinbeck, Grundy Co, IA 9-3-1983 Joyce Ann Block born
12-28-1945, daughter of Elizabeth Alice (Hinson) & Leo John
Block.

Children of Robert Lyle Crocker (17181.15152.3.)
& Muriel (Whitman) Crocker:

17181.   *Jeffrey Robert Crocker born Cortland NY 9-18-1945, married
15152.31. 1-23-1971 Madeline Baucom born 10-23-1945.

17181.   Joan Crocker born Cortland NY 5-28-1948, married 8-16-1969
15152.32. Joseph Michael Sheridan Sr, born 6-2-1947.

INSERT ADDITIONS: I, p 178 (GT)

17181.52153.11. Wendy S Toolas born 1-4-1968, married Michael W Luca

17181.52153.12. *Peter G Toolas born 10-27-1969, married Rachael M
                Wirtenen

17181.52153.13. *Jennie M Toolas born 12-21-1971, married Kyle J Manni

INSERT ADDITION: I, p 179 (RLT)
    Robert Leonard Tallman (17181.57311.12.) and his wife, Rose
    (Evans) wish to add the following information: (See I, p 179/186)
    Rose, born 6-26-1966 at Fort Raley, Kansas, daughter of
    Roseweetha (Schuobel) of Germany & Ted Evans of Lacey WA USA.

    After serving eighteen years in the Coast Guard, Robert Tallman,
    Senior Chief Petty Officer, Officer in charge, U.S.C.G Cutter
    Point Hobart, was stationed at Gloucester MA in 1995-1996, then
    transferred to San Diego; he & his family reside at Oceanside CA

156

INSERT ADDITION: I, p 186 (GCN, VCS)
Children of Rachel Lovell (Daniel) Campana (17511.24511.1.)
    & Anthony Campana: (GCN, VCS)

17511.   *Gail Roberta Campana born Osterville MA 12-9-1935, married
24511.   Osterville MA 11-3-1956 Neil Nightingale born Hyannis MA
11.   5-21-1933, son of Gertrude (Hill) & Roy W Nightingale

17511.   *Virginia Daniel Campana born Osterville MA 3-12-1933,
24511.   married Osterville MA 7-30-1955 Richard Rice Stimets,
12.   son of Florence (?) & Edward Stimets

INSERT ADDITION: I, p 181 (JMcKC)
Children of Stuart Hyland Cammett Sr (17511.24532.1.)
    & Belle Constance (MacKay) Cammett:

17511.   *John McKay Cammett born Minneapolis MN 7-8-1927, married
24532.   1st Detroit MI 6-21-1947 Doris Eleanor Darin DePoldesta
11.   born Detroit MI 1-3-1928, div; CLW Almena Holt Jones born
          New York NY 12-4-1931, died New York NY, 5-15-1978; he
          married 2d New York NY 12-22-1967 Sandi Elaine Cooper
          born New York NY 5-11-1936.

John McKay Cammett earned his B.A. at Wayne State University,
Detroit, MI in 1949, and his Ph.D. from Columbia University
New York, NY in 1959. He taught history, especially European
history, from 1952 to 1991 successively at Wayne State
University, Middlebury College, Columbia College, Hunter College,
Rutgers University, John Jay College, and the Graduate Center of
the City University of New York. From 1968-1975 John was Dean of
Faculty and Provost of the John Jay College of Criminal Justice
(CUNY), and from 1991 to the present (1997) has been Professer
Emeritus of History there.

John McK Cammett is the author of several books and many articles
and reviews especially in the area of modern Italian history.

17511.   *Stuart Hyland Cammett Jr born Detroit MI 1-27-1931, married
24532.   11-24-1954 Barbara Louise Dewey born Milwaukee WI 9-3-1931,
12.   daughter of Marion Louise (Coke) & Lewis William Dewey.
         (Barbara Dewey Cammett's brother, Lewis William Dewey Jr,
         born 6-16-1934, died July 1988, had six children: Lewis
         William III, Robert, John, James, Julia, & Thomas Dewey.)

Stuart Hyland Cammett Jr is a proud descendant (on his father's
side) of Cape Cod whaling men and of many well-known families in
Barnstable County, Massachusetts, and (on his mother's side) of
Scottish ancestors including Stuart, Hyland, and MacKay clans.

Stuart Cammett Jr is a graduate of the Literary School of the
University of Michigan and earned a law degree at that university
in 1954. He began his career as an attorney for Chrysler Corporation, became business/marketing executive and president of the
real estate subsidiary of Chrysler Realty Corporation.

As a founding member of the National Association of Corporate
Real Estate Executives (NACORE), he served as chairman of that
organization from 1979 to 1981. He is a long-term member of
Grosse Point (MI) United Church of Christ, and holds social
memberships in Gowanie Golf Club of Mt Clemens MI, and the
Indian Village Tennis Club of Detroit MI.

17511.   *Joanne Elaine Cammett born Detroit MI 12-11-1934, married
24532.   New York City 6-21-1970 Robert Albert Hansen born Madison,
13.   WI 6-23-1934

Joanne Elaine (Cammett) Hansen earned her B.A. in sociology in
1975 from Hillsdale College, MI; her M.A. in Curriculum and
Teaching in 1960 from Columbia University, NYC; and her M.Ed. in
Psychological Counseling in 1979 from Columbia University, NYC.
Her early career centered on social work research; since 1979 she
has been employed as a vocational rehabilitation counselor in the
city of New York, NY.

INSERT ADDITION: I, p 186 (LL)
Children of Linda (Lovell) Smith (17511.29422.1.)
  & Lawther O'Dell Smith:

17511.   Scott Lovell Smith born Tachikawa Japan 3-6-1962
29422.11.

17511.   Sabrina O'Dell Smith born Washington DC 5-12-1967,
29422.12. married Edgartown MA summer, 1995...

Thirteenth Generation

INSERT ADDITION: I, p 181 (RJG)
Children of Maxine (Hinckley) Goode (11131.13111.11.)
& Robert Joseph Goode Sr:

11131.   Robert J Goode Jr Rev born 12-10-1938
13111.111.

11131.   *Ruth Marilyn Goode born 5-26-1940, married Curtis M Gifford
13111.112.

INSERT ADDITION: I, p 181 (GA)
Children of Idona Rae (Scholes) Pope (11272.11112.22.)
& Alan Roy Pope:

11272.   *Michael Roy [Pope] Lambert born Mountain Home AFB ID
11112.   12-5-1956, adopted by his mother's 2d husband, Howard D
221.   Lambert, married 1st 1977 Donna Earnest, div 1980;
          married 2d 12-3-1992 Anita Pryor. He has custody of
          children of 1st marriage; no children by 2nd marriage

11272.   *Gail Ann [Pope] Lambert born Langley AFB Hampton Co, VA
11112.   8-6-1958, adopted by her mother's 2d husband, Howard D
222.   Lambert, married Hermosa Beach CA 8-18-1984 Scott Adams
          born Los Angeles CA 3-19-1955, son of Ora (Sauber) &
          Joseph Adams

INSERT ADDITION: I p 181 (GA) (REC)
Children of Ronald Eugene Caddy (11272.11118.11.)
& Gerry Lou (Scheuneman) Miller Caddy:

11272.   Michael Timothy Caddy born Grand Island NE 12-11-1949,
11118.   married 1st Nov 1970 Jane DeBush, div Phillipsburg KS 1972;
111.   married 2d Hastings NE 5-2-1988 Renee Goehring born 1967,
          div Kasaney NE 1991

11272.   Patrick Dennis Caddy born Offutt AFB NE 5-12-1958, married
11118.   1st 1979 Dorothy Griess, div Hastings NE 1982; married 2d
112.   Hastings NE 6-5-1992 Dawn Klingenberg born 2-27-1971

11272.   Colleen L Caddy born Elmendorf AFB Anchorage Alaska 8-7-1961,
11118.   married Air Force Academy, Colorado Springs CO 7-31-1987
113.   Michael Reinert; div. 1996

11272.   Ronda Lee Caddy born Andrews AFB MD 9-9-1967, married
11118.114.   Columbus NE 7-7-1990 Dana Bokelman

INSERT ADDITION: I, p 181 (LGW)
Children of Joyce Winifred (Hartwell) Pelletier (14211.18511.12.)
   & Larry Pelletier:

14211.18511.121. Janee Michelle

14211.18511.122. Cara Joy born 6-30-__

INSERT ADDITION: I, p 181 (LGW)
Children of Gerard Allen Bastow (14211.18511.21.)
   & Cynthia (Myers) Bastow:

14211.18511.211. Benjamin John Bastow born 3-26-1974

14211.18511.212. Janine Allen Bastow born 6-7-1977

14211.18511.213. Zachary Aaron Bastow born 12-2-1982

INSERT ADDITION: I, p 181 (LGW)
Children of Beryl Jean (Allen) Anderson (14211.18513.13.)
   & Richard C Anderson:

14211.18513.131. Christine Elizabeth Anderson born 7-15-1975

INSERT ADDITION: I, p 181 (LGW)
Children of William Frederick Allen (14211.18513.15.)
   & Cheryl Ann (_____) Allen

14211.18513.151. Jennifer Ann Allen born 9-5-1979

14211.18513.152. Sarah Kristine Allen born 9-21-1980

INSERT ADDITION: I, p 181 (LGW)
Children of Rosemary (Allen) Booth (14211.18513.16.)
  & Terry Gale Booth:

14211.18513.161. Kristen Marie Booth born 6-2-1983

14211.18513.162. Eric Mitchell Booth born 12-31-1984

INSERT ADDITION: I, p 181 (LGW)
Children of Robert Cedric Allen (14211.18513.14.)
  & Donna (_____) Allen:

14211.18513.141. Robert Dale Allen born 12-20-1977

INSERT ADDITION: I, p 181 (LGW)
Children of Linda Jeanne (Goettman) Wilson (14211.18521.12.)
  & James Thomas Wilson:

14211.18521.121. Russell Bradley Wilson born Orlando FL 12-23-1976

INSERT ADDITION: I, p 181 (LGW)
Children of Diane Shirley (Goettman) Towe (14211.18512.24.)
  & Robert Charles Towe:

14211.18512.241. Farrah Leslie Towe born 3-7-1988

14211.18512.242. Lisa Natalie Towe born 4-24-1993

INSERT ADDITION: I, p 181 (LGW)
Children of Andrew Thomas Goettman Jr (14211.18512.25.)
  & Melissa (Farless) Goettman:

14211.18512.251. Robyn Lynn Goettman born 4-25-1985

14211.18512.252. Everett Mark Goettman born Roanoke Rapids NC
                3-12-1990

162

INSERT ADDITION: I, p 181 (LGW)
Children of Thomas Saunders Allen Sr (14211.18513.11.)
& Vicki Ann (_____) Allen

14211.18513.111. Kimberly Ann Allen born 6-4-1970

14211.18513.112. Tracy Allen born 1-1-1972

14211.18513.113. Thomas Saunders Allen Jr born 10-25-1976

INSERT ADDITION: I, p 181 (LGW)
Children of Janet Ruth (Allen) Machula (14211.18513.21.
& Paul Machula:

14211.18513.211. Amy Machula born Globe AZ 4-2-1977

14211.18513.212. Laurel Machula born Globe AZ 3-8-1979

14211.18513.213. Hyla Machula born Globe AZ 6-__-____

INSERT ADDITION: I p 181 (JMV, MTH, JOB Jr, Family Tree prepared 1996
                 by James Oliver Brooks Jr)

Children of Carol E (Brooks) Warren (16344.21111.21.)
& Kenneth Lynn Warren:

16344.21111.211. Julie Warren born 8-24-1975

16344.21111.212. Neal Warren born 10-17-1977

Children of Paul Arthur Brooks (16344.21111.22.)
& Joan Halpert Brooks:

16344.21111.221. Ann Elizabeth Halbert-Brooks born 11-13-1987

16344.21111.222. Nicholas A Brooks born 3-30-1991

INSERT ADDITION: I, p   (BWS)
Children of Harold Duncan Shaw III (16344.21422.21.)
  & Mary Leonore (Mattern) Shaw:

16344.21422.211. Heather Danielle Shaw born Englewood NJ 7-27-1986

16344.21422.212. Harold Duncan Shaw IV born Englewood NJ 4-5-1988

Children of Sword Crocker Shaw (16344.21422.22.)
  & Delia (Feliciatti) Shaw:

16344.21422.221. Sword Crocker Shaw II born Westwood NJ 8-2-1983

Children of Ian Lee Shaw (16344.21422.23.)
  & Lisa Florence (Favia) Shaw:

16344.21422.231. Corey Ian Shaw born Englewood NJ 9-4-1991

16344.21422.232. Cayli Elizabeth Shaw born Teaneck NJ 9-10-1993

CORRECTION: I, p 182 (LBL)
16344.   Rachael Lena Miesen Leonard born Minneapolis MN 10-4-1972
   31232 married Chicago IL 10-4-1994 Robert Smudde
   321.   born Chicago IL 4-12-1965

INSERT ADDITION: I, p 182 (AL)
Children of Jack Thacher Leonard (16344.31232.44.)
  & Marina (Visser) Leonard:

16344.31232.441. Nicole Corina Leonard born Boston Ma 6-18-1995

INSERT ADDITION: I, p 184 (AL)
Children of David Thomas Holloway (16344.31474.12.)
  & Maureen (McMahon) Holloway:

16344.31474.123. Anna Christine Holloway born 1-31-1995

INSERT ADDITION: I, p 184 (AL)
Children of Jennifer (Holloway) Peatman (16344.31474.21.)
& Robert Peatman:

16344.31474.211. William Ryan Peatman born Wellesley MA 4-21-1996

INSERT ADDITION: I, p 185 (TAC)
Children of Glyndon Harry Crocker III (17181.15152.11.)
& Janet Rae (Schaefer) Crocker:

17181.15152.111. Beth Lucille Crocker, b 1963

Children of Tracy Ashley Crocker Sr (17181.15152.12.)
& Patricia Amy (Mangold) Crocker:

17181.   *Tracy Ashley Crocker Jr born Cortland NY 6-29-1967 married
15152.   Florissant MO 6-13-1991 Kathleen Anne Truetken born 4-1-1970
121.   daughter of Audrey Agnes (Wray) & Libroy Alfred Truetken.
         Kathleen has a daughter, Diane Leeper, by previous marriage.

17181.15152.122. Carolynn Amy Crocker born Syracuse NY 5-20-1970

Children of Jeffrey Robert Crocker (17181.15152.31.)
& Madeline (Baucom) Crocker:

17181.15152.311. Wendy Marie Crocker born 12-27-1971

17181.15152.312. Sarah Alice Crocker born 9-26-1977

17181.15152.313. Robert Charles Crocker born 8-28-1981

17181.15152.314. Jay Michael Crocker born 7-11-1983

Children of Joan (Crocker) Sheridan (17181.15152.32.)
& Joseph Michael Sheridan Sr:

17181.15152.321. Joseph Michael Sheridan Jr born 6-1-1970

17181.15152.322. Bryan Francis Sheridan born 6-19-1974

INSERT ADDITION: I, p 186 (GT)
Children of Peter G Toolas (17181.52153.12.)
& Rachael M (Wirtanen) Toolas:

17181.52153.121. Emily S Toolas born 11-26-1995

Children of Jennie M (Toolas) Manni (17181.52153.13.)
& Kyle J Manni:

17181.52153.131. Troy C Manni born 2-9-1990

17181.52153.132. Travis J Manni born 4-30-1993

17181.52153.133. Katrina L Manni born 12-1-1994

INSERT ADDITION: I, p 186 (RLT)
Children of Robert Leonard Tallman (17181.57311.12.)
& Rose (Evans) Tallman:

17181.   Charlotte Georgia Tallman born Hyannis MA 12-26-1993
57311.121.

17181.57311.122. Joseph Carl Tallman born Salem MA 12-13-1995

INSERT ADDITION: I, p 186 (TTC)
Children of Terri (Tallman) Corbett (17181.573.14.)
& John F Corbett:

17181.57311.141. Kristen Alice Corbett born Hyannis MA 3-1-1994

17181.57311.142. Sean Patrick Corbett born Hyannis MA 7-18-1996

INSERT ADDITION: I, p 186 (GCN)
Children of Gail Roberta (Campana) Nightingale (17511.24511.11.)
& Neil Nightingale:

17511.24511.111. Scott Anthony Nightingale born Boston MA 9-28-1963

17511.14511.112. Keith Michael Nightingale born New Bedford MA
                  10-14-1964

INSERT ADDITION: I, p 186 (VCS)
Children of Virginia (Campana) Stimets (17511.24511.12.)
  & Richard Rice Stimets Sr:

17511.   *Lisa Margaret Stimets born Hyannis MA 10-6-1957, married
24511.121. 1st 1981 Paul Wilcox; div; married 2d 1994 Richard Thomas

17511.   *Richard Rice Stimets Jr born Hyannis MA 5-24-1959,
24511.122. married Sturbridge MA July 1983 Stacey Stratton

INSERT ADDITION: I, p 186 (JMcKC)
Children of John McKay Cammett (17511.24532.11.)
  & Doris Eleanore Darin (DePoldesta) Cammett:

17511.   Lisa Anne Cammett born Detroit Michigan 11-24-1952
24532.111.

Children of John MacKay Cammett (17511.24532.11.)
  & Almena Holt Jones:

17511.   *Ann Marie Cammett born New York City 5-15-1961
24532.112.

Children of John MacKay Cammett (17511.24532.11.)
  & Sandi Elaine (Cooper) Cammett:

17511.   Melanie Claire Cammett born New York City 12-18-1969,
24532.113. married 6-29-1996 Angelo Manioudakis born Chicopee MA
                  11-10-1966

INSERT ADDITION: I, p 186 (SHC Jr)
Children of Stuart Hyland Cammett Jr (17511.24532.12.)
  & Barbara Louise (Dewey) Cammett:

17511.   Stuart Hyland Cammett III born Detroit MI 7-19-1956
24532.121.

17511. *Bryan Dewey Cammett born Detroit MI 4-6-1958, married
24532.122. 10-24-1981 Briggette Carr born East Towas MI 7-15-1955

17511. John William Cammett born Detroit MI 8-10-1962
24532.123.

INSERT ADDITION: I, p 186 (JMcKC)
Children of Joanne Elaine (Cammett) Hansen (17511.24532.13.)
  & Robert Albert Hansen:

17511. Marc Edward Hansen born New York City 3-17-1971
24532.131.

NOTES:

Fourteenth Generation

INSERT ADDITION: I, p 187
Children of Ruth Marilyn (Goode) Gifford (11131.13111.112.)
  & Curtis M Gifford: (RJG)

11131.13111.1121. Craig Marshall Gifford

11131.13111.1122. Curtis Mars Gifford II

INSERT ADDITION: I, p 187 (GA)
Children of Michael Roy (Pope) Lambert (11272.11112.221.)
  & Donna (Ernest) Lambert:

11272.11112.2211. Christopher Lambert born California 5-9-1978

11272.11112.2212. Jason Clyde Lambert born California 6-13-1980

INSERT ADDITION: I, p 187 (GA)
Children of Gail Ann [Pope] (Lambert) Adams (11272.11112.222.)
  & Scott Adams:

11272.11112.2221. Joshua Scott Adams born Los Angeles CA 5-28-1985

11272.11112.2222. Rebecca Adams born Los Angeles CA 8-26-1987

INSERT ADDITION: I, p 187 (EPR)
Children of Gregg Stafford Levinson (16344.31111.133.)
  & Karoline (Sherberg) Levinson:

16344.31111.1332. Daniel Levinson born 1995

INSERT ADDITION: I, p 187 (TAC)
Children of Tracy Ashley Crocker Jr (17181.15152.121.)
  & Kathleeen Anne (Truetken) Crocker:

17181.   Nicole Evelyn Crocker born Florissant MO 12-9-1993
  15152. (Nicole's arrival may have been two weeks late; the
  1211.   reason for this was given by her (half) sister, Diane,
        "There was nothing good on TV.")

INSERT ADDITION: I, p 187 (VCS)
Children of Lisa (Stimets) Wilcox (17511.24511.121.)
  & Paul Wilcox:

17411.24511.1121. Paul Ryan Wilcox born Summit NJ 7-5-1984

17511.24511.1122. Courtney Daniel Wilcox born Akron OH 7-23-1988

Children of Lisa (Stimets) Wilcox (16511,24511.121.) I, p 187 (VCS)
  & Richard Thomas:

17511.24511.1123. John Henry Thomas born Cleveland OH 10-7-1995

INSERT ADDITION: I, p 187 (VCS)
Children of Richard Rice Stimets Jr (17511.24511.122.)
  & Stacey Stratton Stimets:

17511.24511.1221. Jaquelin Nicole Stimets born Worcester MA 3-11-1989

17511.24511.1222. Richard Rice Stimets III born Worcester MA
10-29-1990

17511.24511.1223. Amy Elizabeth Stimets born Hyannis MA 8-29-1992

INSERT ADDITION: I, p 187 (JMcKC)
Children of Ann Marie Cammett (17511.24532.112.)

17511.24532.1121. Mena Aunelah Cammett born New York City 3-2-1987

INSERT ADDITION: I, p 187 (JMcKC)
Children of Bryan Dewey Cammett (17511.14532.122.)
  & Briggette (Carr) Cammett:

17511.   Barbara Catherine Cammett born Cincinnati OH 10-18-1984
14532.1221.

17511.   Elizabeth Anne Cammett born Cincinnati OH 9-8-88
14532.1222.

NOTES

EXCERPTS FROM DIARY (1861-1866) OF
CHARLES WILSON CROCKER (16344.211.)
1861
BOSTON MASSACHUSETTS

<u>Charles W Crocker</u>, age 17 years, lives in a Boston rooming house
run by Mrs. Ephraim Lewis and pays room rent of $2.50 a week. Mr
Lewis goes to sea. Charles is employed as a clerk by a dry goods
store, Haughton Sawyer's (HS&Co) at a wage of approximately $25
a month. When he has time and the money, he returns to Cape Cod
to visit his birthplace, the Homestead located on Round Pond at
"the Plains," in Marstons Mills. He is the eldest of three sons
and a daughter. His mother died when he was 2-1/2 years old; his
father re-married. His step-mother raised him as her own and is
the only mother he knows. His Aunt Martha, his step-mother's
sister, is an active member of the family. When Cape people are
in Boston for various reasons, they usually visit, and often stay
at, the Lewis' house where Charles lives in the city.

1-1:   Paid for glazed cover for cap: $.30. Busy in store putting
        stock back in place. Received a letter from Aunt Martha.
        Weigh this day 110 lbs, height of self, 5'3". Exciting times
        in So Carolina. President Buchanan begins to know his duty --
        or rather to act it. This New Year finds times rather hard,
        a great many being out of employment.

4-10:   Another splendid day. Quite busy in store. It looks a
        great deal like war in South Carolina.

4-11:   Very pleasant, clear, dusty, a despatch from Norfolk states
        that Steamer SO CAROLINA put in that port and left 25 passengers.
        Horace Crocker called to see me. He is fierce to go to California
        in ship CHARGER.

4-13:   April showers. Telegraph reports that war has begun, com-
        menced by the secessionists, replied by Sumpter. Late report
        states that Fort Sumpter is surrendered to the d---d rebels.
        Exciting times everywhere.

4-15:   Beautiful day. A proclamation issued by the President
         calling out 75,000 volunteers.

4-16:   Rain storm, warm. Steamer SOUTH CAROLINA arrived, having
         been to Norfolk; did not go the Charleston on account of the war.

4-17:   Raining in morn; clearing in PM. Schooner NELSON HARVEY
         arrived. Three companies left the city, two for Fort Monroe, one
         for Washington.

4-18:   Pleasant, cool. Called for coat, pants, vest at Powers. One
         Regiment left the city for Washigton. Major Anderson arrived at
         New York.

4-19:   Pleasant, warm. Qute an excitement at the store. William
         Read hung a palmetto flag out a window. A mob was on hand in a
         few minutes. No damage. News came that the sixth regiment were
         assaulted in Baltimore with (stones?). 3 killed; 10 wounded.

4-20:   Very pleasant, warm. Paid for having pants, vest, and coat
         made $10.50. Louisa Bearse came down to work at Marstons.

         (Marstons, a restaurant run by the Marston family; they had a
         home in Centerville. Bearses were a large Centerville family.)

4-21:   Most beautiful day. Heard a very good sermon in AM delivered
         by Rev Mr Sheppard at Tremont Temple. Went for a walk with
         Floretta (Lewis) in eve. Great excitement in city for a Sunday.

4-23:   Pleasant, warm. Sent Wendell Philips speech to Father.
         Destruction of government vessels at Norfolk by the Union men to
         prevent the Rebels taking them.

4-24:   Cloudy, drizzly, coo, wind NE. Steamers SO CAROLINA & MASSA-
         CHUSETTS sold to the government. Business middling.

5-10:   Pleasant; war, as usual. Steamer PEMBROKE sailed at 11 AM
         with troops and provisions for Ft Munroe. Barnes left for West.

5-11:   Pleasant, warm. Great excitement in St Louis; 800 rebel
          troops taken prisoners of war by federal troops. Federal troops
          assaulted by a mob. Federal troops fire and fell abot 20 of the
          mob. Two women. Steamer GREAT EASTERN arrived New York.

7-11:   Round Pond. [Charles has a week's vacation.] Cloudy & foggy
          most of the day. Cooler. Went fishing in the forenoon. Went to
          Hog Pond in PM with Mother, Aunt Sophia, & Ella. As we were about
          starting for home, the horse took to being ugly and sat down in
          arms to buggy, breaking them. No other damage. All hands walked
          down to the Ponds. Thomas brought us home from the Ponds with
          Uncle Joe's horse & lug wagon.

7-12:   Round Pond. A most capital day. Went to Hog Pond in morn
          with Father to get the buggy. Went berrying a little while in AM.
          Got 1/2 a pint. Helped Father get in hay in afternoon. Over to
          Leonard's cranberry marsh & Mr Woods in eve. Paid Thomas Fuller
          for bringing us home last evening, $.25.

7-13:   Round Pond. Very pleasant, quite cool for season. Went to
          Barnstable in AM. Drew from bank $35. Paid for whip and fixing
          harness, .25 ea.=.50., sugar, 2 lbs, .19., for boots made, in-
          cluding case, $3.75. Stayed at Kelley's in Centerville in eve.

7-15:   Centerville, Round Pond, to Boston. Beautiful weather. Paid
          for having boots tapped, .50. From C'ville home in morn on horse-
          back. Fare, Boston: $2.10. Called on Lydia & at Marstons' in eve.

7-16:   Boston. Very comfortable day. Paid for having suit made, J E
          Powers, $8.00. Commenced work again after vacation. Received new
          suit. Mr Haughton says I may stop in counting until Jacob returns
          -- very kind. Business dull.

7-18:   Boston, warm. Nellie Kelley stopped to Mrs Lewis' last
          night. She & Louisa broke bedstead. Frank Bearse stopped with
          George last night. News came that the Schooner HERBERT MANTON was
          taken by one of Jeff Davis' privateers.

7-21:   A most capital day. This day will be long remembered in the
         ages of the future as one when one of the greatest conflicts be-
         tween army & army occurred. The federal troops are obliged to
         retreat. [Overwritten: The Battle of Bull Run.]

7-22:   A charming day...an awful day. The news comes giving an ac-
         count of the severest battle we have had during the present
         crisis. Was fought yesterday. Mary G Crocker died this day in a
         fit, aged 21 years. Col Cardin supposed to be killed. Sad day to
         the North.

7-23:   Pleasant, right kind of weather for the season. Compara-
         tively good news comes today. Report that but about 500 troops
         were killed at Battle of Bull Run. Mass 3d & 4th Regts came up
         from fort and were disbanded. Webster Regt (Mass 12th) left by
         Cape Cod & Fall River routes for the seat of war. Mr. Jacob
         Childs died, 62 years.

7-29:   Showerey, mugg, dog day weather. Col Leonard's, the 1st Regt
         left for the seat of war today. A noble set of men, too.

7-30:   Very warm day. Wrote & sent letter to David. The Mass 5th
         Regt returned home; a great gathering on the Common.

         [Entries for the balance of the year, much the same.]

                           January 1862
                 Residence: 41 Northfield St, Boston MA
         Employment: Haughton Sawyer & Co, 26 & Pearl St, Boston MA
                 On & After 8-14-1862, Camp Stanton

1-5:   Weather clear, very cold, windy. Did not attend church. At
         home all day writing letters. Not improving the 1st Sunday of the
         year very piously.

1-14:   Forwarded $1 in letter to S B Phinney for Patriot, 6 months.

1-15:   Warm. Snow storm in morn turned to rain about noon. Very
         wet and slippery walking. Mr H came to me just at night with an
         envelope containing $25 saying "Charles, here is a little thing
         for you -- we think you a nice young man." I was so SURPRISED I
         couldn't thank him. Business very fair.

1-20:   Harrison Lumbert & Addie Phinney married; also Elijah Lewis
         & Freelove Lumbert.

1-23:   A most lovely day, clear, warm, capital sleighing. Business
         middling. No news from Mr Ephraim Lewis as yet. Been out a week
         last Saturday for Fortress Munroe.

1-25:   Most stormy day this season, raining very hard all day. Out
         on roof in afternoon, shovelling snow. Very bad passing. Water
         half up to knees in many places. Darius sails in ship SARACIN for
         San Francisco.

2-2:   Shaved, first time.

2-5:   Metropolitan R R Co running on runners.

2-12:   Snow in AM, cleared about noon. Thawing rapidly. Business
         quiet. News of Barnside's expedition taking Roanoke Island &
         3,000 prisoners.

2-13:   Zeno Kelley married to Miss Sarah Bursley.

2-17:   Clear & cold. Glorious war news. Report that Fort Donelson
         on the Cumberland River was taken yesterday; 15,000 prisoners.
         Great rejoicing.

2-21:   Glorious holiday. Weather clear, very warm. Washington's
         birthday generally celebrated throughout the city. Closed store
         at 10 AM. Prescott & Mathews arrived home. Went skating on
         Washington Park, down-town, and to East Boston in afternoon with
         Mrs Lewis. Got pants and vest.

2-24:   Warm with hard showers; in eve snow with terrific wind, very
         cold. Fire broke out about 10 PM in Commercial St. At times dur-
         ing night, the wind blew a perfect hurricane. Ned Wilson arrived
         home from NH and VT. Agricultural Hall in Barnstable blew down.

         [Daily entries in diary continue during spring and early summer.
         We resume when Charles is home again on vacation.]

7-21:   Cloudy in morn, clear in PM. At home in forenoon building
         _____ to ditch. Town Meeting in PM. Attended same which was
         called to raise volunteers and bounty for same. Voted to give
         each volunteer the sum of $100 on entering service and $100 at
         end of service. Joseph M Day gave a very Patriotic speech. Town
         Meeting very interesting, enthusiastic, and patriotic. Four
         enlisted on the spot, among them, Henry Goodspeed. Took tea at
         Mrs Woods; Martha Ann and Martha Freeman, Waterman, and self
         called on Josephine in eve.

7-22:   Round Pond & Nantucket: Clear, cool, easterly wind. Mother &
         I went to Nantucket in Packet from Cotuit. Left Cotuit 8-1/2 AM,
         arrived there 2:15 PM. Rough; both seasick. Nellie & Ella carried
         us to the Port. Found Aunt & Uncle at home. Called on C B Jagger.
         Cruising about the island. [This would be Aunt Martha.]

7-23:   Nantucket. Clear, cool, easterly wind. Called on C B Jagger.
         Loafing about. Called on Capt Charles Luce & wife; took order
         from them for goods. Saw Rachell Cormick and sister in eve. Also
         the Coleman girls.

7-24:   Nantucket; via Hyannis & West Barnstable to Round Pond.
         Very pleasant, warm. Went from Nantucket home, very smooth across
         Sound. Slow boat. Cars to West Barnstable, Bursley's barge home.
         Went to C'ville (Centerville) in eve.

7-25:   Cloudy, showery in AM, clear in PM. Fishing in morn. Henry,
         Ella, & self went berrying in PM. Got about a quart apiece. Sail-
         ing in eve with Mrs Jepson, Martha Ann, Georgianne Baker.

7-26:   Home, Marstons Mills. Good weather, quite warm. Went to
Barnstable in morn. Drew from bank, $50. Town Meeting in PM. The
Town have tonight 16 volunteers out of the quota of 48. Eve at
Marstons Mills. Went up with load to meeting at Abram Fuller's.
Called on Mr & Mrs Bassett & Capt Jas. Hamblen's family.

7-27:   Round Pond. Fair weather. At home until after noon, then
went to C'ville afoot. At Mr Kelley's in PM. In eve called on Mr
Jona. Kelley's folks. Left C'ville for home a little after 9 PM
and walked through the woods alone.

7-28:   Round Pond, Boston. Very warm. Went to Boston, found all
well. Met Charles Lincoln in cars bound to Boston from vacation
in Brewster. At house in eve. At store PM. Met Daniel Hamblin on
street. He works on Tremont St. Think strongly of enlisting.

7-29:   Another warm day. At store. I decided to volunteer my services to my country. Spoke to Mr Haughton about it, meets his ap-
proval. He offers to give me $100. The firm regrets to have me
leave the store, yet glory in my pluck and say "GO!" Called on
Willie Whelden in eve. Saw William Buckley. Aunt Clorida Bearse
at house. [Note: Charles' step-mother's first husband was a
Bearse. Clorida (Hinckley) Bearse, wife of Nelson Bearse, was
Oliver & Louisa (Crocker) Hinckley's daughter; one of Clorida and
Nelson Bearse's sixteen children must have been his step-mother's
first husband.]

7-30:   Thunderstorms all day and rained powerfully. Left store this
day to enlist in U S Service. Lewis took me to dinner at Ken-
dall's. Sixteen boys & salesmen in store made me a present of
$29, a reward for my patriotism (which is not as great as should
be.) Bid all hands at store good day. At home in eve. Called on
Lydia. Alice & William Bearse and Frank Parker at house in eve.

8-3:   Round Pond. At home in AM. Warm. Mr Fisk & Susan at house
last night. Took Susan home. Went to C'ville in PM, took tea at
Jona. Kelley's; attended Meeting in hall in eve. Saw large number
of girls. Henry C Lumbert married to Sophia G Howes.

8-4:   Barnstable volunteers appear to be clever nice men. Consi-
         dered by people generally a very warm day. Walked from C'ville to
         L L Lumbert's, then rode with William S Lumbert to Barnstable to
         be examined before Dr Smith at Court House. There nearly all day.
         Passed muster. Took a good dinner at Eldridge's at expense of
         town. Called at Phillips' house as went home. Home in eve.

8-5:   Clear. Quite warm. Twenty-four Barnstable Volunteers left
         home for Lynnfield (Camp Stanton) via Boston. Took dinner at
         Marstons. Went out to Camp about 3 PM. Called on HS&Co. Heavy
         shower in eve. To commence Camp Life bread & coffee for supper.

8-6:   Pleasant, very warm. Fifteen of 24 from Barnstable accepted
         and mustered into service; 9 rejected. Day and Bearse left for
         Cape. I am patiently waiting for uniform. Bread & coffee for
         breakfast and supper. No dinner. Camp very crowded.

8-7:   Pleasant. Barnstable boys got furlough signed last night.
         Left camp about 1 PM and got dinner at House outside. Went to
         Boston in 3 PM train. Boys went home in eve. Went to Museum &
         Copeland's with Etta. Called at store.

8-8:   Thunderstorm in morn; clear during day, thunderstorm in eve.
         Went from Boston home. Had 50 photographs taken at S&L. Called on
         Lydia. Took breakfast & dinner at Mrs Lewis. Train detained in
         Quincy about 1-1/2 hours. Did not get home until after 9 PM.

8-9:   Both cloudy & clear; warm. At home in morn. To C'ville with
         Mr Bursley. Also to/from Town Meeting with him. West Barnstable
         Depot, and at the meeting at Marstons Mills in eve. Good meeting.
         Walked from M Mills to C'ville with C B Jagger to spend night.

8-10:   Lovely day. Stopped with Jagger last night. Arose 7:20 and
         hurried up to Jona. Kelley's house for breakfast, then Mr Crosby
         with Sylvia & self to Steamer ISLAND HOME to go to Camp Meeting.
         We arrived at steamer wharf 8:20, just one hour after stepping
         out of bed. Arrived Camp Grounds about 11 AM, travelled about
         grounds and saw many friends in the boat and at the Ground.

8-10 (Cont'd): Listened to a good address from Governor. Left Ground about 5 PM. Had a pleasant day. Influenced George Collins to put his name on paper as one of the volunteers from Barnstable.

8-11:   Pleasant. Stopped at Mr Kelley's last night. Called at Mr Bacon's, Capt N Bearse's, Ann Maria, Mr Jona. Kelley's and bade the folks good day.

8-12:   Arose 4-1/2 AM and with horse took Father and Mr Nathan down to marsh. Came home, took breakfast, and went to the Ponds, Marstons Mills, and at Goodspeed's before dinner. At home in PM until 4 PM, then to C'ville and bid all hands farewell. Friends feel very bad about me going.

1863

[Charles W Crocker continued keeping a daily record throughout his first year in service as a private in the 40th Regiment of the Massachusetts Volunteers, and through several moves; he went with his regiment to Virgina and spent several months near the front there; then was moved to Long Island in Boston Harbor. Most of the year Charles was company clerk, keeping records, ordering supplies for the men, filling out payrolls, etc. On New Year's Day, 1864, he reviews the year 1863...]

January 1864
Long Island, Boston Harbor, MAss.

1-1:   This New Year's day finds me on duty as Company Clerk, Co A, Provincial Guard (Conscript Co.) commanded by Capt. Wm A Phelan of the 9th Mass. Vol. Infantry, living in a double tent with a stove. Tentmates: C P Smith, William E Horton, and Ezra Heines.

The mud on this island almost equals that in Virginia. A happy year may this prove to all. At work transferring clothing account from Memo's to book. Received a note from a Miss Emma _____ of Worcester through Abellino S Bart wishing me (an entire stranger) a Happy Year. I answered same. All quiet in Virginia, Armies in winter quarters.

1-1: (Cont'd): The prospect of putting down Rebellion a sure thing.
I think peace will dawn before the year expires. Prosperity and
good luck have attended me during the past year; have been favorably blessed with good health. My finances are getting low , not
increased as much as should have owing to expenses incurred by
being on duty in Massachusetts, going on furloughs, etc.
Reported: William S Lumbert died.

1-10:   Another clear cold day. As I look out seaward beyond Boston
Light, whose white tower looms up from the misty deep and sheds
its warning light, I think to myself, I have no desire to take
a sea voyage.

1-19:   Disagreeable weather, wet & rainy. Letters from home report-
ing the death of William S Lumbert. No particulars. William
Lumbert's death sems to me almost impossible to be a fact, and
I do not realize it.

1-23:   Boston & New York: Attended to usual morning duties on Long
Island and about noon started for New York from Boston as guard
of a detachment of Maine Recruits. Arrived in Boston at 1 PM and
marched from Long Wharf to Beach St Barracks where we left the
recruits and had liberty until 4 PM. I improved the time in
visiting Mrs Lewis at 41 Northfield St and Nellie Kelley, 27
Tremont Row. Was at the P C Depot when the Cape train left and
saw E E Bearse, Joseph R Hall, Capt J N Hinckley, Asa Jenkins,
& Gus Scudder. Left Boston with recruits at 5-1/2 PM for Fall
River where arrived at 8 and took the BAY STATE for New York;
touched at Newport.

1-24:   On steamer BAY STATE last night. Up until about 12 midnight,
having done but little guard duty. Turned in on a board and slept
by jerks coolly until 7 AM. On guard from 8 until nearly 10 on
the deck in rear of the Saloon. Had a beautiful view of the
islands and shore. Passing up to NY at 11 AM and immediately
proceeded with our recruits by steamer PORT ROYAL to the steamer
ATLANTIC for Charleston SC where we left the recruits. The full
number we left Long Island with. Very easy guard duty this trip
and the men behaved very good.

1-24: (Cont'd): Landed by steamer PORT ROYAL at New York and proceeded at once to New England Rooms where we obtained permission
to grub, stay, & sleep while in the city, and were dismissed by
Lt Beaumont, Comdg Guard, until 2 PM tomorrow. Had a good dinner
on soup at N E Rooms. Broadway. After dinner & boots blackened
proceeded with Chandler P Smith to his sister's on Tompkins Pl,
Brooklyn, where we spent the PM and took tea. In eve went to
listen to Henry Ward Beecher. Good as ever. From church went to
N E Rooms for the night.

[Charles made several similar trips to & from Boston to southern
ports in the next few months. We pick up his entries in June.]

6-14:   Called on Capt Mitchell, Chelsea Hosp; he was wounded at
Drury's Bluff and left with an arm amputated close. About 8 AM
everyone went aboard steamer for Bermuda Hundreds. Arrived there
6 PM and got to Regt 18th Corp near Point of Rocks about 10 PM.
Found the company greatly reduced by the late battles. Those that
are with the Regt looking quite well. Turned in about 11 PM after
a weary day. Boys all say, "Sorry to see you back at this time;
such dangerous work."

6-15:   On the Field, 18th Army Corp. Arose 1 AM from my bed (Mother
Earth) cold and tired. Regt moved about 3 AM (Co E number 12 men
for duty, viz: Sgt Stocker, Corp W D Holmes, Pvts Albert Finney,
C G Tinkham, Geo W Ryder, E N Baker, W Nickerson, E Holmes,
Lyons, Crocker, Jones, Wrightington) across the Appomattox River
toward Petersburg. Lay in woods in sight of church spires of the
city till night, under fire usually from their works. The colored
troops led the advance & skirmishes with the enemy and drove them
from their first line of field to the protection of their works.
About sundown our troops charged, took an earthwork, several
guns, and a number of prisoners, about 100. Our whole line advanced. We lay tonight by the captured earthwork on a pleasant
plantation, in an orchard of apples & peaches, close to a large
pleasantly-located house. Have had shot & shell as near me as I
wish. I got into the work pretty quick after joining the Regt.
We lost quite a number of colored soldiers; wounded today, about
200. Captured 15 or 16 pieces of artillery.

6-16:   Very warm. During the day we make three or four moves, to
occupy during the heat of the day our position of yesterday in
the wood near the railroad from Petersburg to City Point. In the
evening the ball again opens, and our Brigade moves to the front,
on the extreme left of the 18th Corps, and before the Rebel works
in front of the city. Lay flat on the ground under fire from
infantry. The Johnny balls fly overhead, singing merrily.

6-17:   Weather extremely hot and grease tries from one freely. Lay
on belly all last night. Slept some, but we have heavy dew and
chilly nights. Move early to support the skirmish line, but relieved before noon by 1st Mass. Heavy Artillery, and taken back
to the works. Sgt Herrick, Co K of Beverly, killed almost in-
stantly while sleeping in his tent within 10 feet of me by a
spent solid shot from the enemy. About sundown moved to the rear
and back to campground across the Appomattox which we left Wed
morn. Heavy firing in eve from infantry & artillery. Grant's army
before Petersburg. Entrenched. Good position.

6-20:   Letters from home. Nelson reported David B Coleman's marriage to Miss Caroline E Phinney.

6-22:   In trenches about 1/2 mile from Petersburg and near the
enemy's skirmish line. Shot, shell passing over most of time all
day. The balls just passing overhead, and many striking the
earthwork. No one injured today in our reg't.

A PARTIAL REVIEW OF MY LIFE 1864
DECEMBER 31, 1864

It being the close of the year 1864, one which will prove an
eventful one in history, it is well to cast a look over the same
and derive what benefit one can from his experiences of good or
bad deeds or acts of the year just ended. I have witnessed more
thrilling scenes, passed through greater dangers, seen more of
human nature, and it has been a more eventful year for me in
every way than any previous one of my existence.

The beginning of the year found me a private of E Co., 40th
Mass. Volunteers, in the U S Army serving on detached service

at Draft Rendezvous, Mass., Long Island, Boston Harbor, as clerk with a drafted company commanded by Capt W A Phelan, 9th Mass Vols. Here I was situated where I could visit home and my friends in Boston often and with pleasant associates. If not immediately surrounded by good moral society, I was near its influence.

In February the Rendezvous was transferred from Long to Galloups Island, General Charles Nevins Commanded Post, and at the close of the year, 3rd Div. 24 AC, to which I belong. I continued as Clerk with aforesaid Co until May 2 when I was relieved per Special Order & ordered to report to my regiment in the Field, Virginia, via Hart Island NY.

On 5-3 reported at Hart Island for transportation to my regiment; was delayed there for same until June 11th. While awaiting transportatiion, made a pleasant vsit to Brooklyn NY.

Arrived at my Reg't near Bermuda Hundred VA June 14th and found it sadly reduced by battle & disease during my eleven month's absence. June 15 marched upon the enemy's fortifications before Petersburg VA and the enemy's fire. Here I begin to see and realize the fruits of war. Men wounded, dying, dead.

Continued with my reg't in the trenches before the Rebel City until July 2d when I was detailed as clerk with Capt Elder, AAIG at Brigade HQ. Continued until July 11 when I was detached for duty with Capt Wetherbee CSV of the Division and with whom I remain at present.

While at Brigade HQ in July had dysentary quite severely for about two weeks, the only sickness during the year. With Capt, a fine man, from July to present, and with Armies operating against Richmond under command of Lt General Grant. In November received a 15-day furlough; arrived home Thanksgiving Day. Stopped 12 days; a delightful visit. Visited Boston. But one incident I regret -- an accident which happened to Mrs F G Kelley being thrown from my carriage Thanksgiving eve and from which she is now an invalid. Lost no friends during the year nearer than Cousin James G Crocker and the Wright boys. I never commenced a year with a more contented mind than 1865.

Have not made any advancement toward matrimony as I don't think it prudent for one to do it while in service and living at great risk. And again my circumstances, financial and otherwise, are not in proper condition, and I have no definite lady in view.

In my estimation I stand before the world, honest & truthful,
cherishing no ill feeling toward anyone. Am satisfied with the
performance of my duty and feel as if it had been done properly
and satisfactory. Have to a considerable degree acquired a habit
of profanity which I deeply regret and which I must determine to
dispose of. That is the only fault of importance that I possess
to my knowledge that a young man of good character should not
have. I can but feel grateful to the Giver of All for the health
and numerous blessings bestowed upon me and my friends during the
past year. Feeling satisfied with the results of the year, the
performance of every duty properly and promptly, I bid 1864 adieu
and enter upon the new year with a clear conscience and the
experiences of the past to guide me.

April 1865

4:16:   Fine weather. Drew stores & bread in AM. Rode over to Man-
         chester in PM. C P Smith dined with me. Took a walk with him.
         Reported: assassination of President Lincoln.

4-17:   Lovely weather, but sad news. President Lincoln died
         Saturday morning, April 15 between 7 & 8 AM from wounds received
         by pistol ball, the weapon being in the hands of J Wilkes-Booth,
         the actor. The Richmond Whig appears in mourning.
             Every thinking mind feels this blow greater than if his own
         father had been stricken down. It is the most awful event of any
         one incident during the war.
             I never had anything to arouse my passions to such an extent
         ... I can but feel that every traitor, so proved, should be hung
         without comment. Let the war be prosecuted with renewed energy,
         and show no mercy to the traitor no matter in what form he comes.
         The Great and Good mortal who would have shown and tendered to
         the South every mercy and kindness has been brutally murdered,
         and now may the guilty suffer accordingly. I feel as if I would
         enlist for life today in defense of the Government, Right, and
         Liberty. We are yet to learn the good which is to result from
         this severe calamity. A Generous and Liberty-loving people must
         deeply feel and mourn the loss of their fellow man, the Guiding
         Star, the Magnet, of the United States and its people.

Merciful God, teach us to look calmly upon thy works and not to cherish too bitter feelings toward our treacherous enemies.

Butler ought to be Military Governor of Richmond and make use of these beautiful shade trees by suspending the guilty authors of this Rebellion to them by the necks with hempen cord.

4-22:   Another very warm day with abundance of business. Since the death of Abraham Lincoln nearly every U.S. officer has worn a piece of black Crepe about the arm. No military news of account, but during the week news has come of the capture of Mobile.

4-23:   Attended worship at the M.E. church with Capt Wetherbee. Officers & soldiers of both Federal and (so called) Confederate Armies. Men, women and children in civil garb. Many haughty, proud-looking young ladies, I suppose they wish to be called. Well, they did possess beauty, if that makes a lady, but I fear little heart or principle were in attendance.

Dined at 3rd Brigade Commissary. Called at my Company. The brave lads are well. They, many of them, harbor the idea that they go home soon. Many rumors in regard to it. If affairs progress favorably elsewhere, they may go home 'ere their time expires, and I think they will, but I doubt if any official steps have been taken that way as yet.

5-1:   Clear cool beautiful weather. Finished up muster rolls. Met a number of my reg't on the street. All of them going home soon.

6-5:   Hot. Supplied 3rd Brigade with food. Stevens goes to City Point today. Called at Reg't a few moments. All have home fever.

6-9:   Thermometer 93 in the shade. Called at Reg't in eve. They have received muster rolls but as yet not commenced to make them out. It appears the officers wish to delay the matter as long as possible. The fact is, they get $5 per day for doing nothing while the private gets but 50 cents.

[The Civil War ended and Charles W Crocker was mustered out with an honorable discharge from the U S Army.]

REVIEW OF THE YEAR 1866

In reviewing the year just past there seems but little of general interest worthy of comment. To realize that another year has departed one must feel that he has taken another long stride toward the brilliant yet unknown future. Place the average age of man at sixty, and then, to illustrate that time flies, we will suppose each year a step in our earthly journey of joy, sadness, and ignorance. The child at birth has the journey before him and has to make it in sixty steps, more or less.

Each year a pace forward, and but sixty of them to complete our earthly career; does not life seem short, and a "fleeting show?" Can I realize that I am making my twenty-fifth advance? Comprehending the fact that life is brief, one can but ask himself these questions: Am I making the best of life? Do I lead a life that is beneficial to myself and others? Should we live for ourselves or for others? Do we ever keep the Golden Rule before us?

Are we controlled by the higher and better element of the man (the mind and reason, soul, conscience, and heart) or by the lower and baser element? The passions, appetites, and every sensual, selfish, ambitious desire? Look well to it, and see which element should control the man, his words and acts, and see that the right power prevails and holds supreme control.

The Situation

At the opening of the year in the employ of Messrs Haughton Perkins & Co, Boston, on a salary of $600 per annum. My duties after February 1st being to enter and look after the entire sales made in the store. Boarding with Ephraim Lewis, 41 Northfield St, $4.50 per week. Continue in this situation and at the same boarding place until September 1 when I leave the employ of HP&Co, my year, for which engagement having been made, expiring, and cannot make satisfactory arrangements with them for the future, so accept an offer from F G Kelley for one year at $300 per annum and board, which is by far too little. But I accept this proposal with the feeling that Mr Kelley will do better than this by me.

If all is satisfactory, he gives me to understand that an interest with him shall be given me when the year is up.

HP&Co desired that I should continue with them in the same vocation and for a time on the same pay, but they having failed so many times in fulfilling their promises, I have no faith to accept their promise of "We will do better by you by-and-by." Therefore I begin the year as clerk in a wholesale dry goods house, and at its close, find myself comfortably situated in a retail country store in Centerville.

Investments

At the close of the year built on Father's premises an Ice House costing about $70 and holding about 20 ton. Not having made any other investments, there has been but little increase in my finances. The only method I can adopt for gain is: "Live within your means," and my experience teaches me that the Country is preferable to the City for economy.

REVIEW OF THE YEAR
December 1867

With F G Kelley in Centerville during the year. Endeavor to better my situation, but he thinks he cannot afford to do better by me. Therefore, at the close of the year, I decide to move West and make arrangements accordingly.

The year in a business way has been a dull and monotonous one to me. Trade dull throughout the country. Visited Boston in June, November & December. In December started for the West, but owing to detention by snow, could not meet my appointment with Seth Lewis in Cleveland. Stopped in Boston a week with Emma Crosby who was very sick which created intense talk at the Cape.

Mother, Susan, Mary, Lizzie, and self visited Nantucket in September and enjoyed a pleasant visit.

In the Spring invested $50 in Centerville Fish Weir Co (5 shares), which the past year has not been successful.

My disappointment with Sylvia has been very keen, although she engaged herself to W.A.P. in August. She and others have very many times wronged me by not understanding me and misinterpreting me, etc., which has caused many unpleasant feelings at times, but I do dearly love her as a sister, and hope someday she may know me truly. I have been pained to learn that Ella had formed an attachment for me. Upon learning these facts, I held interviews with her, telling her my present and past position, and I think she is quite well reconciled to her disappointment, as she had loved W.A.P. heretofore. I pity her and sympathize with anyone whose hopes have been thus swamped. But we should all learn the lessons these disappointments teach us.

May good will from their many friends and happiness dwell with my dear friends, Ella & Sylvia, as also with all my other friends and relatives. (Learn to Live Right.)

# # #

NOTE

Throughout Charles W Crocker's diary, and in particular during the years he was in the Army, he referred again and again to "Aunt Martha" without ever mentioning her surname or saying how she was related to him. In earlier times people often referred to a neighbor or close friend of the family as "Aunt" or "Uncle" or even "Grandmother" when there was no blood relationship. Descendants have been wondering just who Aunt Martha was. With thanks to Barbara (Wissing) Shaw, I am pleased to include the following, written by Henry Ellis Crocker upon the occasion of Martha's death, published in The Barnstable Patriot.

DEATH OF MRS MARTHA C STARBUCK

The death of Mrs Martha C Starbuck at the home of Mr Nelson W Crocker, Plains, Osterville, on Friday evening, April 18th, removed from earth a most estimable woman, whose unselfish life and many lovable qualities greatly endeared her to a wide circle of friends.

Mrs Starbuck was born at Pondsville near Marstons Mills, May 25th 1813, and was therefore at the time of her death nearly eighty-nine years of age. She was the daughter of Mr Benjamin Wright, and one of a family of fourteen children, most of whom lived to mature years. Among her brothers were Capt Asa Wright, formerly of Hyannis, Capt Benjamin Wright of Pondsville, and Mr William Wright, one of the survivors of the ship ESSEX which was destroyed by an angry whale in the Pacific Ocean, about three-quarters of a century ago.

Mrs Starbuck was married in early life to Capt William Crocker, a brother of Mr Aurin B Crocker, a well-known citizen of Hyannis. Capt Crocker became a shipmaster soon after attaining his majority and was lost off the Azores shortly after his marriage. A daughter, born after his death, was buried in the cemetery at West Barnstable where the body of Mrs Starbuck was laid to rest a week ago.

Mrs Starbuck lived for many years with her sister, Mrs George C Hussey, at Nantucket, and several years after the death of her sister, married Mr Hussey.

Some years subsequent to Mr Hussey's death, Martha married Capt Obed Starbuck, a successful whaling captain of Nantucket, whose voyages form one of the most interesting chapters in the history of the industry which made the island town one of the leading whaling ports of the world.

The vessel of Capt Starbuck, on one of his many voyages, was captured by pirates, but was afterwards retaken by him and his men, and the pirate crew were conveyed to a South American port where some of them were executed.

Mrs Starbuck's home in Nantucket was greatly prized by her, and here she received for many years her relatives and friends from far and near who were always glad to avail themselves of her generous hospitality. While not a native of Nantucket, she was devotedly attached to the island and its people.

About four years ago, on account of advancing years, she removed to the home of her nephew where she received the most devoted care. In the house where she died had lived for nearly a half century her sister, Mrs Wilson Crocker, who died seven years ago, aged nearly eighty five years. Here Mrs Starbuck lingered, the last survivor of her father's family, or as she sometimes quaintly expressed it, "the last leaf on the tree," until her sudden transition from earth to Heaven.

To the last she retained her faculties to a wonderful degree. Possessing a gift of rare humor, her conversation and letters were a source of delight to her friends. Her unselfishness of spirit as manifested in unnumbered acts of kindness, her uprightness of life, and her nobility of character will long remain as an influence for good with those who loved her and cherish her memory.

Funeral services conducted by Rev Charles N Hinckley of Osterville and Rev E B French, pastor of the Congregational Church at West Barnstable, were held Monday afternoon. The remarks of Mr Hinckley, who was Mrs Starbuck's pastor at Nantucket, were based upon the text, "Thou shalt come to thy grave in full age, like a shock of corn cometh in in his season."   --H.E.C. [Henry Ellis Crocker, a nephew.--ED]

# # #

www.ingramcontent.com/pod-product-compliance
Lightning Source LLC
Chambersburg PA
CBHW061724270326
41928CB00011B/2107